LEGACY
LIT

Praise for

A PLACE CALLED HOME

"Riveting…A haunting, inspiring chronicle of fortitude and persever-
ance."   —*Kirkus*, Starred Review

"[A] captivating debut…Galvanizing and compassionate, this personal
account of survival should be required reading."   —*Publishers Weekly*

"I love a true story where the downtrodden triumph over hardship—and
A Place Called Home delivers. David Ambroz, through grit, courage, and
integrity, overcomes obstacles beyond my imagination. I found myself
cheering for him and the siblings he steadfastly protects, wondering how
they were going to survive. David does more than that—he thrives—and
then he pays it forward. *A Place Called Home* is an awe-inspiring story that
will lift your spirits and soften even the hardest heart. It's a beautifully
told, captivating memoir."   —David Crow, author of *The Pale-Faced Lie*

"A story destined to end in tragedy that magically rewards an indomi-
table determination to succeed. Beautifully written."
                                —Ted Koppel, veteran ABC anchor and
                          New York Times bestselling author of *Lights Out*

"A heartbreaking, gritty, and inspiring personal testament to the burden
that is placed on a child in poverty. David's elegantly written memoir
is an ode to the millions of families who are struggling to survive and
provides the immense hope that is needed to."
                          —Keith Ferrazzi, *New York Times* bestselling author
                                   of *Competing in the New World of Work*

"In *A Place Called Home*, Ambroz shares his personal journey out of a child-hood marked by poverty, homelessness, and years in foster care—a story of courage, tenacity, and the power of education to transform lives."
—Barbara Bush Foundation for Family Literacy

"David Ambroz faced seemingly insurmountable challenges his entire life and emerged with the grace and wisdom to tell the story. His dreams of a better life via education carried him through childhood abuse, homelessness, foster care, and finally to adulthood, where he leveraged his against-all-odds success to advocate for children living in poverty and foster care. This book is an inspiration to anyone who has encountered hardships, encouraging us to tackle them head-on with courage and determination."   —Madeline Di Nonno, president and CEO of the Geena Davis Institute on Gender in Media

A PLACE CALLED HOME

A PLACE CALLED HOME

A Memoir

DAVID AMBROZ

LEGACY
LIT

New York

Note to Readers: What I have written here is true to what I believe happened. Names and identifying characteristics of individuals and place-names have been changed to protect the privacy of others. In places, I have reconstructed the chronology to the best of my recollection, and to aid the narrative I have combined the sequence of some events. Where dialogue appears, my intention was to re-create the essence of conversations rather than verbatim quotes. Others who were present might recall things differently, but this is a true story.

Legacy Lit, an imprint of Hachette Books
Hachette Book Group
1290 Avenue of the Americas
New York, NY 10104
LegacyLitBooks.com
Twitter.com/LegacyLitBooks
Instagram.com/LegacyLitBooks

First Edition: September 2022

Grand Central Publishing is a division of Hachette Book Group, Inc. The Legacy Lit and Grand Central Publishing names and logos are trademarks of Hachette Book Group, Inc.

The Hachette Speakers Bureau provides a wide range of authors for speaking events. To find out more, go to www.hachettespeakersbureau.com or call (866) 376-6591.

The publisher is not responsible for websites (or their content) that are not owned by the publisher.

Library of Congress Cataloging-in-Publication Data
Names: Ambroz, David, author.
Title: A place called home : a memoir / David Ambroz.
Description: First edition. | New York, NY : Legacy Lit, 2022. |
Identifiers: LCCN 2022019466 | ISBN 9780306903540 (hardcover) | ISBN
   9780306875212 (ebook)
Subjects: LCSH: Ambroz, David. | Homeless children—New York (State)—New
   York—Biography. | Foster children—New York (State)—New York—Biography.
Classification: LCC HV4506.N6 A43 2022 | DDC 362.7/75692092 [B]—dc23/eng/20220511
LC record available at https://lccn.loc.gov/2022019466

ISBNs: 978-0-3069-0354-0 (hardcover); 978-0-3068-7521-2 (ebook)

Printed in the United States of America

LSC-C

Printing 2, 2022

To my mother, who taught me to understand and forgive . . . to conquer one impossible thing at a time.

To my brother, Alex, and sister, Jessica. My left and right, forward and backward. Their lives inspire me to reach further than I think I might.

"illegitimi non carborundum"

PART ONE

Chapter 1

I'M HUNGRY. I'VE WAITED AS long as I can, and now I scoot past my siblings to tug on my mother's jacket. She swats me away.

"Walk straight," Mom commands, her voice deep and robotic, the voice of a stranger.

If we stop walking, we will freeze to death. It's Christmas in Manhattan, and the Midtown department store windows glow, each one a framed fantasy. My neck swivels as I pass, entranced by the rich golds, reds, and greens. My eyes fix on a display with an electric train chugging in a circle around a tree. It weaves through snowy heaps of presents, some wrapped, some with pictures of toys on the outside. I'm only five, and all I know about Christmas is the stories I've heard at the churches where we go for free meals...and that in December music drifts from the doorway of every store, and their windows fill with magic. I want, more than anything, to get my hands on that train.

A man crosses between me and my brother, bags brimming with gifts hanging from both arms, his pale face flushed with cold. He steps into the street and hails a taxi. I watch for a moment as he gets in, feeling a longing I don't understand. I want to be part of his life, to be his child, to be him, to be blissfully unaware of the luxury of a warm taxi.

I pull my eyes away, returning them to the backs of my mother and siblings. From behind, Mom's jacket looks like a puffy sleeping bag with arms. The three of us follow her like ducklings, eyes locked on that jacket. Jessica, the oldest, is right behind Mom. She's seven and sometimes holds my hand when the streets aren't so crowded. Then comes Alex. He's six, one year older than me, and balances on curbs and jumps up against walls when it's not so cold. Then there's me.

Tourists shove in all directions, still warm from wherever they got their last hot chocolates, the winter air bringing a holiday pink to their cheeks. I dodge them without pausing. No matter how alluring that window is, the most important thing is not to lose my family.

On the fringes of this shiny holiday wonderland, in the dark alcoves and corners of the night, are people like us, passing like ghosts around and through the bright, clean tourists. We drift in circles, making our home everywhere and nowhere. We hunker down in the colorless crevices of the city, in the gray shadows of gray buildings where the gray snow is piled; we are gray people fading to nothing.

We head farther uptown, and as Times Square bleeds into the Upper West Side, neighborhoods shift in character. I know this area by its sidewalks. My favorite, they are embedded with mica, sparkling like diamonds. The sun sets over the apartment buildings, and darkness begins to spread over Manhattan. Night is the worst time to be outside without a home. My mother stares straight ahead into the eve of the night, lost in her own thoughts. It's cold, getting colder, and we don't have a destination.

"Mom." I try to get her attention, but it's futile when she's in this mood. She flatly repeats her refrain: "Walk straight."

Hours pass and the temperature drops. Every puddle has a skin of ice. The snow heaped on either side of the shoveled sidewalk is hard as rock. The city is frozen solid. My feet are stubs. I stare down at them to make sure they're still there. My dirty sneakers, plucked from the trash, are clownishly large. The laces are wrapped once around the sole, then tied in a bow on top to help them stay on. Each time I take a step, my foot floats up in the shoe, then reconnects with the sole and the pavement. I count as high as I can to pass the time—forty-one, forty-two—but I keep losing track of my count and switch to songs and stories. Last night we had dinner at a church—macaroni and a sermon on the side. We heard the story of the three kings bringing gifts to the baby Jesus. Gold, frankincense, and myrrh. They walked all night, too, following a star. We need a star. Instead, our homelessness stretches on forever, in all directions, studded with temporary refuges—a bus station, a subway car, a shelter, a hospital waiting room, a Bowery slum. I'm angling for one of those now.

"Mom, how about there?" I've spotted a subway vent and can see steam rising from the familiar metal grid.

It's unclear whether she hears me. Regardless, she doesn't answer. Her eyes dart left and right behind her fogged, red-framed drugstore glasses. She's checking to see if anyone is following us. This time, in spite of her suspicion, she stops, and we know this means we're allowed to pause above the grate. Warm air seeps out. My exposed hands feel it first, then my body, and finally my toes start to prick back to life. This must be what it felt like when the three wise men found the manger.

I hear the rumble before I feel it and sneak a glance at Alex. We make eye contact, and the corner of his mouth turns up: He hears it too. The rumble surges to a roar, and a subway car shoots through the station below. A welcome blast of damp heat envelops us.

"Yes!" Alex whispers. Jessica hears him and smiles.

I could stay here all night, but the respite is tantalizingly short. A gray figure emerges through the steam.

"Good evening," he says, politely enough, but Mom hears danger.

"Get over here," she says, shooing us off the grate. He's not the only one—others are emerging from dark corners to usurp the subway grate. The only people brave or lost enough to be out on the streets tonight are also wrapped in mummy-like layers. Their breath floats from unseen slits in colorless cloth. Whatever plumage any of them once had is fading. They step toward us, and my mother propels us onward.

"Enough, let's go," Mom says. *To where?* I wonder.

We end up right back where we started, walking.

Mom must be getting cold. Does she even feel the cold? I can't be sure. I look at my brother and sister. Jessica's steps drag; Alex, the troublemaker, is silent. My siblings have not spoken for hours—there is no joking around or whining, no annoying each other, no pestering Mom about where we are going. We know to be quiet and obedient when she's in this state, but I have to try something.

I take a deep breath. "Mom, we're close to the Port Authority, can we go inside?" I venture.

"Walk straight. They're after us." Mom is always worried about people coming to get us, but they never come, and the three of us already understand that although there are real dangers, "they" are only in her mind.

Now Jessica trips, slumping to the ground. Alex and I stop short. I want to help her, but my thoughts are muddled, and I move too slowly. She silently drags herself to her feet. She breathes puffs of mist. This might be the coldest night we've ever walked, and through the fog of my brain, it occurs to me that my sister might not be okay. Alex is too quiet. My own mind doesn't feel right. We are disappearing into ghosts. We've done this before, walked with Mom all night. We've never had a place to call home, never stayed in one place long enough for me to remember it, but for the first time in my life, though I don't have the words for it, I think we might die.

There is a calculation I make whenever I talk to Mom: Will she hit me, and is it worth it? Asking for a candy bar isn't worth it. That's a mistake I won't make twice. But when she's challenging an authority or beating up on one of us too much, I take the risk. I need to keep us going.

I try again. "Mom, we should go inside." In my head I am saying all of it: *We're too cold. I love my sister! You're killing us. Wake up!* I want to slap her with my words. *I can't feel my feet. I can barely breathe. I'm not even shivering anymore. We're dying.*

Mom stops and looks at me for the first time in hours. She's going to hit me. Is she going to hit me? I can usually tell, but not tonight.

We wait in front of her. We can't navigate the world on our own. Not yet.

"Okay, okay," Mom relents.

Victory! We're going inside. Somewhere, somehow. With new vigor we march past fast-food restaurants, hair salons, metal roll-down doors. She must have a destination in mind now. Does she have a destination in mind? Her mind is a riddle I'm constantly trying to solve.

We find ourselves at a box of a building with black painted metal doors. Hunkered down on the street, the building looks like it's avoiding eye contact.

Mom rings the doorbell. The street is completely silent, asleep or abandoned.

Mom rings and rings, then bangs and bangs. Finally, she yells, "Hey, open up! Answer the goddamn door!" This is our warrior mom, breaking through the voices in her head, fighting for our lives.

The door opens, and heat flows toward us like a dream. We surge forward, ice zombies.

"Lady, this is a men's shelter," the man at the threshold announces, blocking our way.

"What the hell is wrong with you?" Mom roars.

"Excuse me?" the man says. "Don't speak to me like that."

She says something about clouds from a bombing in Ireland and nuclear waste. "It's all around us out here and you're exposing us to it."

The man looks startled and is suddenly speechless. They are at an impasse. I feel a surprising warmth move down my legs. Then the warmth quickly cools, and the smell of urine rises up to my nose. I hadn't realized that I had to pee or that it was happening.

"I peed my pants," I announce to no one in particular.

The man looks at me for the first time. His dreads are neatly pulled back, his eyes bright. Like the man I saw getting into a taxi, I want this man, too, want him to protect me, want to be the person who owns the warmth and lets people in from the cold. His glance flits from me to Alex to Jessica. His pause is an eternity.

"Fine, come in. But you can't let the kids out of your sight," he says to my mother. "This place isn't safe for them."

"You think I don't know that already?" she says.

"The guys in here are fucked up."

He ushers us into a warehouse-like space, and I see what he means. Other shelters are bright and clean with space for children. This room is dark, and I don't see any other children. Ahead I see only the outlines of rows and rows of coffins. On top of each lies a single body.

"Are they dead?" I ask.

"Nearly," he says. "Here." He points at a single empty cot.

"That's all?" Mom asks.

"What the fuck do you want? This isn't a hotel," he snaps, suddenly sharp.

"Okay, okay," Mom says.

"Like I said, don't let them out of your sight," he reminds her and leaves.

"Sit," Mom tells us.

We sink down on the cot, not ready to shed any layers. I am in the middle, between my brother and sister. My eyes adjust to the dark, and details of our neighbors emerge. They are surrounded by bags of all sizes, belching their contents out onto the floor. Sometimes we have bags, but not tonight. We are wearing everything we own.

I smell my own urine, but now it's dominated by the stench of funk, sweat, and vomit that brews in the overheated room. If outside was hell frozen over, then this is hell defrosted. I wonder, looking around, what has brought each man here. Did they come here with their moms too—and stay until they were grown?

My mother stands above us. As my eyes get used to the dark, I see something in her face shift. Another mom is emerging—this is the one who knows what to do. This mom hugs us as often and as easily as the other mom hits us.

"Is this what you want?" Mom asks, gesturing to indicate the roomful of lost souls, strung-out, drunk, miserable specters of their imminent deaths. Mom doesn't usually talk about the future. Poverty is never about the future; it's obsessed with the now, as it must be. We walk the high wire of trying to survive, and I sense more than understand exactly what my mother is asking.

"No!" I cry. "This is not what I want." I catch only glimpses of other lives, spotting them and speeding past them like an express train, but I am certain that I don't want *this*. I begin to weep. I'm starving. I'm afraid my mom might hit me. I don't want to see Jessica fall again. I don't like it when Alex is quiet and still. I don't want to be here, surrounded by the nameless, homeless masses, sitting in my own urine. My brother and sister lean into me from either side as I cry, wanting to comfort me but not quite able. I don't know what I'll have to do to escape this life. It's all I've ever known. But somewhere in the darkness my mother has unleashed a spark of hope. She is asking me what I want, and in that question is the implication that I have a choice. She is asking me to believe in something better. I'm five, but I already know this: I want a roof to sleep under for more than a night or two, with furniture and blankets and toys. I want to protect my older siblings. I want to protect us from Mom, and I want to protect Mom. I want to be the man getting into the taxi with gifts for his family. I want to be the man in the shelter, with a warm space he decides how to share. I want to be another man, one I haven't met yet.

I have no idea what life could be like, but for the first time I know what I want: *not this*.

"Okay, good," Mom says. She doesn't want this for me, either, the chaos inside her that spills out to encircle us. She sits down next to us.

I lie back, horizontal across the cot, feet dangling off the side, squeezed between my siblings with a woman who, for a brief moment, has come as close as she ever gets to being a real mom. I curl into the dogpile of my family.

Chapter 2

I KNOW TOO MUCH," MOM tells us. We're all in a row behind her, riding in the back seat of a forest-green Volkswagen Beetle that shudders whenever she hits the gas. "I helped the Irish. Your mother is at the table. We need to end the Troubles," she says, referring to the Northern Ireland conflict. It is two years after the coldest night of walking, people are pursuing my mother again, and we fled Manhattan this morning. Mom chain-smokes Marlboros, lighting the next with the last, until we arrive in Albany. Our first stop is the state welfare office so Mom can apply for rent and food stamps.

All the welfare offices follow the same labyrinthine process that makes securing help a job in and of itself. Sometimes the meeting is brief, but usually we arrive and wait for hours before and after talking to a social worker. The rent voucher provided limits our options to the poorest areas, and we inevitably run out of money and food stamps toward the middle of the month, at which point we turn to food banks, foraging, church meals, and thieving. The end of the month ticks by slowly until the next allotment comes.

Mom figures out when and where we need to go to reapply. This is our first time going to the Albany County Department of Social

Services, but the waiting room looks just like all the others: worn and spiritless, with a familiar whiff of poverty and hopelessness. The flooring is shiny around the edges but dulled to exhaustion everywhere else. The seats are attached to each other. I scan the other families. Many of them sit guard over all of their possessions. Every mom has brought all of her kids—even if they're school-age, they have to be here in person to prove that she's taking care of them. The room is full of brown faces, but to me, they all look like us—tired, hungry, in need of a bath, and too familiar with this routine. Some of the younger kids run wild, but none of them talk to us.

There is nothing to do or to play with, so I study the brochures that are scattered on the side tables. One of them is called *Healthy Nursing*. From it, I learn how vital it is to breastfeed a baby. There is a line drawing of a breast that I know Alex will appreciate. When I show it to him, he glances at Mom to see if she is looking, and then says, "Give me that!" and snatches it away from me.

When the social worker finally calls our name, she greets us with a forced smile and leads us into her office. I sit on a chair, and the social worker starts asking questions.

"Are you actually looking for work?" Her tone is skeptical. The welfare worker is as much a part of the system as we are, except that she is paid to robotically ask us a series of questions while we are given money for answering them correctly. Her role is not to be a helper but to be a gatekeeper. Her goal is to make sure we don't abuse the system—that Mom truly doesn't have the money to feed us, that she's trying to get a job, that she'll use the money the way the government wants her to. She's going to ask for papers we don't have—pay stubs, proof of how much rent we pay—and I know Mom won't appreciate her skepticism. I brace myself for a reaction, but she is in control of herself. She wants the money. Mom gives the woman the warm smile that she uses when she wants something.

"What's your name, dear?" Mom asks.

"Vaynessa," the woman says.

"That's beautiful. Vaynessa, this is my son, Hugh," Mom responds. "Say hello, Hugh," she orders, so that Vaynessa will know that she's the kind of mom who raises her kids right. My name is Hugh John David Ambroz, and my mother will start calling me David next year, when an unexpected shift happens. But until age eight, I will be Hugh.

"Hi, Vaynessa," I say, and Mom introduces Jessica and Alex.

Vaynessa's face softens when she looks at us. In all likelihood, she lives in the same neighborhoods we do. Her church is probably one of the ones that feed us between checks. "Hi, sugars, are you hungry?"

I don't know the right answer. Mom has taught us to lie when we're asked questions. After she hits us, she says, "You got this bruise fighting with your brother," feeding us the explanation to give if anyone asks. Giving the wrong answer could ruin everything. The authorities could take us away from Mom, breaking up our family. No matter how bad things get, being separated from my siblings would be worse.

I am very hungry, but Vaynessa might be checking to see if Mom is taking good care of us. I think I'm supposed to say I'm well-fed. But if I say I'm hungry, will she deny us the food stamps? Or do I need to be hungry to get them? I can't tell, so I stay silent.

Vaynessa holds out a bowl of mixed candies, including Reese's Peanut Butter Cups. Nobody ever gives us candy, and here's a whole dish of free candy being held out in front of me. I can smell the chocolate. It's like Halloween. Or is it another test? I look at Mom for permission.

"That's so kind, thank you, Vaynessa. Children, pick one treat," Mom says.

We each take a single piece of candy, careful not to grab.

"Did I say thank you?" Mom asks, making direct eye contact with Vaynessa and smiling. She says this a lot when she's trying to charm people.

Vaynessa looks down at the form in front of her. Pen in hand, she asks, "Are you taking care of these children? Are you feeding them three times a day? When did they last see a doctor? How are their grades? Do they have their own rooms, or do they share?"

I've heard these questions before. Vaynessa is trained to be wary of the people who come to her for help. The system doesn't trust people in poverty. If my mother isn't feeding us, it must be her fault. If she can't support us, it must be because she doesn't care. She must be doing something wrong. She must be shirking her responsibility. This culture of blame makes it harder to get benefits, forcing the needy to look for loopholes and work-arounds. The more we use these tactics, the harder it is to get benefits. The harder it is, the more we connive, and so the system teaches us the very qualities it condemns.

And yet, right now, our survival hangs on the razor's edge of Vaynessa's own mood. Did she get enough sleep last night? Did she have a fight with a loved one? Was her boss mean to her? What if she feels sick today and just wants to be done with us? The subjective nature of this process is our crucible.

Mom's quiet worries me more than Vaynessa's state of mind. She is remarkably still, a placid smile on her face. I'm always afraid that feeling disrespected could set Mom off, and something bad could happen. Is this the eye of the storm? Will having her mothering and work ethic questioned make her explode? I'm protective of her dignity. We need this money. If Vaynessa denies us benefits or, more likely, tells us to come back when we have more paperwork, we will walk away with nothing.

The silence stretches out, and I inch forward to the edge of my chair, ready to intervene. If Mom throws something or yells, I'll shepherd us all out of here before security has time to react.

Then Mom says, "I am taking care of them, Vaynessa," as pleasant as can be. I'm relieved and relax just a bit, sliding back into the scooped seat of the chair. "I try to give them balanced meals," she continues, "but as you can see, they do enjoy sweets too." Mom reaches over and puts her hand on top of Vaynessa's, breaking the unspoken rule that says there is no touching in this environment of us versus them. I'm worried, but then, when Vaynessa doesn't pull away, impressed. Mom is doing this for us.

Then she asks, "Are you a mother, too, Vaynessa?"

Vaynessa says, "Yes, these are my boys." She rotates a picture frame to show us. Now there's a big smile on her face.

"They are so handsome, how old?"

"That's my husband. Our oldest is fourteen, then our middle son is ten, and our youngest is six," she says, gesturing to the image of the husband in the picture.

"I love my children, Vaynessa. I know you understand as a mother," Mom says. She deepens her imploring eyes and rueful smile. "I am looking for work, but I can't find childcare, and the jobs I do find don't pay enough to cover all the bills if I have to hire a babysitter."

"Lord, I know it's hard, and I have help," Vaynessa acknowledges. Her eyes blinking with sympathy, she hands my mother a stack of forms.

"Okay, Ms. Mary. Listen. Take these back to your seats and fill them out. Sign here, here, and here. When you're done, come back to me specifically, okay?" Vaynessa says. Mom has won the social worker over. She's on our side now, and, for the moment, she sees Mom as a person instead of a case. She sees us, and it matters. This victory will keep us alive another day.

Mom smiles broadly, giving Vaynessa's hand one final squeeze.

"Did I say thank you?" Mom asks before getting up to leave.

We wait for four hours. It's unclear why. Maybe Vaynessa took lunch. Maybe she was waiting for someone else's signature. Maybe another case distracted her. Poverty is one long line. We wait at welfare offices, food banks, and shelters. At last, Vaynessa returns and summons us back to her desk. "Mary, this is for the balance of this month and for next. These stamps are for you to buy necessities, not alcohol. There is enough here to get you through the month if you spend it wisely. Here is a pamphlet on healthy eating. Here's a pamphlet on self-care, and here's one on anger management with children. You'll have to come back in and talk to us about your efforts to find work in three weeks. I'm also giving you a rent voucher approval form. When you find a place, you need to get your landlord to sign off and then return this form. It can take a few weeks to process, so make sure your landlord understands this." With a beneficent smile, she hands Mom two manila envelopes, one fatter than the other. "You take care of these kids, Mary, okay?"

"Did I say thank you?" Mom asks again, beaming. Just outside the main office, Mom pulls us into the women's restroom, and into the wheelchair-accessible stall. The powerful flush from the adjacent stall doesn't faze her. She tips the contents of one of the envelopes into her other hand. The food stamps come in neat booklets of different denominations. Mom thumbs through them, doing the math in her head. Her expression is half smile, half grimace. It's not enough. It's never enough. But we won't be hungry tonight. Mom puts the money back in the manila envelope, pulls her shirt up, and tucks the bundle into her bra.

We take a bus to a twenty-four-hour Dunkin' Donuts. The Beetle died on the way from the welfare office, and we abandoned it on the side of the road. Mom orders a coffee that she'll stretch to last days by refilling it with creamers. Jessica, Alex, and I take handfuls of creamers and sugar packets, which we mix and eat for a meal. We've just received food stamps that we could use to buy food, but they'll never be enough. This is a regular part of how and what we eat. Taking up two brown faux-leather booths, we each spread out on a bench for the night. It's not as soft as the car, but stretching my legs feels good, and I sleep well under the fluorescent lights and the hum of the ventilation, feeling the warmth of my mother.

The next morning, Mom circles job listings in the newspaper, then starts making calls from the pay phone outside. I see her laughing and gesturing as she talks to potential employers, her smile stretched wide as if they can see her through the phone line. It works, and on our third day in Albany she lands a job interview. She spends a long time getting clean in the bathroom and comes out fresh, washed, and dressed in her long skirt and jacket. She beckons us to follow and walks briskly out the door.

Later, we are waiting on the sidewalk when she emerges from St. Stephen's Hospital.

"I start work tomorrow," she says. "St. Stephen's is very prestigious." Mom is all smiles and warmth, and we bask in her elation.

"That's awesome, Mom. What will you be doing? I mean, I know you're a nurse, but..." Alex asks.

"They have me filling in right now, but soon I'll be back in the ER," Mom says, beaming. She pulls us all into a clumsy hug. I'm crushed into the softness of her arm and chest. She smells nice—it's the perfume sampler she sprayed on at the pharmacy just before her interview.

"Mom, that's great!" I say into her shoulder. It isn't really great. She's better at getting jobs than she is at keeping them, but I want her mood to last.

"This changes everything. We'll get an apartment, get you into school, get things sorted out this time." Alex and I exchange a knowing look. We've been here before.

"Let's go," she says. We track back and forth on neighborhood streets, scouting out FOR RENT signs. When we find one, Mom rings the super's bell and talks to him while we wait quietly, trying to look neat and respectable. Late that night, when I'm beginning to think we're going to have to sleep at a diner again, the building superintendent leads us up two floors to a one-bedroom apartment. The place is broom swept but not clean. On the rug, round indentations left by furniture legs mark out light rectangles suggesting the rug was once white. There are more rectangles of white on the wall, ghosts of the art that captured other people's imaginations. Some of the windows are still hung with blinds. Mom shows the super a letter from St. Stephen's and promises she'll give him money toward the rent at the end of the week. He gives us a once-over and a nod. It's ours, as is. We have a place to sleep tonight, but I don't believe Mom for a minute when she tells the super she looks forward to "a wonderful year." There is zero chance we'll still be here next year, much less next month. I don't let myself hope for anything beyond tonight.

The super leaves, and we bring in our bags. We don't have much, just some clothes. As always, we open every cabinet and closet to see if anyone has left a treasure—we'd be happy to find a few plates, but we fantasize about forgotten piggy banks or jewels that we could sell. This time, no such luck. Mom attempts to force a window open, but it's stuck. She tries the next, and, with a deep, scratchy sound, it rises. Street noise comes in and, with it, fresh air. Only then do I realize that I've been breathing through my mouth, trying not to inhale the lingering scent of wet towels and garbage that permeates this place.

The only piece of furniture is a fold-out metal chair by the open window. Mom sits down heavily and says, "Hugh, get my purse." I bring the purse to her, and she rummages inside until she finds a crushed pack of cigarettes. Lighting one, she inhales deeply, then blows the smoke toward the open window. It circles back into the room, our family's contribution to the apartment's must and funk.

The next day is trash day, and we hurry out early to start furnishing the apartment. One hundred percent of our resources, whether Mom has a job or we're living off welfare, goes to food and shelter. Everything else has to be found or stolen. When we go through the trash, we're looking for clothes—preferably cleaner than the ones on our backs since laundry is only an occasional luxury. We want basic furnishings—dishes and utensils, pots and pans. If we're lucky, we'll be able to drag home a mattress or chairs.

First, we head to the nearest grocery store and help ourselves to a cart.

"I wanna push it," I whine. Gripping the metal bar firmly in both hands, I roll it forward. Proud to be the one pushing the cart, I veer left to avoid a pedestrian, and one of the wheels dips off the sidewalk.

"I'll do it, Hugh," Mom says. "Here, help me out." She taps the side and I put a hand on one corner. I'm definitely steering. We trudge along the uneven streets until Alex, who's running ahead, directs us to a pile of good trash. It looks like someone was evicted—the contents of their whole apartment have been dumped on the street to be picked over, just as ours will be one day soon. Black plastic bags are piled into treasure mounds studded with bulky items too big for the bags. We are early, and most of the bags are still tied so we know the pickings are good, but we aren't the only lookers. Other people are passing by, hoping for good finds, and some grab specialty items, like electronics or materials that they can resell, but we recognize the ones who are like us, whole families here to look for necessities they would otherwise go without. They are our primary competition, so we quickly divide and conquer to get the best stuff. I spot potential around the corner and hurry toward a box of books. Up close, they turn out to be old books with leather bindings. Mom has taught us all to read. Sometimes she makes us read to her for long stretches without stopping. I can't always follow the story, but I like how it calms her. I want all of the books, but we need to save room in the cart for practical items, so I settle for one, *Moby Dick*, which I tuck under my arm. I know better than to get too excited about any find, and we never get attached. We went through this back in January, and a few months before that. When we move again, we will leave our treasures behind. The book in the cart might prove interesting or be so mildewed that it's unreadable, but the one thing I know for sure is that I won't get to keep it.

Mom comes up beside me and unearths the long stem of a standing lamp. "Nice," she declares. There is no shade, but the stem is ornate, and a bulb is still in its socket. It's not a necessity—the apartment already has overhead lighting—but she deems it valuable, so into the cart it goes.

"This might be good," Alex notes as he pulls out a small television. Alex is drawn to electronics—radios, TVs, small appliances. He seems to have a sixth sense as to whether something still works. This one has a cracked white box that has been duct-taped back together. "The tape looks old, so maybe they used it like this until they got a better one. Let's try it out at home." Alex heaves it into the cart. Like me, he isn't excited, even at the prospect of a working TV. This is what we do. This is how we furnish an apartment. If we're still there next week, we might be back for more. Or Mom will have another plan for us that day. Or we'll be on the move again and leave it all behind. There is no rhythm or predictability to our days.

Tearing into the side of a bag, Jessica sorts through clothes and holds up a blue sweater. "Hugh, this will fit you." She tosses it to me, and I hold it up to my front. Close enough. I take a whiff, deem it acceptable, and put it on.

A few weeks later, we've just arrived home from St. Stephen's hospital and are in the lot of our building when I hear someone yell, "Fucking piece of white trash. Are all those kids yours?"

The voice is coming from a slowly moving cop car. The car's lights are flashing, but there is no siren.

"Go inside, right now. Go!" Mom whispers urgently.

I've seen the drunk men in uniform before. Sometimes it's the police, sometimes it's firemen. On weekend nights, they stumble past sloppily, shouting curses, dirty words, and racial slurs, whatever they can think of, "fuck you this, fuck you that." They hate us and all our neighbors because we're poor. I'm ashamed because they're right—we're dirty and helpless. But I'm also angry because I already know I don't want this to be who I am, but I have no power to do anything about it. Can't they see that?

"Go, now. Hugh, take them inside. Go!" Mom hisses again. But Jessica, Alex, and I stay where we are. We don't want to leave her. We're a pack, and packs stick together.

The car swerves to the right and stops. Two cops emerge, and Mom turns to face them. She is wearing her white nursing uniform. Her arms are out from her sides, palms forward. She doesn't want a fight.

"Why'd ya tell 'em to run? What do you got to hide, huh? Fucking piece of shit. How many more you got at home? I bet a bunch. What do you think?" he asks his partner. "Three? Four? Like fucking rats! Just sucking off welfare. Why'd ya tell them to run?"

"I'm sorry, it's late and they should be inside already. I just got home from work," Mom states calmly.

"You are fucking lying," he says with disgust. He strides toward her and gets in her face. "One. More. Time. Why'd you tell your trash children to run? Don't lie to me. It's a crime to lie."

"You seemed angry, and I thought I could talk to you. I didn't want them to bother you while we talked."

He rotates his body like he's about to swing a baseball bat, then whips around, connecting the back of his hand with my mother's face.

Slap.

The sound of the officer hitting my mother ripples through my body. On contact, Mom stumbles backward but doesn't fall.

"Run *now*, fucking run," Mom commands. We retreat backward into the shadows on the periphery of the parking lot, but we still don't leave.

"Stupid lying cunt," the officer says. Suddenly, he grabs Mom by the hair and shoves her against the back of his car.

Our mother has hit us countless times, but I've never seen anyone hit her. Shame, anger, and the instinct to protect my mother combine and combust. Running from the side, I lunge at him.

"Stop! Stop! *Stop!*" I scream. My voice sounds small and powerless, even to my own ears. The second officer swats me away, his hand connecting with my face. I fly backward and land on the ground, the wind knocked out of me.

"Fucking lying piece of shit," the first officer yells as he continues to slap my mother. Her back is against the car, in front of the passenger-side door. There is blood on her white uniform. Near their tangle of legs, I see the Albany Police Department logo emblazoned on the car. My sister is screaming, and faces appear on balconies and in windows. They all see, but I don't expect them to help. What are they going to do, call the cops? I remember, soon after we moved in, the police responded to a neighbor couple who were fighting, screams and crashes echoing through the building. They dragged both the husband and wife out, thrashing them about like rag dolls. We were the ones watching out the window that time, unable to understand what was happening or why. In the neighborhoods where we live— the poor neighborhoods—the cops are always a presence. They feel like an occupying force. I don't think of them as people who want to help me or protect me. I think they want to scare us—either to flex their power or to feel like the neighborhood is under their control.

"Okay, okay, enough. Let's go," the second officer bellows at his partner, putting a hand on his shoulder.

"Get the fuck off my car." The first officer yanks Mom's arm and kicks her in the ass. She lands near me.

I crawl toward her as she slowly pulls herself upright. Back in his squad car, the violent cop looks out the window. He's not done with her yet. He coughs and then, *thwap!* He hocks a loogie at her. It lands on her chest. She looks down, then at the cop. She silently meets his gaze, and I feel momentarily proud of the defiance I see in her eyes. She is unbroken. The car drives away into the night. What just happened?

"Come on, Alex, help your brother up. Jessica, let's go upstairs," Mom instructs. Inside, she cleans herself up, standing at the bathroom sink for a long time. Eventually, she lies down on the used mattress that we salvaged from the trash pile. It sighs under the weight of her body and her distress. Closing the bedroom door behind me, I turn to my siblings.

"Let's go out back. Mom needs quiet." Mom is a tinderbox under any circumstances. We're always careful not to trigger her, and there's no telling how she'll react to this incident. We need to get out of here before we find out.

Behind our building is a run-down playground. We climb to the top of a metal geodesic dome and perch there, shell-shocked. Our lives usually move too quickly for reflection, but this horrific reversal means something, and we're trying to make sense of it. Did Mom do something? Say something to set them off?

"She didn't say a word to them. They just attacked her," Jessica says.

"That's what Mom does to us," Alex says quietly.

"It's not the same," Jessica replies.

"Yeah, it is," I say. There's a long pause. She's our mother. And though she hurts us, we have no doubt that she loves us. Those men had only hatred for her.

"Well, those were *cops*," Alex says. He has a strong street sense of right and wrong. If someone drops something, even if it's just a coin, he runs after them to return it. When we shoplift, he makes sure we don't take too much from any one store. He always tries to do the right thing or the closest he can manage. In his mind, the police are supposed to be the heroes, the saviors. He's already seen evidence contradicting this, but today was absolute proof that they are just as unpredictable and violent as our mom.

We linger on the cold metal bars of the dome, silently watching the darkness descend. Huge, crime-deterring spotlights shine from the corners of the yard, blindingly bright in some areas and casting deep shadows in others. Tall, skeletal monkey bars loom over the blacktop. Nearby, ride-on animals mounted on big springs have half lost their paint, and their grotesque faces leer in the darkness. We stay until we become silhouettes high against the sky, our features and thoughts lost to the night.

Creeping back into the apartment, we are relieved to find Mom asleep, her breathing quiet and regular. She is still wearing her uniform, her white stockings ripped.

"Let's clean this place up," Jessica whispers to Alex. There is temporary peace, and we want to preserve it.

"I'll get cigarettes," I suggest. There is no money, but I'll manage.

For days after that, the mom who landed a job and found us an apartment is gone. Her shadow stays in bed. Her eyes don't see us, and we know not to provoke her.

One day, finally, she gets out of bed and takes a shower. When she emerges, fully dressed for the first time in a week, I quietly ask, "Mom, are you going to work?" She hasn't been back to her nursing job at St. Stephen's since the attack.

She points to her eye, where a shiner has faded from black to blossoms of purple and amber. "I'm a nurse. I can't show up like this."

It's another week before I can convince her she looks better and should return to work. Jessica and Alex have started school, even though the year is almost over, so I'm the only one who accompanies Mom back to the hospital. I'm relieved that she's returning to work. The super knocked on the door last night asking for money, and I know this means we'll be able to pay him.

"Stay here," she says when we get to the waiting room. I nod and sit. I am a pro at this. Waiting is one of my best skills. When Alex waits, he can't keep still. He pokes me and harasses me, energy wiggling out of his fingertips. But when I'm alone, I watch and learn.

The ER at St. Stephen's has hard seats and aggressively ugly beige-purple prints on the walls. It smells like ammonia and vomit. The only entertainment is years-old *Reader's Digest* and *Highlights* magazines, a coffee machine, and a snack machine with shiny, alluring Hostess cupcakes. I fill up on creamers, and every so often I slip into the gift shop attempting to steal a four-piece Whitman's Sampler. I know the flavors it comes with by heart from reading the key in the lid: milk chocolate butter cream, milk chocolate caramel, milk chocolate "Messenger Boy," and dark chocolate coconut.

The ER is crowded, and whenever the automatic sliding doors rattle in their tracks, every neck swivels to triage the new arrival. Some of the patients are kids. Mothers with worried faces hold them on their laps, hugging them and checking their foreheads for fevers. Mom's a nurse but I wonder what it would be like for another adult—a professional—to notice us, to check and see if we're okay. There is something absent in Mom's love for us. I blame her sickness, and when I long for that kind of attention, the person I want it from most is her.

Not enough time has passed when Mom comes back through the door to the waiting room. Something is wrong. I recognize the look on her face. This is the mom who is capable of understanding that we are in trouble.

"They fired me." She takes me by the hand and leads me out the door. I'm not shocked. I don't ask her why. I'm pretty sure that this time it's because she never called in to explain why she was staying home from work. She would never admit she was attacked by cops, and, besides, we don't have a phone. The apartment, the job, the food—it felt like we had risen from underwater to take that two-second gasp of oxygen. We needed it, we gulped it hungrily, but here we are drowning again.

I have a good idea of what comes next. When Mom is employed in any capacity, we are in much better shape than when there is no money for cigarettes, no schedule to follow, no tie to the outside world. Mom's clarity and fear will give way to depression and delusion. Then she might turn her anger and dismay toward us, and we'll have to dodge her blows. At some point she'll get into bed and stay there, smoking in silence. We'll run out of money for food and cigarettes. And then we'll get evicted. What I don't know is that this is the beginning of a slide from poverty to disaster, from manageable to chaos. That's ahead, but right now her family is in trouble, and she cares. She leads me across the street and straight into a dark Irish pub. We sit down on barstools. I quickly discover that my stool swivels, and I'm tempted to push off the bar and get it spinning. I want to go so fast that the room blurs and I can't see Mom and don't have to worry about what she'll do next. But playing on the stool would make her mad, so I twist back and forth in place, slowly, restrained, careful not to brush her knee.

"A finger of whiskey," Mom tells the bartender. Mom never drinks. It's hard to say why she is doing so now. Maybe she knows like I do that there is no place to turn for help.

"We are going to be fine, okay?" Mom says.

"I know, Mom," I reply, but I can hear the fear in her voice, and it scares me. Maybe this time is different. Maybe it's worse.

"I've got twenty-plus years of nursing experience; I'll find another job," she adds, more to herself than me. She sips at the pour, then we walk down the hill to our apartment. She grasps my hand tightly.

Mom returns to her bed, half-wrapped in a toga made from a bedsheet. She stares vacantly at the walls. She chain-smokes, using anything and everything as an ashtray and, in spite of my efforts to pace her, quickly runs through our whole stash of cigarettes.

"Hugh, where are my cigarettes?"

"I'll get them, Mom," I lie. Under no circumstances do we tell Mom there are no more cigarettes.

A moment later, I carefully venture, "I'm going to the store, Mom. I'm going to get fresh ones, okay?" I just want to keep her calm.

"Marlboros" is all she says. I check to make sure Alex is occupied. If he's got energy, he bounces off the walls and it could set Mom off. But he's busy with the TV antenna, still trying to get a picture.

From her purse, I pull the coupon book of food stamps. Flipping through it, I notice there aren't very many left. I bend the book and hide it in my sock, wrapped around my ankle.

Since I can't buy cigarettes with food stamps, I'll have to cash them for change. The upside to this is that it means I can buy a few cheap items for myself. At the grocery store, I grab a caramel from the clear plastic self-serve containers, make my way to the register, put the lonely caramel on the black rubber grocery conveyor belt, place the separator behind it, and withdraw the book of food stamps.

These stamps are the only "money" we have. They are pale beige with dark gray print. Neutral tones, but blatantly not the color of money as if to publicly shame the users. When I use them, I feel like everyone knows I'm poor. Waiting in line, I look down at them. Each ticket reads "Enjoy all foods, just don't overdo it! It takes 20 minutes for your brain to send the signal that you've had enough to eat." The benefits fluctuate, but no matter how much we are given, it is never enough. The quantity they give our family of four can barely feed two people, even if we weren't spending some of it on the cigarettes. Mom shouldn't use food stamps to buy cigarettes, but she's been smoking since she was thirteen, and it's hard to quit a habit like that when your life is unstable and stressful. In line in front of me is a skinny young mother with a baby on her hip and a small child holding her hand. Like me, she is gaming the system. She uses her stamps to buy a single banana, cashing them out so she can pay rent, or get her child a backpack, or get money for any number of things that she isn't allowed to buy with stamps. We stretch each coupon in all directions, as far as it can go.

I'm relieved when the clerk barely looks at me. "That's a nickel." I hand over my food stamp, collect my ninety-five cents change, walk out of the store, and then turn around and come right back in as if I forgot something. I don't know if cashing out is illegal, but I try to hide it just in case. I buy another five-cent item and get another ninety-five cents in change. Now I have enough cash to buy cigarettes at the gas station, where they won't care that I'm underage.

On the way, I glimpse a half-smoked cigarette in the shadow of a trash bin. I scoop it up, brush off the burned bit, and examine the small writing—Camel. Not her favorite, but still useful.

With Mom holed up in the apartment, we spend the first weeks of summer on the stoops of our neighborhood.

"Yessica, girl, get over here," Lissa calls out. Her white short-sleeved shirt is cut off to expose her smooth tan belly. Kids crowd the wide brown stairs in front of the five-story walk-up where she lives. It's a warm night, and the air feels like it's shouldering the exhaust of the whole day's traffic. Music from different stoops thrums and clashes.

"Get the *fuck* off my steps," the neighboring second-floor tenant yells out her window.

"Bitch, shut up, we ain't on your steps anyway," Karl hollers back.

"Karl, forget it," Roberto intervenes, and I can see he's like me, trying to de-escalate. Roberto is the tallest of the group, with dark black hair, deep brown eyes, and full maroon lips. Something about him endlessly draws my eyes toward him. As he talks, occasionally slipping Spanish words into his speech, I take the opportunity to more fully examine the way he fills out his well-worn Lee jeans, how the sleeves of his black T-shirt tighten around his arms, the barest hint of a mustache. I think he's beautiful.

"Garbage, a garbage people. Stay away from him," Mom says about Roberto, and I know she's talking about all Black and brown people. Her frequent racist remarks and delusions stand in stark contrast to what I see in our neighborhood and my friends. Their parents look out for them and sometimes for us when Mom is nowhere to be found. Staring hard at Roberto as he commands the group, I reject Mom's instruction.

Roberto yells, *"Ghetto tag!"* and the trash talk is instantly forgotten. We spring to our feet. The radio drops out. "Stay on the block, and no roofs, *Denise*, that's cheating," Roberto orders. "Stay on the block, everything else is fair game. I'll start. Go get your asses hid."

Ghetto tag is more hide-and-seek than tag. We all bolt, scrambling for hiding spots on the square of streets that make up our block. I pause to consider an abandoned basement-level apartment entrance but reject it—too obvious. It's the first place Roberto will look.

"Bro, there," Alex says, pointing toward a dumpster. It's got one wheel on the curb, so technically it's ambiguous if it's "on the block," but the two of us hop in.

"Alex, this is gross—"

"Shhh. Get a few bags on top of you in case they open the lid."

"Alex—"

"Shut up and dig."

It's dark in the dumpster. The black plastic bags muffle the outside world. I poke one. It's squishy with trash juice.

"Got you, Karl!"

"Rachel, you're safe!"

"Come on," I tell Alex. "I think we won."

"Stay down!" he insists. We stay in the dumpster until the street goes quiet.

Finally, Jessica calls out, "Are you guys still hiding?" and we climb to the top and push our way out. A bag ruptures and my arm is sprayed with a putrid brown liquid. The rest of the kids have gone in for dinner. Jessica wrinkles her nose when we get near. "You stink!"

"We know," Alex says.

"At least we won," I say.

"We killed it," Alex says, and we both crack up, knowing it wasn't worth it.

"I told you to stay away from them. You are better than that," Mom admonishes as we walk into the apartment, still reeking. "You should be focused on schoolwork and learning. Not out with those people," she says, despite it being summer and that we are rarely enrolled anyway. Then she looks at me directly, and says, "And you, honestly, it's disgusting. I don't want to see you on the same block as Roberto, do you understand me? Following him like a fag." The word hangs there, and I stand frozen, not sure what it means. I don't know if I should defend Roberto, pretend I don't know whom she's talking about, or deny her accusation.

The moment passes, but we avoid our friends for the next few weeks, maybe a month, until the day Mom says to us, "I know they are watching. We're leaving."

"Who, Mom?" I ask, somewhat belligerently. I don't want to go.

"Don't be stupid, Hugh." She's right. I know better than to ask her questions.

"The tape is gone. They've been here already. We don't have much time."

Alex and I glance at each other. Wherever we stay, Mom puts a piece of tape at the base of the front door when we go out. If it's not firmly in place when we return, that means the apartment has been searched by the CIA or some other organization. She reuses the tape, and the older it gets, the more likely it is to slip out of place. When it moves, we move.

We are leaving four walls and a roof and walking into homelessness again. I'm not happy to leave, but I never expected to be here long. It's hard to feel attached to any of the places we stay. In this apartment building, for instance, the light has been out in the hallway since we moved in. It's a dark and scary passage, smelling of cigarettes, dried urine, and misery. When I open the door to the garbage room to hurl in a bag, roaches scatter. The man in the apartment next door is disheveled and stares at me uncomfortably hard when I pass. One of our neighbors screams at night.

When Mom says we're leaving, she means *now*. I grab a white plastic

Price Chopper grocery bag and throw in essentials: food, the cigarette supply that I've hidden, and my current stash of salvaged treasures—some coins, a crow's feather, a shiny rock, a pair of argyle socks. I leave *Moby Dick*. Jessica hangs on to a hairbrush. We know better than to take anything heavy. We'll be carrying these bags for a long time. Mom herself gathers six or seven bags that twist around her fingers, turning them purple.

The plastic bags are all we have. The friends we made on the stoop won't remember our names; the schools won't follow up on Alex's and Jessica's brief attendance. River Street could have been a place I called home, could have been where I started going to school. Roberto and I could have grown up as neighbors, and I could have come to understand what I was feeling about him. I don't dwell on those thoughts. I focus on what we need right now. Tomorrow is unknown, unknowable, and uncertain. *Now* is all that exists. It is a hard-wiring of my brain. I live in a cycle: homelessness, hunger, housing, welfare, and homelessness again. Escape requires planning for the future. It requires believing in a future. Surrounding me is the chaos that haunts my mother, the welfare system that doubts and denies, authorities who hate or ignore us—that's all. I see escape and safety in Roberto's world. He's clean. He eats. He smiles. His mother keeps track of where he is. He lives in one place. I'm pretty sure he attends school. He doesn't seem to be abused. His world is out of reach to me. What Mom is doing won't get me there. But I've had a glimpse of what I want, one day when I can look beyond today. I don't know what I can do to make my way there, but I'm going to figure it out.

Chapter 3

I'LL BE STARTING STORY TIME in five minutes," the librarian says, tapping my shoulder. "I hope you'll come listen." I startle awake—I've been dozing while Mom is out looking for a place for us to sleep, at least for a night—but then Alex and I trot over to the children's section and sit down cross-legged in front of the librarian. The reading corner is decorated with a colorful mural of knockoff *Sesame Street* characters, beanbag chairs, and kid-sized tables and chairs. The librarian sits in front, hands crossed on top of the book in her lap, waiting while parents walk their children over.

"I'll be sitting right there," a mom says to her son, and points to a table. "Give me your jacket." She holds the collar of his winter coat while he shakes his arm out.

"Can I have a snack?" he asks.

"After the reading we'll get hot chocolate," she says. I observe this exchange like an alien collecting data about another planet. Children have winter coats. Their mothers hover nearby, keeping watch. Food is provided. Before she walks away, I see the mom glance at me. She quickly looks away, but not before I glimpse a mix of pity and disgust in her eyes. My fingernails are crescent moons of dirt. I'm wearing shorts in spite of the weather.

"Okay, shall we begin? Has anyone read *Where the Sidewalk Ends*? It's a book of short poems. They're clever and simple, but I will go slow. Raise your hand if you have questions." The librarian licks her finger, uses it to turn the page, and begins. Her voice is warm and melodic, and I quickly forget the hot chocolate boy and how his mother looked at me.

When the librarian finishes, Shel Silverstein's world telescopes into the distance and vanishes. I look down at my filthy nails and remember what I wanted to do. I go into the library bathroom, yank a paper towel out of the dispenser, wet it with soap and water, and begin to clean myself. The mirror is low, and I can see my face and hands emerging from the gray filth. I take a fresh wad of paper towels into the stall and clean the rest of my body.

"It's two o'clock," Jessica says when I emerge. "People should be just finishing lunch."

"Let's get pizza!" Alex says, taking her point.

We often collect food from the garbage, but we don't just dive into any old dumpster. Back-alley dumpsters are full of maggots and foul, unidentifiable substances. As far back as I can remember, we've known where, when, and how to look. This knowledge was passed down to us from Mom and everyone around us like folktales, and I learned the hard way not to deviate from the rules. One evening, a promising mound lured me down a dark, dank alley (rule number one: stick to daylight). I promised myself I'd just take a cursory look and go get Alex or Jess if there was anything good. I turned off the main street (rule number two: stay on main streets) and went up to the overflowing dumpster. There were bags of clothes, furniture, and books! Clearly, this was an eviction. I closed in on the books, losing track of my surroundings (rule number three: stay alert).

"Hello," a man said from behind me, his hand touching my

shoulder. I pivoted around, ducked under his arm, and ran straight back out toward the sidewalk. His laugh followed me as I rounded the corner. I never broke the rules again. At least not all of them at the same time.

The rules also call for targeting fresh garbage that is likely to be free of drug paraphernalia. The best food waste comes from grocery stores and restaurants. We cross the street and see a pizza joint we've been to before. "It's not empty yet," I say, meaning they haven't changed out the lunchtime trash. This particular place is tricky—the trash is in front, right outside the entrance. We don't want the staff to bust us and shoo us away. But the windows are plastered with enough stickers, signs, and faded newspaper articles that it should be hard for the employees to see out.

"Stay here," Jessica instructs as she ducks in to scope out how busy the place is.

The trash bin is a large one, with a black plastic bag coming up and over the edges. Even from where I'm standing, I can tell there are plenty of white paper plates and discarded pizza remnants.

Jessica returns. "It's empty, we're fine. Hugh, stay there," she says, pointing. "Block from that angle. Alex, it's your turn."

"Okay, here I go," Alex says. His job is to focus on pizza or calzones, no hunting around, and no drinks because the priority is food, and we need it soon. He's in and out of the bin in a flash. Store owners hate scavengers, and we want the option to return. We scoot around the corner and spread out on the staircase of a brownstone.

"Here," Alex says, handing me and then Jessica a few pizza crusts each. Then he gives me about one-third of a calzone.

"Fuckin' A! Good job, bro," I say. The best crusts are those where people have left little triangles with cheese and sauce between the semicircles of their bites. Today, each crust has ample cheese and sauce remnants.

"Hugh, don't lick your fingers. That's disgusting. And don't wipe

A PLACE CALLED HOME

them on your pants," Jessica instructs. Those being my only two options for cleaning my hands, I'm not really sure what to do.

We return to the library, and hours later, when it closes, we wait in the entrance alcove until Mom shows up.

"This way," she says. "We're going to United Methodist."

"Movie Night!" Alex exclaims, and Mom nods and smiles. We are regulars at Movie Night, a weekly event for the homeless and the poor hosted in the basement of the United Methodist church. We don't care what movie is playing because it's warm and there's always food.

United Methodist is a stately Romanesque building soaring up to the winter stars, its bell tower impossibly high. It occupies an entire city block in a once-noble section of the city. This evening the snow has been pushed from the sidewalk to form a steep slope against its outside walls, making it look like a scene from a Christmas card.

After the movie, Mom comes up to us with Pastor Franklin, Pastor Tammah, and Mrs. Morgan. The Morgans are a family that helps run Movie Night. I think Mrs. Morgan might be the one who chooses the movies. When she's serving food, she always heaps a generous portion on my plate. Now she has a broad grin on her face. The pastors look pleased too.

"We're going to be staying here at the church for a while," Mom tells us. "Did I say thank you?" she asks the pastors and Mrs. Morgan. "This is very generous of you."

The high ceilings of the church make it drafty, but even its chilliest chapels are warmer than outside. Pastor Tammah and Mrs. Morgan bring us to the rectory wing and lead us down a long hallway.

"It's not much, but I hope you'll be comfortable," Pastor Tammah says, opening the door to a long, narrow storage room, a space between spaces. I've passed this room before and seen it full of extra furniture and supplies. Now it will store us. It's been cleared out and there are four neatly made cots placed against the side walls. Some

35

chairs, linens, and flatware for church events still lean against the farthest wall.

Mrs. Morgan gives us instructions without making eye contact with any of us. "You can use the bathroom across the hall," she says, bending down and smoothing out the bedding. "And for showers you can use the bathroom just down the hall in the pastor's office. Now come into the kitchen—this cabinet is just for you. We'll stock it with the same food and supplies we distribute on Thursdays."

Then Pastor Tammah asks about putting us in school. "Oh, I'm so glad you mention it," my mother says. She names one of the local public schools. "It's a wonderful school. The principal is a friend of mine. They offer violin!" She acts like she is in the process of enrolling us and that it's a huge priority for her. She's lying, but she probably believes herself. Pastor Tammah is satisfied.

They leave us to get settled, and we have the run of the rectory. It feels like we have backstage passes. After hours, when everyone else is gone, we can take showers as often as we like. Our hallways have stained glass windows. My sister plays "Chopsticks" on the piano, practicing what we've been taught in Sunday school. Best of all, we have unlimited access to the free donuts that accompany every church event.

It is nearly Christmas. During Sunday school all three classes gather in the multipurpose room, and the Christmas pageant committee comes in to speak to us.

"Listen up, kids. We are going to assign the parts, and then you'll get your lines and head over to Mrs. Richter to get fitted for your costumes. You don't get to take home your costumes, we just want to make sure everything fits. Everyone gets a part, and every part is important," Mrs. Morgan says.

Well, that's a big-ass lie, I think, hoping to be a wise man, or

Joseph. We've learned the Christmas story in Sunday school. Joseph and Mary are forced to travel because an unreasonable bureaucracy requires them to. They have no place to stay and are taking refuge wherever they can find it. The parallels are not lost on me—my manger is a cot in a closet. But then the parable takes a twist, where gifts and salvation are delivered only if you're the son of God. Which means I'm fucked. I'm the son of a very different Mary. Still, I feel personally connected to the story, and also, for no reason, I think I'm an excellent actor. I wait expectantly for them to ask us to raise hands for the parts we want. I practice channeling Joseph's saintly calm.

But then Mrs. Morgan says, "Okay, let's see. Seth Morgan, you are our Joseph." She hugs her son when she hands him his script.

"May Jones, we'll have you as our beloved Mary," Mrs. Morgan continues. It goes on like this, and kids file through, collecting scripts and trying on costumes.

"Hugh, you'll be Shepherd Number Three, and you don't have to worry about learning any lines," Mrs. Morgan says brightly, extinguishing my hope to be one of the wise men. Disappointed, I trudge across the room to the costume racks. Mrs. Richter notices my reaction and kneels down next to me.

"Honey, we'll make sure you are in the front. And you get the shepherd's staff. You'll stand out, sweetie."

"Jessica, you'll be a villager and observer. Alex, you're a shepherd too. You'll get to be with your brother." Mrs. Morgan smiles with genuine warmth. Neither Alex nor Jessica particularly cares, but I wanted a big part. I wanted to be seen, to perform, to be important. I hold back tears as Mrs. Richter pulls the heavy brown canvas costume over my head and arms.

In Sunday school classes leading up to the performance, we rehearse. Then, on Christmas Eve, all the kids gather in the wide hallway that leads to our storage room, using it as a makeshift dressing room. A cacophony of excited voices and nerves echoes off the hard surfaces. I put on my shepherd costume. It feels like sandpaper. My wooden staff is two feet taller than I am.

"I'm itchy," I whisper to Alex. He's in an identical costume, except his ends at his knees and he doesn't get a staff.

"At least you're not cold. Let me hold it," he says, reaching for my staff.

"Fuck off," I say, holding it behind my back.

The line begins to rustle, and I'm moved to the front, part of a small group that will "clear the way and set the tone," as Mrs. Morgan puts it. She gives me a gentle shove. "Okay, Hugh, you are leading the way for Baby Jesus."

We shuffle down the hallway, through the rectory, and then into the sanctuary. I hold my staff high, pointing the way. "Hugh, honey, you aren't Moses, parting the Red Sea. Just use it as a walking stick. Keep it on the ground," Mrs. Morgan instructs gently.

The swinging doors open; I'm standing in the middle of the doorway. I stare straight ahead, up the aisle to the "stage," where the manger scene is set. I don't have a single line, but this is my moment. I walk down the church aisle, slow and deliberate, with all the import of a bride approaching the altar.

The stage has been transformed with bales of hay and life-sized plastic animals. The hay smells pleasantly musty. I head to my left and complete the turn to face the congregation. I'm supposed to stand in place, looking stern and occasionally moving my head to bring the character to life. I follow these instructions with all the gravitas I can muster, planting my staff and dramatically turning this way and that as the story unfurls.

Alex and Jessica are part of the voiceless menagerie on the opposite side of the stage. I try to get their attention, but I don't think they're having as much fun as I am. They're both staring down at the stage floor. Looking out, I scan for Mom and locate her, beaming at me from the third row center. She mouths, "I love you," and, without breaking character, I give her a huge shepherd grin.

After the last wise man has laid his gifts in front of the manger, Mary, Baby Jesus, and Joseph lead the cast out, followed by the three wise men, and then all the other bit players. First in, I'm the last out. The congregation is singing "O Holy Night." I float down the steps, peeking left to get another glimpse of Mom. She is still smiling. I want to stay serious, but I can't help returning her smile, and once we disperse, I hurry to find her.

Retracing our same steps, we ditch our costumes in the hallway and run over to the reception, which is in the enormous assembly hall, adjacent to the sanctuary. Mom finds me before I find her. As she hugs me, we are approached by a pack of adults with their kids.

"Great job, Hugh, you stole the show," one woman says. Then she and my mother drone on and on just a couple of feet above my eye level. Meanwhile, at kid level, it's a dog-eat-dog world.

"You're It, no tag backs!" Seth Morgan calls, tagging his sister overenthusiastically. She stumbles, then starts chasing Jessica.

When we play tag in the neighborhoods where we fit in, it's every kid for themself. But here my siblings and I stand out. We're the only poor kids. We live in the storage closet. We know we're different, and they know it too.

"Get those gross kids," says a kid I've never met.

My sneakers are way too big. I'm wearing a men's button-down shirt, blue with red stripes, the too-long sleeves rolled up, and too-big pants. Still, I give chase to the others, especially Seth Morgan, who has now changed out of his Joseph robes into pressed khakis, a white shirt, a blue blazer, and loafers, all well-fitting. I watched the Morgans, well-fed and warm, arrive tonight in their black Saab, perfect and disgusting. I want to be part of that family. In every gesture they make I see the home that waits for them, cozy and clean, full of toys and clothes and food, a place they take for granted. It comes with two parents, a mom and a dad, grown-ups who provide breakfast every single morning and hurry them off to school. I envy the Morgans, and I hate them for having what I want. So I chase Seth Morgan, because his existence is the opposite of mine, and he deserves to be tagged out for it.

Unlike the other kids, my siblings and I have a side game going. I dart away from the kid who's It and dive under the snack table, on top of which there are Dunkin' Donuts Munchkins, all different flavors, hundreds stacked like gold bars in a vault. A Christmas miracle. I don't know how many we're allowed to take, but the adults don't seem to notice my hand sneaking out from under the banquet table.

Pockets stuffed with Munchkins, my next stop is the coat rack, where I dive into the soft wool and rifle through the pockets. I find cigarettes, money clips, condoms, butterscotch candies, receipts, and plenty of dollar bills. Church is a good place to steal. They talk about helping the poor in our Sunday school lessons, and I'm poor, so it's almost like they've already forgiven me for taking their money.

"Hugh, Alex, Jessica, it's time to go," I hear my mother call, and I immediately obey. She's wearing a tight, donated dress. A statement cross on a thick chain dangles past her ample chest, suspended in midair below it. Her short hair pokes out from under a broad hat, a frosted blond color that comes in a box. I've seen her apply the dye in more than one public bathroom. I know my mother doesn't fit in. I can't imagine any of us ever will.

All the kids are being summoned by their parents, and one by one, they leave the church. I watch the Morgans put on their coats and hats, Mrs. Morgan tightening her daughter's scarf against the night air. Everyone except us is getting into their cars. They are all going to homes with full pantries and Christmas trees and family photos and tightly made beds. The frivolity and laughter and Munchkins and carols dwindle into the night, and the life drains out of the church, leaving it hollow and cold. The last child I see is a little girl with fat chestnut braids. While her father tries to get her arms into her winter coat, she points up at the window and the starry sky beyond. "But I want to see Santa!" she cries. "You promised he would come if I did good tonight!" Her pleading fades as they usher her outside.

It's a lie, I want to tell her. *I've been good and it doesn't matter. There's no Santa.*

We say good night to the janitor and return to our closet.

Christmas morning in our room is startlingly cold. There are no windows, but Alex goes to investigate, and when he comes back, he says, "There's snow. Let's go sledding."

"Bring me back cigarettes," Mom says. We put on all of our clothes and walk down the hallway to the bathroom.

"Hold this," Alex says, handing me the triangular top of the trash bin. It's a swinging lid that reminds me of a seesaw. I rock it to make it swing.

"Seriously, cut it out. Give it back to me," Alex orders. He lifts the half-full garbage bag out of the can. "Score!" At the bottom of the can, the janitor has left a few new black garbage bags. We take one each and walk out to the adjacent park. We are not the only ones with makeshift sleds today—I see trash can lids, cardboard, and flat pieces I can't really identify. Poverty is the mother of invention.

Some of the kids in the park are well equipped. "What the hell is that?" I ask Jessica.

"It's a toboggan, a kind of sled. It's old-school," she responds. The toboggan doesn't go far or fast. The device itself seems poorly designed, and the kids on it quickly topple over.

I see a trio of kids wearing matching snowsuits in different colors. Their boots come up midcalf. I point them out to Alex. "They look ridiculous," I say unconvincingly. I think it would be really fun to match Alex and Jessica.

Alex just says, "Whatever, let's go."

As I watch, each of the matching kids climbs onto their own red saucer with yellow handles, lined up to race. "Ready, set, go!" Their gloved hands grip the handles, and they shoot down the hill, fast and elegant.

"Come on, let's do it. Jess, you first. Get a running start." Alex is in charge. I have one eye on Jess, but the other is on those kids, now making their way back up the hill.

"No, let's go together," Jessica suggests. We walk up to the precipice.

"*One, two, three!*" Alex yells, and we run and jump onto our garbage bags. We fly out and over the hill. Alex manages to land on his butt, while Jessica and I belly dive face-first. We laugh a little too loud to prove we are having just as much fun as the kids on the red saucers.

At the bottom, we smile at each other, brush the snow off ourselves, and walk back up together. My sneakers are already soaked through. As we climb, the three "perfects" sail back down on their saucers, spinning and giggling. The world belongs to people like these three, like the Morgans, and like the little boy at story time in the library. I wonder why I don't get to be a part of it and whether I ever will be.

Then, not long into the New Year, a parishioner, Lee Robinson, takes me aside and says, "Can I ask you a question? Would you like to go to sleepaway camp?" Lee and his wife, Sarah, are always kind to us. Lee is a deacon of the church, and they don't have children. They make a point to ask how we are and to chat with Mom. They remind me of the Sicilian grandmother who runs a bakery and sandwich shop called Carousel's that's around the corner from United Methodist. She's four feet tall in heels. There, Mom runs a "tab," and the proprietress lets us order our pick of Italian sandwiches stuffed with meat, shredded lettuce, and plenty of condiments. For dessert we have napoleons.

"I'll pay you back," my mother always says.

"We got you, Mary," the woman answers, instinctively knowing how important it is to my mother to maintain her dignity.

There are just enough moments of grace like these—being seen by the Robinsons and the Sicilian grandmother, being recognized as worthy of going to camp or ordering the kind of sandwich that I myself choose—to sustain us. Not only that, they always seem to come when I need them most. When I'm hungriest or coldest, a hand comes forward, and with it comes more than relief for the suffering of the moment. There is a message in these kindnesses that tells me there's the possibility for a better life: *You matter. We care. You are worthy.* Once I figured out that these adults existed, I started keeping an eye out for them. While they are predisposed to be kind toward kids, I've figured out how to motivate them from sympathy to action. I ask them questions like: "Do you think Governor Cuomo should run for president?" Being smart and witty seems to get me more attention and support from these angels.

That summer, with the help of United Methodist and some of those caring adults, we go to Camp Hebron, a Christian camp. Lee and Sarah Robinson drive us there. I'm going to be a kid like the other kids for a whole week.

We rise to the morning bugle and trudge out to the bathrooms, everyone toting a shower kit. My kit, as it were, is in one of those ubiquitous plastic bags that reads "Thank you" a number of times from top to bottom. From there, we march into the dining hall. The food is laid out down a long table—wide platters of eggs, dollar-coin-sized pancakes, bacon, condiments—the layout repeating every four feet. I take one of everything, keeping a careful eye on the other kids to make sure I'm not taking too much. When I see that we're allowed to get seconds, I quietly get up and do the same thing again. Nobody pays attention to how much I eat, so I keep going until breakfast ends.

There is a swim test, to make sure we're "water safe." When I was

five, my mother took us to a beach in Florida. She taught us to swim
by throwing us a couple of feet ahead of her and saying, "Swim to
me." Since then we've been in public pools, and sometimes we climbed
down a ladder to swim in the murky Hudson River, which was dark
gray with marbled orange oil at the surface and sewage gathering at
its edges. I love swimming, and I can stay afloat, but I've never had a
lesson. I move my arms in the water, trying to head across the pool,
but no dice. I'm put in the lowest swimming group.

The swim coach, who is wearing short shorts and a tucked-in polo
stretched over his belly, gives us pointers from the side of the pool.

"Hugh, we know you can paddle. Why don't you try the stroke we
are practicing here?" he says. I like the way he talks—I don't have to
guess what he wants or anticipate his reaction. I can tell that all he
wants is to help me get better. I will! And then I do!

From swim practice we go to arts and crafts. The other kids already
seem to know what can be done with wood Popsicle sticks and Elmer's
glue. I wonder if this is something else they are taught in school. Their
structures swiftly rise from the table, awkward but complex. I keep my
dream home at one level, but when I am done there is glue all the way
up to my elbows.

"Hugh, let's go get cleaned up," the junior counselor says cheerfully.
Unembarrassed, delighted by the attention, I follow him out to the
hall restroom. He turns the water on, adjusting it to a comfortable
temperature for me. "Here ya go, really get in there and scrub." I like
how he gives me clear instructions, just like the swim coach. I'm not
worried about upsetting him. I don't have to take care of him. He rubs
my hair, then goes to wait outside the door while I clean up.

The days unfurl like that: prayer, food, physical activity, and everyone so kind. We drink bug juice and play tetherball and sing a song:
"Pharaoh, Pharaoh, let my people go." The counselors treat us all the
same, but I see the ways in which the kids here are like the ones at
United Methodist, the ones who had matching snowsuits and sleds.

The other kids have personal name tags sewn right into their clothes. At night they look through their duffel bags to find warm clothes and bug repellent. Instead of a duffel I've brought some extra underwear in a pillowcase. They are used to getting three meals a day, plus snacks.

At night, in the sleeping bag the Robinsons lent me, I lie awake imagining. I am finally part of the world that I've seen only from a distance, and I want to stay here forever. Camp will end in just a few days, but what if it didn't? What if one of the counselors said, *Hugh, we've talked to your mother, and she would be happy for you to stay another week.* That sounds realistic, even possible. What if the counselor said, *Hugh, we'd like you to stay with us for the rest of the summer.* Or, *Hugh, we're staying open all year. Your mother says it's fine for you to stay with us forever…*

And then it's over. I cry as we pack and clean the cabin. When the Robinsons come to pick us up, my mother is with them in the car. She's glad to see us, like the other parents, and on the drive home she asks, "Did I thank you?" so many times that I see the Robinsons exchange a glance.

"You can drop us here," my mother says when we near the bus station in Albany, and I feel a familiar heaviness descend on me. It's just like the Christmas party at United Methodist. The other kids are going home to parents who will take them out to dinner so they can eat the foods they missed most at camp. They'll show their parents the dream catchers and macramé bracelets they made. They'll unpack their bags, and someone will do laundry.

When Mom tells the Robinsons to drop us off at the bus station, she pretends it'll be easy for us to get home from there, but I know what it really means. There is no home and no plan for where we'll go next. I can tell we'll be sleeping right here at the bus station tonight. I've brought home the lopsided house that I made out of Popsicle sticks, carefully holding it on my lap for the whole ride back to Albany. But when we pile out of the Robinsons' car and walk toward the station, I drop it in the first trash can I pass. I don't need to be told that it's no use to me now. Popsicle-stick homes are too fragile, and carrying one around doesn't make sense anymore. It's a burden. Why would I want to remember summer camp? I'm about to be hungry again. And yet summer camp stays with me, not in the form of souvenir crafts, and not as a fun, nostalgic memory, but as a guiding light.

Chapter 4

"Call me Aunt Flora, children," says an older lady with gray teeth wearing a faded mauve apron over a tired floral dress. To my relief, after a couple of nights in the bus station, Mom announced that she'd found work as a live-in nurse for this woman—and now we're being instructed to pretend she's our aunt. We've often lived with strangers but never in an apartment. We've been taken in at places where people go and come, squats and shelters. This was her home.

"What a lovely place," Mom tells Aunt Flora. "Children, have you said thank you?"

"Thank you, Aunt Flora," we chorus. Mom is on her best behavior right now, but I'm nervous that she will ruin this. I don't want to get kicked out, even though deep down I know it's just a matter of time.

We journeyed from downtown, taking a few buses and traveling far from United Methodist and the neighborhoods we knew. This is a nicer part of Albany, with wider tree-lined streets and no bars on the windows. The apartment is on the second floor of a three-story colonial town house, and from the front hallway I can see dark oak floors stretching into several rooms, each full of tightly upholstered Victorian furniture, china lamps with tasseled shades, Oriental rugs, and pale, long-limbed porcelain figurines on every surface. I've never been in a place with so much furniture. In shelters we usually get a bunk bed and a locked armoire for our belongings, and even when we rent an apartment, we never find much furniture for it. The most fully furnished place I've been is the home department of Macy's—a good place to get warm—and even that is stark in comparison. I am curious, but cautious. I don't know the rules for a place like this.

As if she could read my mind, Aunt Flora says, "This is a Jewish home, no cursing or misbehaving."

"Ms. Rose, they are churchgoing kids. They know better," Mom says graciously. "Did I say thank you? You are a miracle for us."

"Presbyterians are not Jewish," Aunt Flora says, as if she's made a point. "No shoes, please," she adds, and waits while we take them off in the entryway. Then she smiles her gray smile, turns, and slowly leads us down the hall.

Every window in the apartment is draped in dark floral curtains. There are pillows in a similar floral pattern on the living room sofas, and Oriental rugs on the floor. Every surface is covered with teacups, picture frames, and baubles. I have no possessions, and this woman has nothing but possessions. They seem at once valued and forgotten. I move forward cautiously, making sure not to knock over anything. The silence and sorrow make this place feel like a funeral parlor. This is not a person who celebrates life. I am relieved to know that we have a place to stay, but I'm already focused on what I'll have to do to make it last. I need to keep Mom calm. I need to make sure Jessica, Alex, and I don't bother Aunt Flora in any way.

When I inch forward into the front room, Aunt Flora stops me. "Don't go in the parlor, please," she says, with no "please" in her tone. There are more rules as we tour the apartment, and it seems strange to call her "aunt" when she's treating us like boarders, not relatives. Two cats suddenly appear, weaving between my ankles. I start to reach for them—I've always wanted a pet—but when Jessica bends down to pet one, it snarls at her, darts into the forbidden parlor, and leaps up on one of the velvet sofas, glowering at us like a gargoyle.

"My beauties are purebred Scottish folds. Best to just leave them be," Aunt Flora says. "There's a bathroom right here"—she points as we pass it—"and here's where you'll sleep." She opens the door with an age-spotted hand, veins visible through the skin, to a bedroom with hardwood floors, a worn, red Oriental rug, and a queen-sized bed covered with decorative pillows. I already know that Alex and I will end up on the floor. Mom doesn't sleep on a regular schedule, but whenever we stay someplace with only one bed, Mom and Jessica share it. I press down on the bed, feeling how soft it is. I can tell it's not plastic-coated like the mattresses in the shelters.

Aunt Flora calls us into the kitchen, which is yellow and sunny, with a smooth oilcloth on the table. "I'm making dinner," she announces. "Liver. It's full of vitamins." I watch in wonder as the old woman, bent over by a visibly painful spine, springs to life at the stove. Mom steps in to help whenever Aunt Flora needs to get anything down from a cabinet or lift anything heavy, and she does a lot of cleaning, but Aunt Flora's need for a nurse seems to come and go. What she really seems to want is a companion to take her shopping and mitigate her loneliness.

"Set the table, Hugh," Mom says, and points to a cabinet with glass doors.

I open the cabinet and find a full set of matching floral dishes. At the table, I give each of us a proper place setting and a paper napkin from a stack. Mom tells Alex to get us each water, and I help him fill the thick, clear glasses, carefully carrying them one at a time to the table without spilling a drop. At last, Aunt Flora scrapes rubbery slices of liver onto plates for each of us and the cats. I take a bite, chew and chew without much progress, and finally swallow it with a gulp of water. Still, I clean my plate.

"Thank you, Aunt Flora. That was delicious," I say. Jessica washes the dishes and I dry them, figuring out exactly where each one goes.

Mom has landed us in a good situation: a private room with pillows, and a bathroom with a bathtub that I can't wait to try, and now Aunt Flora is giving us free, home-cooked food. It's different from church handouts and soup kitchen meals. It was made right here in front of us, just for us. This is one of the best places we've stayed.

That night, as we're getting ready for bed, Alex and I pull all the extra pillows off the bed. Alex raises one over his head as if to whop me with it, but I glance at Mom, lying in bed. I don't want anything to upset her.

"Shhh. Don't!" I whisper, and he lowers it. The pillows are covered in heavy, rough fabric, but there are a lot of them, and we make them into a nest on the floor.

The next morning, Mom gets out of bed to help Aunt Flora bathe and get dressed. They leave to go grocery shopping together, and I clean up. Leaving a mess could get us kicked out, and it's one thing that I can control. I start with the bathroom, wiping down the sink and cleaning the toilet. Then I try to make the bed. I smooth the sheet and blanket, then attempt to arrange the pillows exactly as they were when we found them. There are all different sizes, some big, some small. I've seen the display beds at Macy's, and I move the pillows around until they look perfect.

With all of my work done, I decide to take a bath. I can't remember the last time I've had a bath. At shelters, we're allotted a time to use the shower, either in the morning or at night, and when we're sleeping in public places, we use the paper towels in bathrooms to wipe ourselves down. But this bathroom is ours to use as we please. Everything in the bathroom is white, covered in white tile, with a little basket of old, odorless potpourri on the sink. I fill the tub with steaming hot water, climb in, and lie there until the water starts to cool. I open the drain and turn the water on again, feeling the new hot water mix with the old. Under the faucet is a circular plate with a lever controlling the drain stopper. The screws above the lever make it look like a face with a long nose. The face amuses me. It looks like it's saying, "Well now, aren't you clean!" I chuckle to myself and raise the "nose" of the face to close the drain. Now the face looks a little surprised, like it's saying, "Haven't you had enough?" I move the lever up and down, continuing the dialogue with the face in my head until I hear Mom and Aunt Flora coming home with the groceries. I hurry out of the bath, throw on clothes, and scramble down the stairs to help them unload the bags.

"You shouldn't run through the house with wet feet," Aunt Flora chastises me.

I nod and apologize. I want to be a perfect visitor, but I'll never know all the rules of this house. Can I lie down on the sofa, or is that rude? Can I help myself to a glass of water, or should I ask first? These safe, clean rooms are rare and special, and I don't want to give them up.

The very best thing about staying with Aunt·Flora is that we're all enrolled in elementary school at PS 22, an FDR-era building that is big, clean, and majestic. It's a brick building with granite ledges under the windows, and there are no bars on the windows. Mom declares it "a good school in a good neighborhood."

I am eight years old, and I join Mrs. Sarno's third grade a month into the school year. Though I missed most of second grade, Mom expects every test, report card, or note from my teacher to be perfect, an A. If not, she'll say things like, "What's the matter with you? The Japanese are going to chew you up. Are you stupid? I told you to study." Mom wants us to be well educated and successful, and I'm 100 percent on board. First and foremost, I want her approval. Also, I realize that getting As is the only way I can get noticed by people outside our family. I want them to see me as a smart, hardworking child. The better I do, the more the teachers praise me, and the more they praise me, the harder I try. Grades are a crystal clear way for me to get their support, whether in the form of a compliment or an extra slice of pizza at the class party. And I believe Mom when she indicates that education is the way out of poverty. I don't know exactly how it works, but I know that if I become a doctor or a lawyer, then I can be the one with the house and the furniture. I want a refrigerator full of food. I want to know what it feels like to wear a shirt that nobody else has ever owned. I want a bicycle. Perfection is the only path I know to get what I want.

After school each day, when Alex isn't staying on the schoolyard to play basketball and Jessica isn't going over to a friend's house, we walk home to an actual apartment now. Up the stairs that creak under our feet, voices still at volume, we come home as if we are "normal" kids. Inside, the house is completely silent and still.

"Aunt Flora is napping, go play," Mom orders, smoking her cigarette at the kitchen table. Her tone is foreboding, so we nod and go into our room. Of the many discoveries in Aunt Flora's apartment is a stack of board games on a lower shelf.

"Clue," Alex says, opening it up on the Oriental rug. The three of us spread around it.

"The murderer is amongst us!" I say excitedly.

"Shut up," Alex says with a smirk. "I'm Professor Plum. Jessica, you be Miss Scarlet. Bro, Mrs. Peacock is calling you out."

Each of us clutches a long, narrow sheet of paper to track characters, weapons, and rooms with a little stub of pencil.

"Bro, go." Alex is all in on this game, nudging me with his socked foot.

"I went; it's Jess's turn," I say, turning to her. She's seated cross-legged, in deep concentration.

"I know who it was," she declares. "It was Colonel Mustard in the library with the revolver."

"You sure?" Alex asks, stalling. But I think she's right.

"*Yes.* Open it," she says, pointing to the envelope with the solution to the crime inside.

Alex opens the flap and pulls out the cards facedown. Dramatically, he flips the first card over. It's Colonel Mustard. The second card shows the revolver, and he pauses.

"*Alex*, turn the card, don't cheat," Jessica demands, bouncing up and down in anticipation.

Alex flips the card. The library.

"*Yes!*" Jessica yelps.

"Quiet," I say, through a big-ass grin. "Let's do it again."

—

Mom is getting up every day, getting dressed, and helping Aunt Flora. The house is clean. We are getting to school on time. This is Mom functioning at her best. I expect the tide to turn at some point, but I am caught unaware when one morning, when we've been living with Aunt Flora for a few months, Mom announces, "Hugh, you are Jewish."

I have no idea what this means, but it's always safer to follow my mother's orders than to ask questions. All I know about Judaism is that temples, like churches, are a reliable source of free food and pleasant places where people sing and talk.

"Aunt Flora is Jewish, and now so are you," she says. I glance at the gold cross necklace that hangs from her chest but keep quiet. "Jews are more successful," she continues. "They're the rich ones. They run the banks. They're doctors. They have all the power."

I'm curious about what she's saying. Is being Jewish, like getting As, something that will help me? I look to Alex and Jessica for a signal, but Jessica looks away and Alex has no expression on his face. This is a bad sign. They don't want her to see them reacting. They want to stay out of it.

Mom doesn't share much about her life, but she has always been very clear that Jessica and Alex have the same father and I have a different father. I have the last name of Alex and Jessica's dad, Alexander Ambroz Sr., and his name is on my birth certificate. He was our mother's second husband, a doctor. She says they lived in a brownstone in Manhattan, and she also accuses him of mistreating Alex and Jessica. Nonetheless, as far as we know, her marriage to him was the last time she was in a stable situation, with a home, a husband, and two babies. It fell apart soon after Alex was born. My father came into her life afterward, soon enough that Alex is only a year older than me, but the details that Mom gives me are fuzzy and often change. I don't know which ones are true. As far as I know, he could be Jewish. He could be a bartender or a doctor that she met at a bar; he could be a general in the army or, I fantasize as I stare at tabloids in the grocery store, a Kennedy. I would like to discover that I'm part of a wealthy American dynasty. Mom doesn't seem to know for sure which one-night stand resulted in me. Every time her story changes, a new version of my father enters the rotation in my mind, each one more handsome and loving than the last. My father is a hope, a hero-in-waiting, the one who might rescue me. In my fantasy, my dad and I are my siblings' saviors too. *We can't leave Alex and Jessica*, I'd tell my father. *They're our family.* But in this moment, the only fantasy about my father that matters to Mom is her new resolution that he is Jewish. Dad hasn't come for me yet, and may never, so for now I play along. I'll be Jewish if that will save me.

"When you are at school today," Mom says, "I want you to look at the other boys' pee-pees. Some are different; those are the Jewish ones." She believes as a Jew I'll have a better chance to succeed, and the first requirement of my new religion is to research penises.

So the next afternoon, while my class is at recess, I dutifully head to the boys' bathroom. There's a line of full-sized urinals across the back wall, rising from the ground to above my height. I hover in front of them, holding my penis as if I were about to pee, or just finishing, and watch the boys come and go. I look at their penises, but I don't know who is Jewish or what I'm looking for, and long minutes pass while I study the porcelain of the urinal, yellow and cracked.

Eventually, a teacher comes in to use the bathroom. He stands at a urinal and pulls out his penis. It is much larger than mine and fringed with wiry black hair. I turn to face him and stare openly.

"What are you doing?" he asks.

"My mom told me to look at boys' pee-pees so I can see the Jewish ones."

He looks at me for a moment. Then says matter-of-factly, "Okay, maybe you've seen enough. Let's wrap this up." With some relief, I let him lead me out of the bathroom.

That night, Mom says, "Hugh, we are going to the doctor tomorrow." This is strange. We don't go to the doctor. The food we eat often makes us sick, and we're in a perpetual state of ill health. Mom handles most of our medical needs, and what this means is that if we complain, she tells us she'll give us something to cry about. Most of our injuries come from Mom's violence, and we give each other aspirin that we take from her purse. We run a rag under cold water and hold it against our bruises or get water with ice at a fast-food restaurant and wrap the ice in a paper towel from the bathroom to soothe the pain. The only time in the past few years that I received medical attention was when Jessica, Alex, and I were each pulled out of our separate classrooms and sent to the school nurse for the lice that were jumping from our heads onto our desks. The nurse told us she was going to call my mother, then came back to the room, lips in a tight line, and said, "I'm going to treat this myself." She washed our hair with foul-smelling shampoo over the sink. I returned to my classroom and avoided making eye contact with my classmates.

We don't have checkups or receive vaccinations or go to the dentist. Occasionally we go to a clinic. But if there is health care that we qualify for, Mom isn't interested; nor is there any way for us to register. We don't have an address or a phone number. We aren't able to make an appointment and then show up for it, and most people like us don't. Any process is beyond our capability. The only system that we could manage would be to walk into a building without an appointment, get treatment, and walk out. When it comes to the ailments of the poor, there is both recognition and judgment, but poverty programs treat the symptoms, never the system that produced them.

I don't feel itchy now or even sick, but I don't ask Mom why she is taking me to a doctor. The next morning, after Alex and Jessica leave for school, Mom and I board a city bus. No matter where we're going or why, this is an exceptional moment. Mom has singled me out for an outing. I'm not her favorite child. She always makes it very clear that Alex is "the brightest, the best, my precious son." Being alone with her, holding her hand, feels special. I still don't sense danger. I just think about how jealous Alex and Jessica are going to be. I might lord it over them. Or maybe I should be more gracious—it's not their fault Mom hasn't selected them for such special treatment. Using transfer coupons, we switch buses twice and end up in a new part of town. We enter a clinic.

"Isn't this a nice place? Aunt Flora found it for us," she says, as if these words can transform the dour, mint-green waiting room. It is run-down, and there is a sickly smell in the air. The TV in the corner of the room, in a metal bib to keep it from being stolen, is snowy, and the sound is muted. Government clinics like this one exist to treat people like us, and it shows. No effort has been made to make it clean, comfortable, or efficient. Sitting next to Mom in a hard scooped chair, I lean over the three-inch gap between seats and snuggle against her. Her arm comes around my shoulder, and I feel her warmth.

"Mary! Mary A.!" A nurse hollers my mom's name, somewhat muffled through the plexiglass. Then I see her step to the side, and the door next to the check-in desk swings open. She leads us down the hall and to the right, into an exam room. There is a bed in the center and equipment on either side. "Here, have him put this on," the nurse says to my mom while handing me a folded blue paper robe. As she leaves, she says, "The doctor will be in in a bit." The door closes softly, and it's just me and Mom.

She sits down and stares at me expectantly. I hesitate to pull down my pants or take off my shirt, not because I'm modest but because the air-conditioning is on full blast. "Mom, no. I don't want to."

She stands up and unexpectedly slaps me. Not hard. A warning slap. I undress.

"Can I keep my socks on, Mom?" She nods, and I put on the robe. Turning away from her, I drop my underwear. The robe feels too big and too thin against my skin, but I gather it around me and climb up onto the examination table, the paper crinkling beneath my body. A man wearing a small, round cap comes in. "Hello, David," he says. I have two middle names, John and David, but nobody has ever addressed me by them, so I have no idea why this doctor is doing so. I look at Mom to correct him, but she stares at me blankly, as if that's my name.

The doctor bends down and takes my penis in his hand. Countless times, Mom drilled it into my head not to let anyone touch my private parts, so I sit in silent confusion and terror as he pulls back the skin at the tip of my penis. I don't understand why Mom is acting like it's okay. I am so scared I can barely breathe.

Papers are shuffled, and he and Mom leave me alone in the room. When the nurse returns, she guides me to another room. Confused, I start to cry.

"This won't hurt," the nurse says gently as she puts a mask over my nose and mouth.

"Breathe in and count backward from ten," the doctor says. I am sobbing too hard to count. When I wake up, I'm in yet another room. My mom is there, stroking my head. The blur of consciousness comes into focus on one spot: my penis. It is bandaged, and a dull pain is beginning to break through the anesthetic.

"You did so well, David. You are Jewish now," Mom says. I barely register that she, too, is now calling me David.

"Your father is Jewish, and now you are too," she repeats. "They are powerful, they own the banks. I want you to thank Aunt Flora when we get home. We are going to call you David now. Do you understand? Because you are Jewish, Hugh...David," Mom explains through my anesthesia fog.

When I'm discharged, Mom leads me back to the bus stop where we arrived. Walking is painful, and a dull pain around the whole area of my groin escalates as we wait for the bus back to Aunt Flora's house. The bus pulls away from the bus stop and rumbles over the street. I gasp in pain, but a single look from my mother silences me. I close my eyes, nauseated. Every single jolt and stop of the bus is excruciating. It's a local bus that stops on every damn block.

I can't ask Mom what happened—my priority is not to trigger her. She's being compassionate now, but there's an edge to it. If I cry, if I even say, "It hurts, Mom," if I needle her with questions, she'll give me something to cry about. Mom hits as often as she hugs, and I'd rather have neither than both.

At home, Aunt Flora smiles warmly and welcomes me to the family.

"Did I thank you?" Mom says to Aunt Flora. They hug, Mom's body overwhelming Aunt Flora's small, hunched form.

It's not clear to me what has been done to me under the bandage. All I know is that I've had surgery and I feel violated in a way that is too big for me to comprehend. My siblings seem to understand that I've been through something bad. Alex doesn't bother me with questions. There is an unspoken truce. Jessica brings me food. Over the next few days, I lie in bed while the pain in my crotch diminishes and then gets worse than ever. I can't stop shivering.

Aunt Flora, who hasn't entered our bedroom since the day we arrived, ventures in while Mom is out. She puts her hand on my forehead and shakes her head. "You have a fever," she says. She pulls a wool blanket out of the closet and spreads it across me.

Then Mom bursts in. "What are you doing with my son?" she demands.

"Mary, I need help with a light bulb in my room, would you

mind?" Aunt Flora says and leaves the room with a quick look back at me. She doesn't seem like the boss anymore. She seems scared of my mother.

Later, I hear the voices of Aunt Flora and Mom down the hall. At first, they're murmuring, then Aunt Flora says firmly, "The boy needs to see a doctor!"

There is a bang—Mom has slammed her hand down on the kitchen table. "I'm a nurse," she yells. "You don't know what you're talking about."

In the bathroom, I pull down my white underwear, sweating and shivering. I sit on the toilet and stare down at my penis, or where I know it to be. The original bandage still encircles it, and I have been peeing through it for a week. That area of the white cotton has turned brown. I can't tell what's going on underneath, so it's the rank, rotten smell that scares me the most. Something is very wrong below the bandage. I'm terrified that my penis is going to fall off, but I can't go to Mom. She'll be even angrier. My abdomen is hot and red, and my pelvis feels like I have ants marching all over it. I know I have to try to clean myself, like I do whenever I'm injured. In my mind this is the only solution. Resting a hand on the wall, I take a wad of fresh toilet paper and gently blot at the bandages, but the pain is too intense. My left hand thrusts out and grabs the counter. I'm spread out now, one hand on the wall and the other on the sink, my feet wide apart. I concentrate on my breath, pulling the air in deep and holding on to that moment. And again, and then again. Steadied, I try again to clean myself with the wadded toilet paper. Each blot is agony.

I have cleaned myself as best I can, but now my bladder demands release. I slowly turn to face the toilet, terrified. It's going to hurt so much. I sit down, and stare at my underwear. The smudge at the front is a rust color—disgusting. I don't want them on me anymore. Using my feet, I shimmy out of the underwear and sit on the toilet nude from the waist down. I count to ten. *One, two, three, four...* Looking down, I concentrate on the white floor tile. *Nine, ten... eleven... thirty-four... fuck...* do it now, Hugh, now! and I release.

Piss and blood stream out of me. "Aaaah, Mom! Mommm..." I scream. She opens the bathroom door, annoyed. Aunt Flora is right behind her. Mom gets on her knees to examine me. I start to shake and whimper. Aunt Flora gasps and runs out of the room. I've instinctively started to pull my legs together at the thighs. Mom pushes them apart and tugs at the circle of bandage and mesh, and I roar.

"*Enough,*" Mom commands. But I cannot stop crying. The cotton bandage comes off with a flash of pain, but the mesh underneath is still wrapped around my penis. I instinctively push her hand away and kick her shoulder. She slaps me. "I said, enough. Sit still. You are making this worse." Blood oozes out of my penis, and Mom, who has been muttering about all this fuss over nothing, sees the damage, and her lips tighten into a straight line. She examines the remaining mesh with deep attention.

"Honey, I need to take this mesh off. It should have come off sooner, but now your pee-pee is healing attached to it. We're going to soak it," Mom says, in a new voice of loving calm. She starts to run a bath. I have enjoyed my baths in this tub so much. Now I watch with dread as it fills. I know exactly what is coming. I remember what she did to me in Miami three years ago.

The accident happened when I was four years old. I was standing on the second floor of an outdoor staircase with a toy fishing rod draped over the white railings. I was busy anticipating a tug on the line when I was bumped from the side, hard, and flipped right over the railing. For a moment I felt like I could fly. I spread my arms, looked down, and saw a flash of giant banana palm leaves on the sidewalk below.

I woke up on a gurney in the hallway of a hospital.

"Hugh, you did it this time. You broke your arm. Are you happy?" Mom asked.

The cast stayed on my arm until it started to itch and smell. It was the same smell I recognize now, and, as with my current situation, my mother didn't take me back to the doctor. Instead, she decided to remove the cast herself.

She took out a big steak knife. I tried to writhe out of her grasp, but she pulled me to the floor and sat on me to keep me still. She wedged the tip of the knife, blade up, under the edge of the cast. Then she jerked it outward, sawing through the first centimeter of the cast. Little by little, she cut through it, poking my skin with the tip of the knife each time she pushed it farther under the cast. A stench filled the room from my bone-thin, filthy arm, which was dotted with blood.

Remembering the cast removal, I continue to weep quietly. She picks me up, plops me into the bath, and leaves the room. I look at the face of the circular plate, its lever nose raised into the expression that had once seemed so goofy and amused. My favorite part of living here has been almost daily baths—no lines for the bathroom, no roaches, no disgusting shared showers. I love sitting in the water, staring forward, and scrubbing, soaking until my fingers look like raisins. But this is not one of those occasions, and my friend the drain plate looks worried and sad.

When the tub is half-full, I turn off the faucet, and my sobs fade. I can hear Mom and Aunt Flora fighting in the other room.

"Mary, are you sure? Don't get upset, but I need to tell you again that you should really take him to a doctor. You're a wonderful nurse, but this is an emergency," Aunt Flora says. I perk up. Aunt Flora is an adult. Mom's boss, technically. She sounds timid, like she's scared of Mom now, but there's still a chance Mom will listen to her.

"These are my children," Mom yells. "You stupid old woman. You fucking piss yourself. Who are you to tell me how to take care of my kids?"

That's it. I won't go to the doctor. And we won't be able to stay here with Aunt Flora for much longer. But I literally can't leave. I can't walk.

I can't even think about this right now. I just know it's over. I'm mad and in pain and terrified of what's about to happen.

Mom comes back in and sits next to the tub on the toilet.

"Scoot up," she says, gesturing that I should move closer to the faucet. "More."

Now I'm squatting at the end of the tub, and my wound, with its attached mesh, is under the faucet.

Without pushing up her shirtsleeve, she reaches into the water and finds my penis.

"Mom, please don't…Mom, please, Mom…" I plead. This is the line my mother has always walked. She protects us and hurts us. She provides and deprives. We survive beside her, despite her, and because of her.

She pinches my penis with one hand, and the other dips into the water. Then she whips her hand back. The pain is excruciating, but the mesh is still there. She does it again. Three times. The mesh rips off. The water clouds with my blood. The pain is a tsunami, and the bathroom goes fuzzy, then dark.

When I come to, she is gone. The water is still running; but because of the overflow drain, it hasn't risen above my chin, and I haven't drowned. The house is silent, except for the thunderous sound of water hitting the tub. I grab the rims of the tub and pull my chest up. A wave of pain surges through me and I slump back.

"Jessica…" I say weakly. "Jess…" No answer.

Leaning forward, I twist the nozzle to stop the water. I get up slowly, step one leg onto the white-tiled floor, and scoot over to sit on the closed toilet seat. My penis is still bleeding, and I press against it lightly with a wad of toilet paper. It quickly soaks up the blood, breaking apart in my hand. On the floor next to the tub is a washcloth, already soiled with my blood. I wring it out into the tub. Pinkish water drains out between my fingertips. I take a deep breath and press the cloth against my wound. My penis, this important, sensitive part of my body, has been touched and cut, permanently changed, and scarred. I'm ashamed and confused and afraid and angry at my mother. But I try to stay above the surface and do what I know needs to be done. I need to stop the bleeding. I need to get out of this bathroom. I need Jessica and Alex. I'm going to survive this and my mother.

Naked and wet, I go to our room and lie down on the rug. It's Persian, mostly red with an intricate pattern. With my head to one side, I can smell its earthy scent and see, up close, the threadbare areas where white knots are exposed. I look up at the ceiling. Centered in a sea of cracked plaster is a sad, square light fixture that holds two bulbs, one of which is out. I focus on the web of cracks instead of the wrenching pain in my penis. I hear no voices, nor any sounds. Not even the cats creeping around. I'm alone.

Lying there, an image of a father, my father, floats in front of me, and I mumble a song I learned in camp. I repeat the song over and over, holding the washcloth and waiting for the bleeding to stop. *You shall love the Lord your God with all your heart, with all your soul, with all your strength, and with all your mind.*

"Hugh…Hugh, come on, get up. I got you." Jessica is kneeling beside me. She slips her arm beneath my head and brings me up to a sitting position.

"Come to bed, come on." The room swirls. "Come on, that's it, Hugh." Her voice is my anchor. She leads me to the bed. I'm naked, and ordinarily it would mortify me for her to see my eight-year-old body, but I don't care.

"Mom changed my name." I start to cry again as she lays me back in bed.

"Drink this, it's just water."

"My name is David now," I tell her before I take a sip and lie back.

She starts to hum the song I had been singing. "Sleep. I'm right here," she says, and I do.

There is no follow-up visit to the doctor's office. No Jewish father appears to lead me to a life of prosperity. Mom gives me some pills and slowly I heal, on the outside.

Inside, I am not completely broken. Violence and pain and struggle have been the white noise of my life, but this breaks through. The pain is so great, the invasion of my body, the change of my name. Hugh is gone, and with him any faith I had left in my mother, any hope that other adults would intervene. In his place is David, who is determined to save himself, to survive this and to protect himself from the people he cannot trust. I feel like I have walked through and out of a fire, and in the heart of the flame was the fundamental break from my mother. I understand that to survive her, I have to escape her.

Chapter 5

I'M JUST STARTING TO FEEL better when Alex and Jessica come into our bedroom.

"Start packing," Alex says.

"Aunt Flora said we have to go," Jessica adds. I'm not surprised. When I heard Mom yelling at Aunt Flora, I knew it was only a matter of time. She wasn't family to us. She tolerated us and thought she was doing a mitzvah by letting us stay, but with Mom, Aunt Flora got a lot more than she bargained for. The only thing I'm sad about leaving is school. There are years when we don't go to school, and when we do, we often arrive partway through the school year, but I've just started to see the value of school. I like learning, the teachers are nice, and they feed me.

"Mom, where are we going?" Jessica asks. We are at the train station, where Aunt Flora dropped us off. Mom told us and Aunt Flora that she had an apartment lined up for us in New York City, but she doesn't.

"I'll figure something out," Mom says. And just like that, we are back at our old haunts, spending whole days in Grand Central and sleeping at the coffee shops inside the station. In New York City there are places homeless people can stay without being harassed by officials: subway cars, buses, some parks, hospital ER waiting rooms, churches, and libraries. Mom has learned where and when it is safe to be in these places. We have only the stuff we can carry—not a lot. Mom finds a place to sit, and we take our places on either side of her, leaning back to sleep in the hard chairs. Penn Station is dirty and lawless, but Grand Central feels regal. I love looking up and around the vast space, though years will go by before the celestial mural on the ceiling is restored, the muck of years washed away. Only then will I realize the beauty that was above me all along.

"I need cigarettes," Mom tells me. I scope out ashtrays and other places people might have discarded cigarettes with enough left to smoke. But it's not sufficient. We also need food, so I stand in a sea of commuters at Grand Central, begging for a dollar. People surge toward me, faceless in crisp navy and pin-striped business attire and winter gear. I plant myself right in front of them, my hand outstretched. Today, however, prospects aren't good. Just a few feet in front of me, the commuters part, and then they pass on either side of me without a second glance.

"Sir...sir...ma'am...excuse me...can I just...please..." I try to address the countless faces that surge past, but I'm invisible to these people, like all the homeless are across the city—just annoyances to be moved out of the way or "cleaned up." I stare up at the gray ceiling and wonder how this is supposed to work.

The morning commuters from Metro-North are often generous, but something is off today. I look down at my hands, my clothes. I am filthy. I inhale deeply, tucking my chin down so I can discern my own scent. I am rank. I want to scream, *Help us!* but I know better. Alone on a packed concourse, surrounded by all of these people, I understand we are not part of their reality. My family and our ilk are a nuisance for these people—if they've even considered our existence. They want to pretend I don't exist. But they will see me one day. For now, I need money. Mom is going to be furious if I come back with nothing. She'll slap me, a casual one without real emotion. Just feedback, her way of saying, "Bad job." I make another round of the ashtray trash cans around the station and manage to collect a number of cigarettes with some tobacco left. It should be enough to mitigate her mood, but it won't do anything to help my hunger.

"This is enough," Mom says when I hand her the cigarette butts. Alex and Jessica must have had better luck bringing in cash. "Let's go," she orders, and exits Grand Central. It's snowy and cold out. Agitated but determined, she leads us less than a mile west to the Port Authority bus station. Without explaining her plan, she guides us with purpose around and through the crowds of the Greyhound bus terminal up to the window.

"Four to Greenwood Lake, New York," she says. "One baby."

Kids under a certain age are free. I must be the "baby." The clerk peers through the glass. I'm not sure if she can see that none of us is a baby, but she looks slightly annoyed.

"Four to Greenwood Lake," my mother repeats. "One baby."

Hearing the total cost, Mom hesitates, but only for a moment. She stretches open the neck of her black turtleneck with one hand, and with the other reaches down it to grab the cash from under her breast. The clerk watches, her eyes widening.

"If you have to go, do it before we get on the bus," Mom says, and all three of us trudge into the women's room. My mother has always insisted that we go into bathrooms together. There is no safety on the streets, at least none that lasts. I'm in a constant state of alertness, on a hair trigger to react to any outside force. I never let my guard down. Homeless prey on homeless; criminals prey on the homeless; officials harass the homeless; and the public insists we stay out of sight. Keeping our little group together is our only strategy to protect ourselves from being hurt or lost.

Mom pushes open the door, checks the bathroom. If she sees two or more pairs of legs tangled in a single stall, then we know to turn around and leave immediately. If the coast is clear, then we go in. Alex leads the way, and I walk in with Jessica, hand in hand.

The bathroom is poorly lit and reeks of piss and dirty mop water. The trash can near the door is overflowing. Graffiti on the tile walls has been painted over, offering a blank canvas to the next "artist." The stall doors are also painted and squeal when Jessica opens one. I follow her in.

"Turn around," Jessica says, and I face the door, marveling at the graffiti. "Suck my dick," "Be here at 4:00 p.m. for…" and drawings of stick figures doing many different things to each other. The lewd words and images echo what my mother has told us goes on in this very bathroom. She's paranoid, but sometimes it's hard to know where the line of reality lies.

"Jess, don't sit all the way down on the seat."

"I know that."

"Alex, do you have toilet paper?" Jessica asks the stall wall.

"Um. I'm peeing."

"Alex!"

"Sorry, no. None here either." I hear Alex finish and go to the sink.

"Bro, wait for us," I say. We walk out together, ready for the bus trip to a destination we've never heard of.

When we find our bus, the driver is standing in front of it, smoking and talking to a couple of other drivers. My mom walks up to the open door, but the driver stops her.

"We aren't boarding yet, ma'am," he says.

"I have children, let us on," Mom replies, and bulldozes onto the bus. In her full-length dress, sweater, and blazer, her short hair, large hat, and big red Sally Jessy Raphael glasses, Mom means business.

The bus is idling, and the heat is on. I sink gratefully into my seat next to Mom. Alex and Jessica sit across the aisle from us.

"He'll help," Mom mumbles to herself, staring out the window.

"They have a lovely house. He kept my parents' wealth. He got it all—
I should have gotten half. He'll help." Then, out of nowhere, she asks,
"You guys hungry?"

Startled, Alex's and Jess's heads whip around and stare. We haven't
eaten yet today.

"Yes," we all say in unison.

Out of her purse comes a king-sized Snickers, plenty for all of us.
She hands it to me, and I tear it open.

I carefully score two lines across the bar with a fingernail, dividing it
into thirds. I hold it up for approval from my siblings. But as I pull the
first third away, I twist it so that a bit of extra filling comes out with my
share. I hand the bar to Jessica. She takes her piece and hands the rest
to Alex. The chocolate melts slowly as I move it around in my mouth.
Mom is watching, and I grin with a mouth covered in chocolate.

"Your teeth are disgusting," she says. I laugh, giddy.

As the bus speeds down the long highway, the metal and stone of
the city give way to more and more green. The dull hum of the engine
lulls me to sleep, and I wake up when the bus lurches into an industrial
parking lot. I look out the window to see a flat stretch of hard, filthy
snow framed by a low wall of plowed snow and nothing else. We
trudge off the bus and follow Mom up the street into a simple café with
a handful of tables and a counter displaying pastries. I don't go near it.
The memory of the Snickers is still fresh, but I don't want to look at a
muffin and awaken my hunger.

"Excuse me," Mom says, getting the attention of a waitress. "I'm
looking for Lake Drive." She gives a street number. This is a new
location for us, but it doesn't register to me as anything different from
what we do every day: We wander. Sometimes Mom seems to have a
destination. I never know where we're going.

Greenwood Lake must be a very small town. This woman seems to
know the address, but she looks like she doesn't think she should give
directions to my mother.

"It's fine, he's my brother," Mom says.

The three of us stare at Mom. Brother? We've never known ourselves to have an uncle. Mom is an island. I've never thought of her as having anyone but us.

She rattles off the names of his wife and kids, names we've never heard before.

"It's not far," the waitress says, "but you should get the cab. I can call him if you want."

"No thanks, we want to walk. We just took that endless bus ride," Mom says.

The town is nestled against a long lake. As we walk out of the town center, the modest houses are spread farther apart. The front lawns are blanketed in snow, and tall trees, heavy with snow, frame the houses. Each has a garage, and I can see that in the backyards some of them have swing sets, covered in snow. There are few cars on the road and no other pedestrians. The quiet of the streets brings me a good feeling, but I'm not sure why. It almost feels like we'll come to a magically warm gingerbread house full of cousins and food.

I've wondered about my father, but I haven't ever thought about my mother's family. If she has a brother, that's exciting. I walk beside my siblings, perky and quick. Perhaps her family—my family—doesn't know our condition. Maybe they've been looking for us.

Mom leads the way, and when we find her brother's home, it looks like the others. It's a yellow one-story home with vinyl siding and a driveway leading to a side porch. My heart speeds up at the thought that we could have family who live in a house like this. Mom bangs on the door and rings the bell. There's no answer. There's no car in the driveway, and the curtains are closed.

"David, go around the back. See if the door is unlocked," Mom says.

I can't see a walkway, so I trudge through the snow between the house and the fence to the back. Walking along the fence, I see odd bulges distorting the shape of the surface of the snow—perhaps there is a bicycle underneath? I notice how big the yard is. It doesn't even have a back fence. The rear is bordered by a dense forest. Halfway back, I can see the snow-topped shapes of a patio set, a table and four chairs. This is where the family—my family—sits in nicer weather. I stare out and can picture Alex and me exploring that forest. I can almost smell the pine.

Reality intrudes, and I turn left and go up three stairs to a patio covered in snow. I try the screen door, pulling my sleeve over my hand so I don't have to touch the cold black handle directly. It's locked.

I follow my own footprints back to my mother. The damp is soaking through my sneakers.

"So?"

"It's locked."

With a frustrated grunt, Mom strides past me around to the back of the house. Confirming that the door won't open, she suddenly pushes her hand against the screen door, tearing the screen. Jessica, Alex, and I look at each other. We've never seen her break into a home. But is it breaking in if it's her brother's house? Family would want us to be warm. I decide it's okay and watch as she tries the handle of the door behind the screen, but it, too, is locked. I sigh and see my breath float in front of me. It's going to be a long walk back to town. Even as I think this, Mom takes off her scarf, wraps her hand in it, and punches a small pane of glass. It breaks easily. With the scarf still wrapped around her hand, she reaches inside and unlocks the door.

We gravitate to the kitchen and look around. There are children's books and toys. There are photos in frames. *This is my family*, I think. In the kitchen, Mom moves quickly through the cabinets and fridge, pulling out bread, bologna, peanut butter, and jelly. Soon there is a bounty laid out on the table. We descend on it, feasting. Mom finds the Chock Full o'Nuts and makes herself a pot of coffee. We use the bathroom, and Mom asks Jessica to sweep up the glass from the back door. Then, when I am starting on a second sandwich, I hear the front door unlocking.

"Stay here," Mom says, and goes into the front hall.

We hear voices—a man, a woman, children, Mom. This must be my uncle and his family. The voices intermingle and elevate. It's not the warm welcome I imagined. Not even close. The female voice says, "You can't just fucking come into our home."

Then the male voice, my uncle: "Mary, what are you doing here? I can't give you money again."

"Again? What do you mean again?" the woman demands. "We have our own problems and you're giving her money? Get her and her trash the hell out of our home, or I'm calling the police."

"Fuck you. We are not trash. We need help. We are your family." Mom sounds outraged, but she barely raises her voice.

"The hell you are," the woman retorts.

"Calm down," says my uncle.

"Don't tell me to calm down. You need to get her out of here."

I hear the sound of a child crying.

"Let's calm down. Mary, where are your kids?" he asks.

"In the kitchen."

He walks into the kitchen, and I see him for the first time. He's taller than Mom, plump like her, with rounded features, thinning gray hair, and a line in the middle of his forehead that makes him look worried or shocked. He smiles at us. I study his eyes. They look bright and concerned. Does he want to help us? Jess, Alex, and I are a team. We wouldn't kick each other out of the house. But behind him is a woman, her features distorted with anger, and next to her are two boys, pale and dark-haired, scared. They might be around our age. They live in this house, and they have a right to this house and all that food.

"Look at that; she fucking broke in," the woman exclaims, pointing at the door.

There's a standoff, all of us waiting silently in the kitchen. I'm not sure what's going to happen. This woman might call the police, and my mom broke in, so it's very possible that we'll have to run and hide. I glance at the door where we entered—that's where I'll bolt if this turns dangerous or violent.

"Get out of my house," the woman yells again.

"Let me talk to her. We'll figure this out. Take the boys into the living room," the man says. Reluctantly, she herds the boys out of the room.

"This is Jessica, Alex, and David," Mom introduces us.

"Hello, guys, I'm John. I'm your uncle." He gives us an apologetic smile, and I know right then that he's not going to help us. We say hello, then he turns back to Mom. I see her relax, so I know the chance of a dangerous outburst has passed. "Mary, what are you doing? You can't just show up like this."

"John, we have nothing, I have nowhere to go. You have to help us while I get back on my feet. We can stay in your basement for a while..."

"Mary, no. She won't stand it. You have to go," he says.

"Go where?"

"I'll take you into town. You have to go back to the city."

"Can't we stay tonight? It's late. There are no more buses."

His wife reappears in the doorway. "You need to get out of my house right now, or I'm going to report you for breaking in."

"Alice, I'm handling this." He turns back to Mom. "Mary, I can't. I'm sorry."

Something turns in our mom. Her posture straightens. "Fine. We'll go."

"Let me drive you into town," he says.

"No, we walked here, and we can walk back," she says to him. Then, to us, she says, "Let's go." I look at the window. It's dark out, and I know how much colder it will be when we step out into the night. I wonder if the bus terminal is still open.

My uncle reaches into his jacket. "Here, take this."

"No, you can't half help us, John. You are throwing your family out on the street," Mom yells, angling her voice toward the living room where his wife is. She gestures for us to follow. As we walk out, he puts a hand on my shoulder.

"Take this." He shoves money into my hand. "I'm sorry."

I hold the money in disbelief. Is he really going to let us leave? Doesn't he see what's going on with our mom? Why won't he help us? I wonder if he knows who my father is. But he gives me a nod of dismissal and releases my shoulder. I put the money in my pocket and hurry out the front door after my family. I will never see my uncle again.

I hurt for Mom. I know she is offended, embarrassed, shattered. Her brother rejected her in a moment of need. I couldn't imagine Alex or Jessica doing that to me. I'm mad at him for being a bad brother. But part of me knows that there's more to the story. My mom is different. She explodes, like she did with Aunt Flora, and once she does, other adults don't want to help her anymore. But what about us? Why won't anyone help us?

Mom is standing in the driveway, waiting for me, erect and proud.

I reach up and take her hand. "Let's go." We turn and walk away.

"God bless you," Mom calls out over her shoulder as a farewell, her voice dripping with sarcasm.

I look back once, and the whole family is watching us. I'm angry at that woman, and that man, but especially at those children. They get two parents. They get food. They get a house. Why them, and not me? Mom is quietly crying, and I ache for her. I hate seeing her hurt. I squeeze her hand tighter. We have nowhere to go, and it's going to be a cold night.

I reach in my pocket and palm the money. Maybe it's enough for some food. I separate a couple of bills and hold the rest of it out to my mother. "Mom, I took this," I lie. When I'm not trying to escape her, I love her. When she doesn't scare me, I want to help her. When she feels abandoned, I am her family.

She pulls her sweater down from the neck, stuffs the money into her bra, and we walk on and into the night.

Chapter 6

"Damn it, not a fucking dime," she says, rooting in her purse. We're at a bus stop along Madison Avenue with no destination, just squatting and passing time. She closes the purse, bowing her head for a moment, the remnants of a cigarette bobbing up and down between her fingers. She stands up and starts walking south, so we follow. It feels like we've walked miles, down boulevards, past stores and people, eventually arriving at a Midtown branch of the New York Public Library.

"Alex and Jessica, you stay here," she instructs. In the city, when we leave Alex and Jessica behind like this, it means we're paying a visit to Cyd Donahue, a wealthy man she says used to be a nursing patient of hers. I'm almost always the only one she brings to see him. This may be because I'm the youngest, but I can't help wondering if he's my father. He would be a good one—he's kind and he has money to take care of me. I can't think of anything else to want.

Cyd runs a flower shop near Lincoln Center, where he sits like a king at a huge steel desk in a back room. While we wait our turn to see him, the men who come in and out to talk to him don't seem to be buying flowers.

Finally, Cyd invites us into his office. Mom takes a chair across from him, and I sit on her lap. He leans across his desk to greet me warmly, using my former name and asks, "How is school, Hugh?"

"It's good," I lie. I'm pretty sure I should be in the fourth grade, but I haven't been to school since my surgery at least six months ago.

Cyd looks directly at Mom with pursed lips. "Mary, they have to go to school."

"Of course they do," she says. Then she starts to plead her case. "I don't get any child support...The money from the state is never enough...Just one more time—I'm going to find a nursing job..."

Cyd leans back in his chair listening with his arms crossed. I look behind him, where there are glass-doored refrigerators full of flowers of all sorts: orange with black centers, big white bulbs that explode from their stems, and roses bleeding from one gorgeous shade of red to another. Whatever the season outside, it's always spring at Cyd's.

The silence snaps me back into the moment. Mom nudges me. I lean forward and place my elbows on the desk, chin on my hands. Cyd's chair creaks as he leans to a drawer and pulls out a wad of cash the likes of which I'd never seen. It's folded in half, stuffed in an overtaxed money clip. I see only hundred-dollar bills and twenties. He counts out a pile of bills, then neatens the pile and taps it twice. "Mary, you got to get it together. These kids—come on, Mary."

"Did I say thank you?" Mom turns slightly and pulls down her sweater to tuck the money away.

After we get the money from Cyd, we pick up Alex and Jessica, and head to the Port Authority Bus Terminal. We end up back in Albany's South End, not far from Aunt Flora's apartment, but in a neighborhood with fewer trees and taller apartments packed close together. Here, the paint on the windowsills is peeling and there is garbage on the streets, crushed into the corners of the curbs. The governor's mansion is at the top of a hill, and nearby is the Rockefeller Plaza. It's a congregation of state buildings surrounding a reflection pool. They look a lot like the

World Trade Center towers, except for one that is shaped like a huge concrete egg. Where the hill slopes down to the Hudson River is a little neighborhood of leftover, run-down buildings including our four-story walk-up. We're on the parlor floor, which has tall ceilings and scraps of furniture left by the previous tenants. Across the street is a Chinese food store with a weatherworn GRAND OPENING sign that will stay in place for as long as we live here.

We're no longer in the right district to attend our old school, PS 22, but Mom has bulldozed our way back into it. I've already missed the beginning of the year, but this is the first time I've returned to a former school. I hadn't made friends with any of the kids, but I'm excited about the comfort of a familiar school, where I already know that the lunch ladies will let us come back for seconds, and I remember that if the students don't open the potato chip bags or bite into the apples that come with their school lunches, they put them on a giveaway table, and I can help myself. Kindnesses come to me more quickly since the faculty are aware of my situation. Instead of the nurse being shocked and asking questions when I'm sent to the health office for lice, she greets me warmly and gives me the treatment herself instead of sending me home. When kids arrive hungry or with behavioral problems from homes where there is violence and unsanitary living conditions, schools are the most logical place to have the resources to address these issues. But teachers shouldn't be expected to be social workers. Everywhere I went, teachers did the best they could to help with the resources they had.

After our first day of school, Mom takes us to Price Chopper and promises us a fresh start. "I'm going to cook a nice, healthy dinner for you," she says, cigarette butt hanging off her lip. I'm glad that this mom is here, the one who talks, who wants to nourish us. In New York City over the last few months, we spent too many nights in Port Authority, where I was constantly on alert to every approaching footstep, afraid someone would mess with me. I've been begging for cash and stealing food from bodegas, but now we have the school food and a new supply of food stamps. It's a moment to breathe. Though even when Mom is trying her best to provide, I'm still on guard—it's in moods like this that she's fed us raw garlic and cod-liver oil to prevent us from getting colds, which I don't want any part of.

In the meat section of Price Chopper, she picks up a package of bone-in chicken sealed in a yellow Styrofoam rectangle. It's slightly gray, but it's on sale. "The dark meat has more protein," she says, adding the chicken to the cart. Alex gives me a skeptical look. She doesn't cook. She's never cooked. Sometimes she leaves a coffeepot on the stove for hours until the grounds ignite; she has boiled water until the pan collapses. She sends me to find potatoes. "Get the big ones," she says. I take the opportunity to sneak caramel cubes from the candy bins into my pocket. Then I walk along the aisle eating caramel and planning my entry in the egg drop competition. It's our first school project, and I want to win.

Mom is working as a lunch lady the day of the competition. This is her first time volunteering at one of our schools.

"I'm an involved parent," she tells us. "It's important that the school knows that. Your teachers will challenge you appropriately." The lunchroom is in the gym, with preprepared lunches in white paper bags lined up on folding tables. When I enter, I see her in action. A kid is standing on a chair. "Sit down, Jeremy!" she commands, hands on hips. She knows all of the kids' names. He hops down and she smiles at him. She marches through the rows of tables, wrangling the kids with a calm authority that I wish she had at home.

When I get in line to pick up my lunch bag, Mom comes up to me. I'm still at an age where having my mother around makes me proud, but the feeling instantly changes to embarrassment when she uses spittle to wipe a smudge off my cheek. Then, even worse, she turns to a kid named Marco Stiles, who has the bad luck to be standing behind me in line. "You know, Marco, David is a top student," Mom tells him. "He would make a wonderful friend to you. All of my children are excellent students." She knows I don't have friends at school and is attempting to make one for me. Marco stares at her as if she's an alien. I shrink down into my sweater.

After lunch, when all the classes in the fourth grade assemble at the side of the building for the egg drop challenge, I'm delighted to see Mom there in the group of teachers and other staff who have gathered to watch. When Mom is at her best, her warmth radiates on me, and in these moments, I want to make her proud. I hope she'll get to see me win.

We've each been given an egg, a shoebox, and a sheet of rules for the challenge. The goal is to configure the box to protect the egg from breaking when it's dropped from increasingly high windows in the school. Whoever's egg survives the longest will be the winner. I've laid my egg on a soft bed of torn-up newspaper, then filled the rest of the box with more scraps of newspaper.

The teachers are the ones who are going to drop the eggs. There are fire stairs going up the side of the building, so they climb up to the first flight and start dropping the boxes, one by one.

"David Ambroz," my teacher calls, then drops my box. I run forward to open it and find a splash of yellow yolk. I grimace and throw the contraption in a big garbage bag that one of the teachers is holding open.

"Good try, David!" my mother cheers. She comes up behind me as I watch the teachers begin to drop the surviving boxes off the second story. "Try looking at some of these other structures to see what the other students have done."

The girl who won put her egg in a stocking, which she then suspended between the two sides of her box to prevent it from ever hitting the ground. "See that?" Mom says. "That's using your brain."

The following Saturday, Mom is still in a good mood. We walk over to Rockefeller Plaza, where there are free concerts and a natural history museum. She signs Alex up to be a Cub Scout. Then she disappears into the Egg, which is a performance art space, and when she emerges, she tells me that she has enrolled me in a children's theater group. Just me, not Jessica or Alex.

"You did? What? When...whaat?" I'm so excited that I'm barely coherent. I love lip-synching to songs, reading books aloud, being in church plays or school choruses. This is the best news I've ever heard.

"Honey, it'll be good for you to be part of something so prestigious."

Mom is doing better than she has in a long time. Shopping for healthy food, volunteering at school, cheering me on at the egg drop, signing me up for an after-school program. Through the veil of her mental illness, this is a glimpse of the mother she wants to be. She understands what it means to be upwardly mobile, and she tries to plant seeds: sending us to church, camp, school, and talking to us about how important it is for us to one day go to college.

Then she makes a move that I never dreamed was possible. In late October, on the walk to school, we pass a sign for free kittens. In the neighborhoods where we live people can't afford veterinary care. They don't get their animals spayed or neutered, and as a result, there are lots of unexpected and unwanted kittens and puppies. There are always flyers for animals needing homes.

"Please, can we get a kitten, Mom?" I beg, as I always do when I see the signs.

Alex and Jessica each chime in. "Please, Mom?" "We'll take good care of it."

I am shocked when Mom yields, saying, "Let's take a look on the way home." This is the closest she's ever come to saying we can get a pet, so I dream about the kittens all day.

After school, we find the sign again and go downstairs to a basement-level apartment. The door is open, but there is a locked iron gate.

"Hello in there," Mom calls out. "We're interested in the kittens."

I can't believe this is really happening. I have never wanted anything more than I want a kitten in this moment. I stand right next to her. Jessica and Alex are behind me.

A woman emerges. Her hair is in a neat twist of braids on top of her head, and a toddler is pulling at her skirt while she grips the waistband to keep it in place. She turns to him and patiently says, "If you want to hold my skirt, you gotta move your hand down here, Sammy, like this." She points to a lower spot on her skirt, and he obediently moves his hand. She straightens her skirt, then points to a cardboard box in the corner of the room. "Over there." Mom stays where she is, talking to the mother, but Jessica, Alex, and I surround the box. It's full of tiny kittens, probably too young to leave their mother. They all have different colors and markings. I immediately pick up the one I want. It's gray and white, sleepy and adorable.

"It needs a name," Jessica says. "How about Elizabeth?"

"That's a human name, not a cat name." I stare sternly at Alex and Jessica. "Besides, are you going to change the litter box? Didn't think so." We all know, without saying anything, that I will be the kitten's primary caregiver. It's always been my role in the family; in a thousand small ways it's expected that I will take care of Mom, clean our space, mitigate conflict where I can, and absorb the punches when I can't. I'll be the one to feed and care for the kitten. I decide on the name Snickers. It's my absolute favorite candy bar. Alex and Jessica don't protest. Jessica might even like the name—a smile plays at the side of her mouth.

"Well, that's certainly a unique name," Mom says. She scoops up the cat and hands it to me. I inhale deeply. Snickers smells earthy and feels warm and even softer than the crushed velvet sofa at Aunt Flora's, which until now was the softest thing I'd ever felt.

On the way home, Mom takes us to the bodega where she sometimes buys liverwurst. She scrounges up enough cash for kitty litter, toys, and canned cat food for the kitten. We have no furniture, but we have a litter box. I scratch Snickers behind his ears, and he makes a strange motor-like sound. "Mom, listen to Snickers!" I cry. "Is he okay?"

She smiles and says, "That's a good thing. It means he loves you."

Once I realize my touch can make Snickers happy, I am in constant pursuit of the purr. Every day when I come home from school, I hurry to find him. Either he's tucked in a tiny ball on a towel, or he staggers toward me, mewing. He curls on my lap while I do my homework. At night, I put him next to me on my towel tucked into my neck and scratch behind his ears. He sleeps with me until morning.

Rehearsals for *Peter Pan* start a week later. I walk by myself to the theater. The Egg is a large building, and the main doors are closed and locked. There is no clear sign of where to go. I pull out the schedule that I found in Mom's purse to confirm that I have the right date and time. As I walk around the building, a security guard approaches. "Can I help you, son?" he asks.

I hold up the forms toward him. He walks me to a stairwell that leads down to a sunken hallway. There's an open door at the end of the hall. As I step inside, someone says, "All right, Moms, we need you to say your goodbyes. You can wait in the room over there or return in two hours." With that, all the moms exit past me, and the kids are left in a semicircle surrounding a woman dressed all in black, her hair pulled back.

"Okay, I'm excited to share our program. As you all know, this year we'll be performing *Peter Pan*." She spends the next hour leading us in vocal exercises. I take deep breaths and exhale while chanting, "Mooooo," exactly as instructed. We start to learn songs and some dances, and I enthusiastically thrust my arms into the air and belt the songs at the same time as I'm figuring out the lyrics. I am in my element.

At the end of rehearsal, she gives us our parts. I've been cast as a lead Lost Boy. "David, here are your words and your solo song. Loved your breath work, real commitment. Keep that up," she tells me. Clutching my precious script, I walk toward the refreshments. The only thing I love more than rehearsing is free snacks.

That night, lying on a mattress that came from the welfare office, I watch the headlights of passing cars swoosh across the room. I've already memorized the song "I Won't Grow Up" and proudly sing it to myself. The cars slide past. I watch them move across the ceiling, the oceanic rhythm lulling me to sleep.

After a few weeks in the neighborhood, we start to settle in. I start to think that maybe I can keep Mom stable for longer if I just manage all the situations that are most likely to set her off. This means I'll need to build up a large collection of cigarettes. I'll try to keep the apartment clean. I'll report only good news to her, telling her when I get an A or when a teacher has given me a compliment. I'll run interference between Mom and anyone who wants to talk to her. If the landlord wants to ask her about rent, I'll promise him we'll have it next week. If a neighbor has a question for her, I'll say she's asleep or unavailable. I'll make sure Jessica, Alex, and I keep quiet. Even if Alex gets pee on the toilet seat, I'll remind Jessica not to yell about it. If Mom can stay in this mood, maybe we can stay in this apartment.

One of the best things about staying in a place for more than a few nights is the chance to make friends. I don't bother trying at school, but the neighborhood kids are my people. I've seen other kids around my age on our street and in our building waiting in the same welfare lines that we do. After school one day, Alex and I walk up toward the park and start up a game with a bunch of them.

"It's called ghetto Frisbee," Alex explains. It's a game we played in New York City, but the kids look confused. Alex directs them to throw the metal trash can lid into traffic like a Frisbee, hurling it low into the traffic. The money shot is when the disk goes under a car then floats back up into the arms of a teammate across the street. We've never seen it happen—the physics aren't there—but we relish the default play, which is to hit the car and sprint away as fast as we can. At the time,

I didn't know where the name came from or what the word "ghetto" implied, but if you'd told me it referred to the spaces where poor people and minority groups are relegated, I wouldn't have been surprised. That described what I knew about my community, and what my day-to-day life was. This neighborhood is different from Aunt Flora's because most of the people who lived near her were white, and most of the people who live on our block are people of color. The people in her neighborhood had nice cars and well-maintained buildings, green lawns, and shady yards. In our neighborhood every surface is hard and there is no greenery. Visually, everything is in a state of decay or disrepair—the cars, the paint, the people. There are bodegas instead of grocery stores, fast-food joints instead of restaurants, schools that my mother doesn't want us to attend. I know that our neighborhood is poor, but it's where I feel most comfortable.

Walking home from a few rounds of ghetto tag, two of the kids we've been playing with head right to our building.

"You live here too?" the older one says as we all approach the same door.

Alex and I pause, not sure if this is some sort of trick. "We're on one. What about you guys?" Alex asks.

"We're up on four," he says. "This building is shit. I'm Hugo, and this is my brother, David."

"Ha, that's his name too." Alex laughs and lightly punches me on the shoulder.

If they're on four, then I know who their mother is. Aurora is a big presence in the neighborhood, either leaning out her fourth-floor window or hanging out on the stoop talking to and at everyone.

"Boys, watch out for each other," she hollers as we leave the building together the next night.

Our friendship with Hugo and David brings our moms into contact with each other. They aren't friends, but where Mom usually avoids all other adults, she acknowledges Aurora's existence with a smile and a nod. She might have a brief conversation with her instead of averting her eyes. Once or twice I even see them smoking cigarettes together on the front stoop.

"Mary, how can you smoke those things? Disgusting," Aurora says about Mom's Marlboros, even as Aurora lights up her own menthol cigarette.

One time, we're entering the apartment and Aurora calls to Mom from her window. "Mary, can the boys stay at your place for now? I have a gentleman *visitor*."

Mom mumbles, "She's got a lot of gentlemen visitors." But to Aurora she says, "Of course." But when the boys show up at our door, Mom sends us all outside.

This time, instead of staying on our block or going to the park, the four of us head over to the Knickerbocker Arena, just a few blocks away. The Grateful Dead are playing tonight, and in the parking lot, a pothead in a tie-dyed shirt looks at me with lidded eyes. "Wanna miracle, kid?" I ignore him and hurry out of his view. David and Hugo are the lookouts, and Alex and I approach the first car together, one on either side. I look in the window, check over my shoulder, then tug the chrome handle on the driver's side. It opens. I dive in and hit the glove compartment: There's a crumpled dollar bill and a nearly full pack of gum. I move to the ashtray area, quickly collecting the coins. I grab a few cassette tapes off the floor and throw everything in my backpack.

I learned to steal because I was hungry, and I know hard times will come again, so I am always looking for food or money, even when we have just enough. But I am also looking for ways to have fun. There is excitement in the hunt. Are we crafty enough to succeed? Can I haul in more than my brother? The game of it, like ghetto Frisbee or exploring the farthest corners of Grand Central in New York City, is something I also need to survive.

We decide to go for more.

"Bro, this one," Alex directs, and we move down the line, two cars over. "Damn, the door is locked. Yours?" Alex asks.

"Mine too, damn. Wait—" I've found a triangular window that is tilted outward. I stick my hand through this funny window and reach down to unlock the door. "First dibs!" I holler. It's a bust, just a crappy sweatshirt and car papers in the glove compartment.

My pulse throbs as if I'm in a race. I'm thrilled but scared. I try door handles, and open compartments, knowing I'm doing something wrong but necessary. Today I have an apartment; in a few weeks I most likely won't. Today I have food; tomorrow I most likely won't. The owner of this car has more than me. They'll be fine. I try not to think about that person coming back to their car, seeing what we've done, and feeling violated and angry. Instead, I focus on feeling justified.

"Onward, bro, come on," Alex says, while we walk along the rows, looking in all directions to monitor for owners or cops. A few cars away, I try the passenger-side door of a blue VW Beetle with rust creeping up from all the seams. It's unlocked, and I pull the door open. It creaks. To me the sound is a bullhorn, and I freeze, holding my breath. "It's fine, move," Alex says, urging me forward.

I grin nervously across the car at him, and we resume our work. There are duffel bags in the back seat, and we tip them upside down—spilling their contents onto the dark green leather. It's mostly clothes. "Search the pockets, bro. I'll do the front," Alex says, and we divide and conquer.

"Sweet!" he crows. The change drawer is stuffed with crumpled ones and quarters. Emptying that into our bodega bag, I also snag some Slim Jims from the floor. Satisfied that we've taken all there is of value, we back out of the car. I close the door as quietly as I can.

Moving through the cloud of pot smoke, we discover that the next car is also unlocked, and the next. It turns out Deadheads don't lock their doors. We burglarize the cars quickly until we notice people are starting to trickle back into the parking lot. I don't want to get caught.

If the cops were to bust us and call Mom, we'd be in real trouble. Once Jessica got caught stealing makeup at Duane Reade and the drugstore called Mom, who beat the crap out of her.

But I'm not too worried about being arrested. There is a sea of cars in the middle of a dense cloud of pot smoke. The cops are just as likely to harass these hippies as they are to care about our thievery.

We're supposed to split our takings evenly, but on my way out of the stadium parking lot, I surreptitiously take a few dollar bills and shove them into my underwear. I'm sure the other boys are doing the same. We head to the parking lot behind the Chinese restaurant, our agreed-upon meetup spot. The lot's black tarmac is broken up. The smell of an open dumpster mixes with hot exhaust that pours from the fan above the restaurant door. We sit down in a corner and count out the bills and coins. After a brief pause, we hoot with delight. It's an incredible haul, perfectly executed. The total comes to ninety-two dollars, plus more spare change and gum than I've ever seen.

"Fuck, let's go to Crossgates!" Hugo hollers. We've been to the mall with Mom before. It's far, but not so far away as to be forbidden.

"Dude, nah. We got to get some stuff for Ma," David says.

"Not with all of it. Arcade?" Hugo asks.

"Whatever, let's split it and get out of here," Alex says. We carefully divide the money into equal piles. It's getting late, but we all head to the corner store. My first priority is a large stash of cigarettes for Mom, some for now and some for darker times. After that, I pick Doritos, Big League Chew, Clearly Canadian fizzy water, and a huge tub of cheese balls for ninety-nine cents. With just a little left, I splurge on some Garbage Pail Kids trading cards, which are the going currency in the neighborhood.

"We should get back home," Hugo says. "My mom will be wondering where we are." And he's right—when we come back up our street, Aurora leans out of her window. "Where were you? I thought you were staying downstairs."

I'm impressed that Aurora knows and cares where her boys are—and notices when they aren't where they're supposed to be. Her sons start to mumble a lie about where we were, and I step in. "Oh, we went to see the hippies smoking pot. I hate that music. They're all so high."

Aurora looks at us skeptically and raises an eyebrow. "Mmmm-hmm," she says, making sure we know she doesn't believe us. Alex and I go into our apartment where Mom, who was supposed to be watching the four of us, is lying on her bed with her eyes open. She doesn't greet us or ask where we were.

Aurora is her own brand of crazy, but it's obvious that she loves her boys. When she calls them in for dinner, we all go inside. They go up the extra three flights to their apartment, and when their door opens, I can hear the clatter of dishes and Aurora saying, "Dinner's ready, what took you so long?" In our apartment, Mom is either in bed or in the folding chair by the window. Nearby, she has books that she scavenged and uses to reinforce her narrative that she is a woman of intelligence, but I've never seen her read them. Other than volunteering at school, she isn't looking for a job. And she never makes dinner. The chicken that she bought is still in a bag in the refrigerator. But we have our own ways of feeding ourselves.

"David, we're going to Ponderosa," Jessica tells me when, at the end of our second month in the apartment, our food stamps start to run low. Ponderosa Steakhouse, a chain restaurant, has become one of our go-tos when we're out of money. It's relatively close to the apartment.

The restaurant has a Wild West theme—the building is painted in earthy tones with wood rails, and its logo is in a signature cowboy font. A superfluous split rail fence surrounds a tiny wedge of grass in front of the building, and there is a single sad tree near the entrance.

The parking lot is full of family cars—Ponderosa is a place to celebrate on a budget.

At Ponderosa, customers pay a fixed price at the front cashier when they enter. They lay claim to a table, then help themselves to the all-you-can-eat buffet. Our hustle is to pretend to be part of a family that has already paid. It begins outside, where we wait under the red awning until we see a family that looks like us.

Alex and I simultaneously point as one, two, three kids around our size tumble out of a wood-paneled station wagon. We'll wait for them to eat, and then, when they emerge from the restaurant, we'll hurry in to take their table before the servers have a chance to clear it. They look enough like us that the servers will assume we're the same kids, returning from the buffet with our third or fourth course.

The family enters the restaurant, and we stare at the door hungrily until finally they emerge. Then we spring into action, entering the restaurant one at a time. "Can I help you?" the host asks as I buzz past her station.

I pause midstep. "Just bringing Mom her glasses. She forgot them in the car," I answer, the lie rolling off my tongue. She nods. Security is not tight. These are minimum-wage hosts employed at a chain buffet— the way I see it, they care in proportion to their meager wages.

Once I make it past the host, I quickly assess. It's easy to spot the table that the family just left. It's still covered in their dirty dishes. Good. The service staff hasn't noticed that they're gone. The three of us hit the buffet, grabbing new plates at the start of the line. Mac 'n' cheese, chicken nuggets, pizza. I pile my plate high, then take my seat.

"Should we say grace?" Alex jokes, and we all say, "*Grace.*"

"Look how much steak they gave me," I say, proud of our ingenuity. No one gets hurt by this trick, and we get to eat as much as we want of whatever we want.

"David, eat your greens," Jessica says with a smile, pointing to the green Jell-O cubes on my plate. The three of us eat quickly. I'm full after the first plate, but I want more, as if I could hoard it somewhere inside me for winter. When I make my way back up for seconds, Alex is right behind me.

After the second helping, Jessica says, "Enough, guys. We have to go. Here, let's wrap some in napkins and put it in our pockets for Mom." We're stuffing our pockets when everything almost goes downhill.

"Honey, where is your mom?" a woman asks, walking up to the table. She is clearly the manager or someone in charge.

We're prepared for this. "Mom is getting the car warmed up. We're just finishing up," Jessica says.

"Hmmm, yeah, okay," the woman says. She looks at us for a long moment, her eyes lingering on our ill-fitting, dirty clothes. "Yeah, well, get your fill and get going, okay?" she says with a kind smile. We scarf the last scraps from our plates before leaving, hoping to show that we are not in a thieving rush to exit. At the front door, I turn back and catch the manager's eyes, and I smile at her. She smiles back and gives me a little nod. She cares, I can see it. It is the best she can do, and, for today, it is enough. Another angel.

Ponderosa is one of the ways we fill in the gaps. We need food, a mother figure, community, safety, and education. Mom inconsistently provides some of these needs, and the rest is up to us. When one of Aurora's gentlemen callers accidentally knocks on our door, I say, "I think you're looking for Aurora. Let me walk you upstairs."

When I deliver him to her door, she winks at me and gives me a toothless smile. "Thanks, David," she says. "I got you." An hour later, when he leaves, she gives me a dollar and says, "Nice doing business with you." Aurora makes sense to me. I see her wheeling and dealing, just like me, both of us using what we have to survive.

The more I go out of my way to charm Aurora, the more attention she gives me. One night at dinnertime, she comes downstairs and tells Hugo and David, "Let's go get us some fried chicken." Then she gestures to me and Alex. "You too."

"We don't have any money," Alex says.

"Don't you worry. Just bring your stamps."

Fast-food restaurants ordinarily don't take food stamps, but Aurora knows how to work the system at another level. We walk a couple of blocks downhill to a Popeyes-style restaurant near an eighteenth-century house, the Quackenbush House. We can smell it a block away. The warm, buttery chicken is the best food I've ever tasted. I look at Aurora and her boys with a sense of wonder. It seems like heaven to have a mother who provides chicken like this.

"Hugo, cariño, you want more?" Aurora says, pulling Hugo in closer. He is almost as big as she is, but he responds by throwing his arm around her and nuzzling his head into the crook of her neck. He usually acts so tough.

"I'm good, Ma," he says.

"You're good, and . . . ?" Aurora responds.

". . . and thank you," David says quickly.

"Dang right, David." She reaches across the table and puts her hand on his. The easy affection impresses me. They are completely off guard, and she is unabashedly loving toward her sons. In the halo of their love, I can imagine the warmth of what might be with my own mom.

I'm nine, old enough now to know that this is what parents are supposed to do—they are supposed to care for their kids, give them food, talk to them about good manners, guide them into adult life without neglect, abuse, and violence. I've seen parents do this—Mrs. Morgan from United Methodist made sure her children were nicely dressed and had roles in the Christmas pageant, and it was a safe bet that she made them a home-cooked meal every night, but Aurora is different. Aurora and her sons are poor like us, and yet she still manages to take care of them. She feeds and clothes them. She cares where they are when they roam around at night. She gives them a home that is stable in all the ways I've ever dreamed. Resentment toward my mother blooms in my heart.

Then, a few days later, Mom and I are headed to One Dollar Thursday at the used clothing store. I come out of our apartment with bruises on my arm and neck, and Mom shoves me forward to go faster. From her window Aurora yells at my mother, "Mary! I see you, Mary. You leave those kids alone."

I am stunned. I've never seen anyone call out my mother for hitting us. Priests, rabbis, teachers, shelter directors, church members, welfare employees, and Aunt Flora have all been witnesses to our bruises and lice, our hunger, a ceaseless tide of neglect and abuse. I can't stop my mother, and none of the adults around me have ever intervened on my behalf. The moment Aurora leans out the window to confront my mother in her busybody, queen-of-the-neighborhood way, she becomes my hero. She doesn't call the police, and nothing will change, but she's telling the truth about something that everyone else pretends they don't see. To see Mom being held to account for brutalizing us, and realize that it is possible, feels to me like an invisible shift, and I breathe deeply. In that moment, for just a moment, what I've experienced—being hit by my mother—aligns with what someone outside our family sees. Her words are our dark secret revealed. Aurora speaks the truth loudly. I want to be seen, and I feel seen by her.

"I know what you do," my mother threatens Aurora, her voice rising into a yell. "I know how you earn money. *Whore*. You watch out, talking to me like that. I'll tell the landlord." Never mind that the landlord is probably one of Aurora's clients. Turning theatrically, Mom puts a hand on the small of my back and ushers me quickly toward the bus stop. She doesn't say a word about the confrontation, but she is quiet at the store, and I am worried. My goal has been to protect Mom from interactions like this. She is upset, and when she's upset, our precarious living situation easily collapses.

Later that night, Mom's anger toward Aurora spirals. "Stay away from that woman," she rants. "She's dirty. Trash. She is a whore, and she's got AIDS." The level of vitriol in her tone sends up a warning flare. She has insulted Aurora before, but now she is tense and sweaty, her face flushed. Pacing the room, Mom mutters, "Bitch..." and the rest is a mumble. Her fists are clenched as she paces back and forth across the living room.

Backing out of the room, Alex, Jessica, and I sit in a triangle in the bedroom, looking at each other, while Mom still fumes in the other room, behind the closed door. Alex is on the floor, his back against the wall. Jessica is perched on the window ledge. I'm on the bed.

"What the hell was that?" Alex asks.

"Mom's losing it again," I respond.

When Mom gets angry, there's always a risk that she will descend into catatonia, and this time it happens quickly. The next day Mom sits near the front window, loosely wrapped in a bedsheet, smoking. She doesn't move. She doesn't speak. Days pass, then weeks. I trade food stamps for cash, keeping the cigarettes coming. I quietly put coffee in front of her, then slip out of the room. We go to school and come home to find her in the same position.

On a Saturday morning, I sing as I get ready for *Peter Pan* rehearsal. We're going to be fitted for costumes this week. I know all my lines in the song and get so excited singing them that I forget to be quiet for Mom: *"I don't want to grow up, I don't want to grow up. I don't want to wear a tie, I don't want to wear a tie..."* I hop and jump around, having fashioned a cape and sash from Jessica's clothes.

"What are you doing? Stop it. What are you doing in Jessica's dress?" Mom demands.

"It's not a dress, it's a cape," I start to say before the slap connects with my face.

"Take that off," Mom orders. "Is this what they are teaching you? I didn't sign you up to be a sissy, singing and running around in your sister's clothes. Enough, you are not going back."

"But we have dress rehearsal," I whisper, quietly so she can't hear. I know it's too risky to try to convince her. The play is in my life, then out of it, like apartments, neighbors, and schools.

Two weeks later I'm eating the last of the Rice Krispies, and I notice that the cereal isn't snapping, crackling, and popping. It's squirming with maggots. I scream and drop the bowl. Then I quickly check to see if I've disturbed Mom, but she doesn't seem to have heard me. Jessica comes into the room to help. When she opens the refrigerator, we see the raw chicken that my mother bought at Price Chopper. Maggots are crawling out of the plastic bag. I flee to the wooden fire escape at the back of the apartment. Jessica comes after me.

"I think I swallowed some," I sob. "They're going to grow inside me."

Jessica hugs me and says, "You're fine. It's going to be okay."

When I calm down, we go into the kitchen, and Jessica sweeps the broken cereal bowl into a garbage bag. With two fingers, she picks up the corner of the chicken package and drops it into the bag. Then I hand her the bleach. She shakes the open bottle toward the refrigerator, hoping the splashes of bleach will kill the maggots on contact. We use an entire roll of paper towels to dispose of the dead maggots. We are on tenterhooks until it's clear that Mom isn't going to notice the missing chicken or paper towels.

Our next batch of food stamps runs out halfway through the month, and there is no more food for any of us. Snickers meows plaintively when I come home, and I open the cupboard, knowing it's empty. Over the next few days, I go to the grocery store and request deli meat samples, which I put in my pocket and bring home. I steal cat food from a bodega. I pick up handfuls of creamers at Dunkin' Donuts and empty them all into her bowl.

But whatever I give her isn't the right food, and it isn't enough. I try to save some of my school lunch, but it's all I'm getting right now. The food never makes it all the way home. We are all hungry at this point, and we can't go to Ponderosa or ask Aurora for help every night. We find Snickers eating his own poop.

"He'll choke on it," Mom says matter-of-factly, then walks out of the room. It's my problem to solve, and I try, but one day after school, no little kitten staggers out to greet me. I start looking for him. There's very little furniture in the living room. His favorite spot is where the sun comes in the front window and meets the gray carpet, but he's not there. Increasingly worried, I creep quietly into Mom's room. She's on the bed, awake, but she doesn't acknowledge me, and I don't ask if she's seen Snickers. I look under her bed—no kitten. Backing out of Mom's room, I go to our bedroom and check the corner where I've been sleeping, but it's empty. Moving more quickly, I go through the kitchen toward the back sunroom where we keep the litter box. I find Snickers slumped next to the box as if he's tipped over. His paws are frozen in motion. Stunned, and then suddenly sobbing, I drop to my knees and scoop him up in my arms, hoping it's some kind of trance and he'll snap out of it, but he is lifeless. "Nooooo. I'm sorry," I cry out loud enough to rouse Mom from bed. My siblings follow her into the room.

"He ate his own shit and died," Mom says neutrally.

I kneel down, his body still in my arms, and sob.

"Give him to me," Mom commands, putting her hand on my head, in a gesture not of love but of annoyance. "Enough whining, David. You should have taken care of him. I'll handle it now."

I want to run at her and pound with my fists. This is her fault. She's the adult. She could have done something. I can't take care of everyone and everything all the time. I can't take it anymore. *I don't want to grow up.* I want to be a Lost Boy, like Peter Pan, without a parent. I want to hurt her so she can feel what I feel, but knowing what that might bring holds me back. Days earlier, without warning, she had reached up and pressed a hot iron against my thigh. I screamed and fell backward, scooting away on the floor, terrified that more was coming, that she would iron my face. She didn't yell or cry out or tell me what I'd done wrong. It was just an inexplicable moment of brutal, casual cruelty. If she could do that for no reason, then what would she do if I showed her how I felt? I am powerless. I've always been powerless, and any hope I had that I could save us, keep us alive, keep us safe, is gone.

I watch Mom put Snickers in a garbage bag along with the cat toys and the litter box. She tightens the sheet that's wrapped around her body and puts a sweater on over it. I've never seen her take out the trash. Mom does not take out the trash. But now she dumps the bag in the metal garbage can in front of the building. I don't move. "I'm sorry, Snickers," I whisper. "God, please take care of Snickers. He didn't do anything wrong."

The next morning I hear the garbage truck before I see it. A man is hanging off the back and drops to the street before it comes to a complete stop. The metal bin with Snickers is the third one in. It goes up in the air and tilts toward the yaw of the truck. Bags tumble out, and I'm not sure where Snickers is. My heart clenches and closes into a tight fist. I pace, watching the truck take him away. Jessica comes up behind me and puts her arms around me, holding me. Jessica is good at making friends, finding ways to spend time away from the apartment. She doesn't play ghetto tag with us. She does her best to escape. But when I'm at my lowest, she's the only person I have. She cares for me when I can't care for myself. She holds me as I cry for Snickers. I cry as quietly as I can, knowing that if Mom sees me, it could set her off again. She could get us kicked out of the apartment tonight. The fewer shocks to her system, the better. I cry because I can't stop crying, and when I finally stop, I don't feel better.

A couple of weeks have passed when Alex wakes me up on a Saturday morning. I sit up in bed and remember, as I have every morning, that Snickers is gone.

"Come on, I need help with my race car," Alex says. I had to give up *Peter Pan*, but he has continued to go to Scout meetings. Before Snickers died, Alex came home with a kit to build a small race car. With their dads, the boys are meant to use the materials in the kit to make the car, decorated however they want, which they then will race against the other boys' cars. It's the quintessential American father-son activity.

"Tomorrow is the Pinewood Derby," he says. *We have no tools, and no dad*, I think to myself. But I stand up and follow him to the living room. We open the kit. It contains a block of wood, four plastic wheels, and two metal axles.

I hold the wood steady while Alex uses a kitchen knife to hack out a trough for the axles. We jam the tires in.

"Maybe you should tape them," I suggest.

"It didn't come with anything," he says. "I think they're just supposed to stay there."

"Glue?" I venture. But we don't have glue. Alex takes two pieces of gum from our Grateful Dead haul and hands me one. I chew it until Alex sticks out his hand.

"But there's still some flavor left!" I protest.

"Give it."

I hand it over.

"Here, you can paint it with this." Jessica appears with a bottle of nail polish. Alex attempts to paint the car, settling for a few uneven stripes down the sides.

The next morning, Alex and I walk to the school gym where the derby is being held. I watch him place his car on his troop's table. It looks jacked next to the others—they are slick race cars, uniquely carved and custom painted with racing numbers and flames running down the sides. Some father-son teams have chosen to model their cars after real race cars, with signature colors and brand sponsors. Most of the cars have weights on the bottom and are built for speed. Dads and sons mill around the room, checking out other cars, and it is more fathers than I've ever seen in one place, all in clean, fresh clothes. They lean over to talk to their sons, dropping an arm around their kids' shoulders. Alex gets in line to race his car, standing alone stiffly. Mom hit him pretty badly with a shoe last night. He's wearing long pants and a long-sleeved shirt, but I know that he is bruised from head to toe.

When it's time for his heat, Alex places his car on the track, a steep hill with a long runway at the end. At the starting bell, the boys release their cars, and they zoom down the hill. Alex has to give his an extra push to get it going. The wheels are uneven, but eventually gravity wins out. The car slides more than rolls to the bottom of the hill and comes to an abrupt stop. Alex grabs it off the track without a word. "That was stupid," he whispers angrily. "Let's go."

"But there are cookies," I say, pointing.

"Fine," he says, and while the awards are announced over a loud-speaker, we are at the potluck table, shoving food into our mouths. We eat, looking around at the vast array of active fathers. Lost in our own thoughts, we eat more than our fill, seeking to quench a hunger that is not satisfied by food.

"Where do you think our dads are? Do you think they know about us? Maybe they are looking for us?" I say quietly.

"Nah, bro, this is our family. We got this; I got you," Alex says, putting his arm around me. We linger as long as we can, knowing that at home the rent is unpaid and soon we'll be homeless again.

Chapter 7

DOING LAUNDRY AT A FAST-food restaurant is always dicey—a manager might kick me out or a patron might scare me off with a glare of disgust—but I don't have much choice. Since we were evicted from Aurora's block a couple of weeks ago, we've been wandering through public spaces and shelters, and public bathrooms are my only opportunity to get clean. I turn the silver lock on the door, hear it click, and relax slightly. I probably have fifteen minutes before someone complains that the door has been closed for too long.

This Wendy's has vintage fixtures, some of which have been updated with the indestructible surfaces of anti-crime design. The mirror has the fuzzy cast of anti-graffiti film, but people have carved through it with an obscene invitation reading "Call 212-555-5555 for a fuck."

At the sink, I crank the hot water to its max and then jam a wad of paper towels to plug the drain. With the water climbing, I open the plastic grocery bag holding our clothes. The mixed odor of dirty clothes stuffed in a plastic bag is a powerful funk, and I wrinkle my nose as I dump them in the sink.

Mom's big, beige, menstruation-stained underwear tumbles out of the bag, followed by her underwire bra and her go-to turtleneck. The rest is a mix of our socks, underwear, and cotton shirts. I hold a cupped hand of the pearlescent white soap under the faucet, letting the suds fill the sink, then step back to let the laundry soak. After a few minutes I scrub the fabric against itself to really work out the odors and stains. I hope the hot water will kill the lice that have been feasting on me. Most kids get lice at some point in time. It's annoying, it's treated, it's over. Me, I've had lice for months on end, on and off for a decade. If a school nurse doesn't step in, it goes untreated. For homeless kids, life is just brutal. It's uncomfortable and unhealthy, day after day. It's a constant state of fear, insecurity, violence, and sickness, and the reprieves are rare. Kids in poverty may not have my exact story, but their stories are all too similar. And almost nothing has changed.

I take off all my clothes except the shorts that are serving as my underwear, and add them to the sink. My own scent wafts up to me, stronger now that I'm fully exposed and in a closed environment. Being filthy is a horrible feeling. I feel like Pigpen from the *Peanuts* comics, with a constant cloud of dirt hovering around me.

I moisten another folded bunch of paper towels, add soap, and rub my face, wincing at the vigorous scouring I know I need. I work down my body, using a clean paper towel for each limb. Last, I let my shorts drop, lean forward on the sink, and clean my butt crack. The angle is awkward, and I meet my own eyes in the fuzzy mirror.

"Disgusting," I tell my reflection.

When I'm done, my body feels tingly and fresh. I pull the paper towel from the drain, releasing the water. I carefully rinse each item with hot water, then wring it out as hard as I can, especially the shirt and pants I'm about to put back on. I sloppily fold the rest of the clothes and put them back in the plastic bag. The clothes I'm wearing are still damp, but this is as clean as I'm going to get before we find a new living situation.

A few days after my Wendy's bath, Mom brings us to a two-bedroom basement apartment in a rough neighborhood in Albany. More than ten people drift in and out—it's probably a squat—but it's a ceiling over our heads, a floor to sleep on, and a bathroom to clean our-selves. I'm always grateful for a bathroom, but it's there where a new problem begins.

"We can share it, but you can't tell Mom," Jessica says, holding up a pretty decent-looking toothbrush.

"Where did you get that? Did you steal it? Do you have toothpaste?" I ask in quick succession. I hate the film that builds up when my teeth go unbrushed—it's chalky against my tongue. When my mom talks, a white stringy saliva sometimes yawns between her lips. My mouth feels sticky, and I'm sure I have the same.

"Someone left one of those 'dignity kits' that the volunteers hand out on the bathroom sink. It looks almost new, and there's lots of toothpaste left," she says. We might not be the first or the only ones using it, but it's better than nothing, or so we think.

Soon thereafter, Jessica develops an enormous angry sore on her upper lip. It seems like a zit at first, but it spreads and crawls across her lip. Unthinkingly, with her sore in full bloom, I share a strawberry milk-shake with her. The straw is still in my mouth when my mother slaps me. "Now you're going to get it too. You idiot. Look at her." It hadn't occurred to me that the sore on Jessica's mouth was contagious.

I already have what I think are canker sores inside my mouth, but I haven't given them much thought. My teeth are yellow and rotten; my breath is bad. A few sores don't register as significant. But now I make a connection between the blisters in my mouth and what is happening on Jessica's face.

When herpes reaches my face, I have it even worse than Jessica. Probed by my worried fingers, the blisters leak and spread all the way around my mouth. I pick my nose, and the sores creep up into my nose.

"Mom, it hurts and itches—can we get some ointment or some-thing?" I ask.

"You're disgusting. You're going to get scars. Nobody will ever want to look at your face. I told you to be careful," Mom yells at me. "Stop touching your damn face, wash your fucking hands, and this will clear up. Do you understand?"

Hoping Mom's instructions are enough, I do stop touching my face and picking at the sores. I wash my hands whenever and wherever I can. Eventually, the sores turn a plum shade and then scab over. My face stiffens, and I can barely move my mouth until the scabs start to fall off. The skin underneath is pink and new.

As a child in poverty, I live in a sustained state of ill health that manifests in daily traumas of illness, infection, infestation, and unmet needs. When health care was established as a social service, its founders didn't consider the hurdles between having that right and accessing it. No one thought about kids like me who have to find the rare dentist who takes welfare and a parent who has the time and money to get us there. Every step in health care is harder for people in poverty. Why don't public schools have free clinics where every child can access free health care without being embarrassed, without their parents having to take time off work to get them there?

The herpes is nearly gone when I am jolted awake by an electric bolt of pain, like a nail being driven through my tooth.

"Mooommm," I wail. It's day five of this, and she's giving me over-the-counter painkillers, but nothing has helped.

We are all on the couch of our squat, a different squat than the one with the toothbrush. At least in this one it's just us. I crawl toward my mother, trying to get into the cradle of her arm. I'm ten, too old for this behavior, but the pain is overwhelming. I haven't been able to eat or drink anything for days. Alex and Jessica, now awake, stay where they are, but they watch with rapt attention. It's risky to complain to Mom, and it's anyone's guess how she will handle the trouble with my mouth, but I have no choice.

"Mom, my tooth—"

"I know, I know," she says. She is silent for a moment. Then, with surprising resolution, she says, "Okay, kids, let's go. Get ready." To get ready sounds absurd, given that we slept in our clothes, but we all stand up and go.

The bus shelter has been colonized by a homeless person. His boxes and bags cover the bench and ground, and he is rocking and mumbling to himself. A few people are waiting outside the shelter, keeping their distance, but not Mom. The bus can take a long time, and she is not a stander. She pulls me over to the bench, brushes his trash right off the end of it, and sits down. I'm immediately on her lap.

"The bus!" Alex yells, and we turn to look. After a beat he adds, "Will be coming soon." It's a joke we play—pretending we see the bus before finishing the sentence with the disappointing truth that it's still nowhere in sight. It usually devolves to a game of tag within sight of the bus stop, but I'm in too much pain to play along today.

This March morning is not as cold as yesterday, but the area around the bus shelter is littered with big white grains of deicing salt left over from the last snow. Intrigued enough to be distracted from my pain, I crawl off Mom. I step on the salt, and I like the crunch that it makes. Jessica and Alex come over and we systematically crush all the salt around the shelter until the bus arrives.

When we step onto our third bus of the morning, Mom says, "This is the one that will take us there. We're going to get your tooth fixed." Her warm hand encircles mine. Alex and Jessica sit in front of us. "Hold hands," Mom tells them. We need to stay together. Alex turns around to make a face at me. I ignore him, but he does it again. He can't sit still. Eventually, he rotates until he is on his knees facing me. The semicircular metal handhold that projects from the top of the seat frames his face as he mouths insults at me.

"*Faattyyyy,*" he mouths silently, drawing each letter with his finger in the air. Mom stares out the window, and he stops whenever she glances in his direction. I stare straight through him until he turns his attention to my sister.

I'm expecting to see a doctor's office, so I'm confused when we disembark at the Crossgates Mall, where we've spent many hot afternoons walking in the food court and sneaking into movies. The parking lot is full of cars nosed into piles of plowed, dirty snow. The lampposts rise, skeletal, into the sky. Outside the bus, the cold is shocking, and we hurry toward the mall doors, entering through Sears. Mom walks with purpose through the mall toward a storefront that says ACME DENTAL in red letters. It's next to a hair salon. Mom and I step up to the check-in window.

"My son has a dental emergency," Mom says to a woman in mauve scrubs.

"Okay," she says, handing Mom a form. "Take this over there and fill it out completely. We don't take Medicaid, so it's either credit or cash, no checks." She taps a sign on the plexiglass screen that says this.

Mom may or may not have enough money tucked in her bra, but I know the drill: We'll get the service and then either pay what we have or leave without paying anything at all. She sits down and begins to fill out the form. I watch as she identifies herself as Susan Grant of Troy, New York, including a bogus address and phone number. She gives my name as Sasha, one of her nicknames for me.

When she gets to a line on the form, "Describe the nature of the emergency," Mom looks at me. "David, the absurd thing here is that I'm asked to fill out a paper form to describe an emergency. Do you understand why that is idiotic?"

"Because it's an emergency!"

"Yes, honey, precisely."

She walks back to the window with the clipboard, and I hear her say, "He needs to be seen *now*."

"Ma'am, I will walk this right back and share it with the doctor. Please have a seat," the woman says. But Mom doesn't move. The woman looks at my mother for a beat, rises, and disappears into the back.

When Mom sits back down, she seems anxious. "Mom, it's going to be fine," I say, reaching for her hand.

"Susan, Sasha, let's head back. We can get you ready. The doctor is going to fit you in before his next appointment."

All eyes in the waiting room rise to look at us, alarmed that we are jumping the line.

"Honey, I can't go back there," Mom says to me.

"Why not?" I ask. She's certainly seen me in pain before—it can't be that. Maybe she's nervous or embarrassed about what the dentist will say when he sees the state of my teeth.

"I can't go back there," she repeats. "Jessica will go with you." Jessica's head whips toward us.

"Alex can go," Jessica says immediately.

"Get up and go. Now." Mom's tone leaves no room for discussion, and Jessica and I rise.

"Ma'am, you need to come with your son," the nurse tells her.

"I cannot. His sister Jessica will go," Mom says. I notice though she changed my name to protect me from some imagined threat, she's forgotten to change Jessica's. I make a mental note to share this with Jessica as evidence that Mom must love me more.

"Okay, hon, hop up," the nurse says. "This is Marcia, she's a hygienist—a helper. She'll get you set up for the doctor."

"Hi, Sasha, pleasure to meet you. And you are?" Marcia asks.

"Jessica, I'm Jessica. And this is David," she says, exposing my true identity.

"Okay, well, it says Sasha here on the intake, but David is fine too," Marcia says. "Sasha, just relax back, okay? I'm going to put this cover over you, so we keep your shirt clean..." She becomes quiet when she sees my shirt. It's not exactly filthy, but far from clean.

"I need you to open your mouth so I can see what's bothering you," Marcia says, slipping gloves on.

Jessica reaches out and touches my leg to comfort me and keep me still. I open my mouth wide. Marcia has what look like metal chop-sticks, one of which has a point at its end and the other a small mirror. She sticks them into my mouth.

"Oh, wow, um, do you remember the last time you went to the dentist?" Marcia asks.

I garble, "No," but I do remember. It isn't hard to keep track of *never*.

"Well, I'm going to just look at the troublesome tooth now, okay? I need you to hold very, very still," she says, lowering the chopsticks toward the tooth that is radiating pain. I jolt fully upright and clamp my mouth shut.

"Okay, let's numb it a bit so it doesn't hurt as much, and we can fix you up. Would you like the pain to go away?" Marcia asks.

"Yes, please," I moan.

"Okay, I'm going to put a little gel on this Q-tip and then dab it on a few places in your mouth. That should numb everything," Marcia says.

"What is it?" Jessica jumps in. "We should check with Mom."

"The doctor doesn't have a lot of time, and we fit your brother in between appointments. I promise you, it's completely safe." She dabs a few places circling the offending area.

"Okay, go ahead," Jessica says, doing her best to be Mom's surrogate.

"Let's give that a minute, David, Sasha...ummm. How old are you?" Marcia asks, looking me at me.

"Ten," I reply.

"What's your favorite subject at school?"

"Art."

I feel a little bit of pressure.

"Does your mouth feel better?" she asks.

"Yes," I admit. For the first time in days, I feel almost no pain. My head is clear. I breathe a sigh of relief. "That's all?" I ask. "That gel is a miracle!"

"No, sweetie, we have to do a bit more work. I need to look

around in there and find out what's the matter, but it won't hurt anymore."

"Okay."

I can feel the instruments tapping lightly on each tooth. "When is the last time you went to a dentist?" she asks again.

"I don't know," I mumble.

"Hi, Sasha, I'm Dr. Simon." A tall, distinguished-looking man with thick white hair comes into my periphery. "What have we got here, Marcia?"

Marcia starts using terminology I don't understand.

"Let's take a look, shall we?" Dr. Simon says. The light dances across my closed lids as the doctor's tools probe and push around in my mouth. After a few minutes, he says, "David, you have a very bad cavity. It's infected, and, well, that tooth needs to come out."

"Come out? But then I won't have enough teeth!"

He says, "It's a baby tooth, and a little loose already, so you were going to lose it soon. Don't worry, you'll get another tooth to fill the space. You can leave this one under your pillow for the tooth fairy."

Tooth fairy? What's a tooth fairy? I start crying, and Jessica stands up. "I need to tell Mom."

"Let's go out there together," Dr. Simon says, gesturing toward the door.

When he returns, he tells Marcia to numb me up. "David, that tooth has to come out, and your mom is on board, right, Jessica?"

"Yes, Mom said it was all right," Jessica says.

I feel a couple of pricks and some pressure. I taste the latex of his gloves in my mouth. Then he leans back, and I open my eyes.

"Okay, that's gonna take a minute to kick in. Let's look at a few more things while it does. When's the last time you saw a dentist, guy?"

"I don't remember," I lie again.

"Okay, that should be enough," he says, bending forward to examine my mouth again. Marcia is on my left, the doctor on the right, Jessica at my feet. I can hear the music from the hallway, some generic jazz station. This time I feel a lot of pressure as his tools move around in my mouth.

"David, hold still," Dr. Simon says sternly. His movement is less and less gentle, and I find my head moving despite my best efforts.

"This one's stubborn...goddamn!" His hands slip, and the sudden withdrawal causes my mouth to slam shut.

I sit upright, blood pouring from my mouth.

Jessica screams and runs out of the room. "*Mommmmmm...*"

"Marcia, gauze, please. David, I need you to sit back."

I struggle to stand up, but Marcia's and Dr. Simon's hands firmly keep me in place.

"Shit. David, lie back now," Dr. Simon demands.

I comply, closing my mouth, which quickly fills with blood.

"David, open your mouth for me."

I hear her coming. I know those clogs. I can't see her, but I can feel when Mom is behind me. Dr. Simon and Marcia stand up.

"Mommmm," I mumble. "Mom, I'm bleeding."

"Mrs.—" He doesn't know her name. "I need you and Jessica to wait in the waiting room."

"What have you done to my son? David, stand up. We are leaving," Mom says. Then she tells the doctor, "I'm going to sue you and this entire operation if you've hurt my son."

"We just need to stop this bleeding and then—" Dr. Simon starts, but Mom cuts him off.

"Don't lecture me, you quack."

There are hard bits in my mouth that I realize are fragments of my tooth.

"You both need to back the fuck up," Mom says, grabbing my hand and pulling me to my feet. She leads me out the door to the waiting room, Dr. Simon and Marcia on her heels.

"Ma'am, give us a minute. We need to help him," Dr. Simon says.

"You've helped enough," Mom says.

On our way out, Mom pauses to announce to the patients in the waiting room, "That monster just crushed my son's teeth and cut his tongue nearly out of his mouth. You should go elsewhere." We go right into the women's room, and she hoists me up so that I am sitting in the sink. "Lean back, and open your mouth," Mom instructs.

I do as told.

"Jesus, what did he do?" she says.

I start to sob.

"Enough, David, you'll be fine. Here, rinse out." She cups her hand and holds it up to my mouth. I rinse a few times, and Mom rips off the bib—throwing it to the floor. I notice Alex and Jessica standing by the door, motionless. Taking off her scarf, Mom wets it in the adjacent sink and begins to gently wipe the blood off my face. As she wipes, she coos, "You are a brave boy. You are going to be fine. It's okay, we'll fix this." This is the Mom I know is always there behind her illness, the one who loves me as best she can.

We get back on the bus and head to another dentist's office. His office isn't as nice as the one at the mall, but this time Mom comes into the exam room with me. She has not let go of my hand since we left the first dentist.

"I'm a nurse," she tells the dentist. "Have I thanked you yet for your availability? Do you recommend a round of antibiotics?" I feel safe under Mom's watchful eye as the dentist answers her questions and extracts the remainder of my tooth. When we leave, he gives us each a toothbrush. He hands my mother a prescription for an antibiotic that we never fill.

My mouth is still healing when we find our way into a new shelter in Albany. This shelter requires us to be in school. Mom puts us back in our old school, PS 22, where I'm placed in the fifth grade, maybe. Other kids track time with birthday celebrations, holidays, Communions, traditions with family and friends, even world events. My family, and so many others around us, don't celebrate. We don't take family trips. We don't have access to media. Our frequent moves don't coincide with the beginnings and ends of school years. There are many places, and time is tracked by high and low points of pain and relief. School is always a relief.

The kids in my class instinctively avoid me. I spend my days bent over a table in the library, running my fingers through my hair. A snow of dandruff and lice drops to the desk. I try to kill them with my thumb or by rolling a Bic pen over them like a rolling pin, pressing firmly to punish them. It's hard to study—my thoughts are interrupted with the insatiable need to scratch. But I do get excited when the school announces a talent show. I really want to be up onstage, but I don't have a plan until I go home. Then Jessica says, "Hey, we should do a lip sync for the talent show!"

Alex half-heartedly agrees, and we gather on the driveway to rehearse. I bring down my tape player, the one I've been using to listen to tapes that I get from the library. They mostly are self-help tapes with subliminal messages—"You are tough. You are strong. You can do anything you set your mind to"—and I listen to them to fall asleep. Now I set the player on the neighbor's car, and we work up a routine to the Angels' song "My Boyfriend's Back."

"Jessica, you be the singer. I'm your old boyfriend. Alex, you're her new boyfriend." We choreograph how we will fight over her while we sing.

"Come on, Alex," I cheer. "Nothing is impossible! You can do it! You can do anything you set your mind to!"

At first, when Mom comes home and sees what we're doing, she says, "That's disgusting. You're brothers and sister, not boyfriends and girlfriend."

Then the wind changes, as it sometimes does, and Mom says, "You're going to need some costumes. Let's go to Next-To-New."

At Next-To-New it costs a dollar for whatever used clothes you can stuff in a brown paper bag. Jessica finds a poodle skirt, but it's too puffy and won't fit in the bag. To make room, she takes out a sweater I liked.

"Hey! That's mine!" I protest.

"No, we're here for this," Jessica says.

"The sweater *is* for this. It's part of my costume."

"Here," Mom says, pulling our food stamps out of her bra. "Alex, go next door and cash one of these."

Jessica and I exchange a look of excitement. Mom is getting an extra dollar. She's going to let us fill two bags this time.

By the time we're done, Alex is wearing a bad-boy leather jacket. Jessica sports a poodle skirt, white athletic socks, and a kerchief in her hair. I am stunning in my creased khakis and beige Ralph Lauren V-neck sweater.

The day of the show, we are corralled backstage along with the other acts. Parents aren't allowed, but Mom doesn't care. She's there, using her spittle to wipe a smudge off my forehead and straightening Jessica's kerchief. Mom, in her way, has always taken an interest in the arts. When we were younger, she took us to see a production of *My Fair Lady* in a park in New York City. She listens to classical music on the radio. When she takes us to museums to get warm, she makes a show of leading us through the exhibits.

Jessica hands our tape to the grumpy janitor turned DJ.

"Is it cued up?" he asks.

"Yes, just hit play," Jessica says.

From backstage we can see the various performances of New Kids on the Block songs. I am riveted, but Jessica wants us to rehearse. We get in position, and Alex starts lip-synching, flirting with and annoying Jessica, and then...*her boyfriend's back and there's gonna be trouble.* I swoop in, the star.

"David, stop." Jessica interrupts my reveries. "Pay attention. Here, like this. Push, then leap back." She shows me the choreography, which I'm having trouble remembering. It doesn't help that it keeps changing.

"I'm not sure I would give in so easily," I protest.

Alex is neutral. This is not his jam.

"Just do it," Jessica orders. "Then, when he punches you in the stomach, you've got to jump back as if the force throws you. Like this, see?"

Our performance is after the NKOTB song "Step by Step," but there are so many groups doing the same song it's hard to know which "Step by Step" we're supposed to follow. Then we hear, "And now we have the Ambroz trio performing 'My Boyfriend's Back.'"

Jessica stands between us, a hand on the back of each of our necks. "Okay, we can do this. Let's win," she says with a squeeze and a gentle push.

We do not win, but when we come offstage, Mom hugs us and tells us she's proud. In those moments, I am proud of myself and my family in spite of our circumstances. I know we can survive anything, and I see us as champions. When one trauma recedes, another rolls in, and often there's a relentless sea of adversity to overcome that leaves marks—both physical and psychological scars—but my anchors are Alex and Jessica, and Mom's love, though inconstant and unreliable, is real. I don't know where we'll end up next, but when the daily burdens bear down on me, these moments lift me back to the surface, where I can breathe enough to kick forward and push my way toward a distant shore, a better place than this.

Chapter 8

W E'RE GOING TO BOSTON," MOM tells the unsuspecting taxi driver after we pile in. She waves a fresh wad of Cyd Donahue's cash at him.

The driver does a double take at the money and Mom, then says, "Lady, I can't take you to Boston."

"Well, who can?" Mom asks impatiently.

"I'll take you to Dispatch," he says, turning back to the road and setting off. All four of us are crowded together on the pleather bench seat of the cab. He drives us to a beat-up garage filled with yellow cars.

"That way." The driver points Mom toward an office desk. She strides up, and without pausing for civilities she tells the dispatcher, "I'll pay someone five hundred dollars to take us to Boston."

"Lady, this isn't Greyhound." His cigarette bops up and down from the left side of his lips.

"All cash, half up front, half when we get there. And some for you," she says.

"Sit. Wait." He points toward a line of chairs attached to each other. A few minutes later, he summons Mom.

"That over there is Frank. He'll do the job for you. You pay him directly. You understand?" He's already turning away. Mom nods her head at us, and we follow her to the car.

"Frank, I'm Mary. This is Alex—"

"Nice, get in. Piss here if you have to before we start. Do you have to piss?" He stares at me. I shake my head no.

We pile into the back and settle in for a ride to a place that I've never heard of. I don't know why Mom chose Massachusetts or where exactly it is. She is paranoid, and this is the dot that her finger has landed on in the spinning globe of her mind.

Most of the day passes in the car; we make occasional pit stops along the highway. I'm dozing against Mom when the driver suddenly pulls over.

"Get out," he says. "Pay the other half and get out."

"This isn't Boston," Mom protests.

"No fucking shit. Pay and get out." There's no chance my mother is going to pay for an incomplete ride. We pile out of the car and take in our surroundings. He's brought us to a strip mall in Brockton, twenty-five miles from Boston.

"Look, there's a Dunkin' Donuts," Alex says. Mom is already heading in that direction.

We camp out at Dunkin' Donuts for several days and then start shelter hopping. As is standard in the shelter system, we have to be out by a certain time in the morning. The next night, instead of returning to the same shelter, we go to another, or to a train station, or we ride a bus. If Mom has a plan, she doesn't share it with us. Like barhopping, we get progressively more bedraggled and disoriented as we go. Then, at a welfare office, Mom tests out a new story.

"I've been in an abusive relationship. The children's father... We need a safe refuge," she tells the social worker, who nods sympathetically. As far as I know there hasn't been a man in her life since a boyfriend she had in Miami when I was five. I know better than to ask her about whether there is any truth to what she's saying to the social worker.

In any case, she is a victim. Of her illness, of herself, and of a society that hasn't found a way to reach her, treat her, or intervene to rescue her or us.

"We have a number of options for you," the social worker says. "This one in Pittsfield is a wonderful place for recovering families."

In New York City, if there were shelters designated for women and children, or long-term facilities, we did not visit them. From what I could tell, the shelters we stayed at primarily served vets, drug addicts, and mentally ill men. When we arrived, someone nameless would show us the bathroom, our cots, and where the rules were posted. We usually had to be out by 10:00 a.m. or sooner.

In Pittsfield, the women's shelter is different. It sits on a tall hill on the main street. It's a big, white New England mansion that has been renovated to house a number of families. We are welcomed by a mostly female staff and the staff facilitator, Claire, a pale woman with dark hair. She sits us down in an office to explain how the shelter works, what they have to offer us, and what's expected of us. In the New York shelters, the employees were weary and resigned, but here in Western Massachusetts, the shelter seems to be full of well-meaning, educated women who are optimistic about our chances for a brighter future. Their program is designed to help struggling families rebuild a stable life.

"Kids, we've enrolled you at Pittsfield Middle School," Claire says. "David, you're in sixth grade, is that right? And"—she checks her notebook—"Alex and Jessica, am I right that you are both in seventh? What's the last full year of school you guys completed? I don't have any school records yet. Mary, do you have their transcripts?"

"No," Mom answers curtly.

"Any immunization records?"

"No."

"I'm sure they'll be able to catch you kids up. We'll make sure they know how special you are," Claire says brightly.

We all nod silently.

"And, Mary, once you've settled in, we'll start thinking about jobs for you, so anytime you have an idea about an area where you can picture yourself working, please let me know!"

"I will do that," my mother agrees. "Did I say thank you?"

After a visit to a local medical center where I receive immunizations that I've had multiple times already, I join the sixth grade at Pittsfield Middle School, a stately brick building with granite columns and large windows. It doesn't matter what grade I was last in or what skills I have. Whenever I go to a new school, they just admit me and hope for the best. But unlike the schools I've been to in bigger cities, there are no bars on the windows at Pittsfield, and there are expansive green athletic fields. The kids seem friendlier, too, and respectful of their teachers. I feel safer here, but I'm still uncomfortable among my peers. At lunch, I hide in the library so I don't have to talk to my classmates.

"Ambroz, you doing the fundraiser?" one of the jock boys asks me in homeroom.

"Sure, yeah," I say, having no idea what he's talking about.

"Cool. It's for the football team, you know."

"Dope," I say, but he looks at me blankly. "I mean, yeah, that's cool." I don't do sports. I'd rather watch the boys play basketball than play it with them, but I don't say that.

The homeroom teacher explains the fundraiser later that day. It's nearly Christmas, and the students are selling holiday wrapping paper to benefit all the teams. The football players smirk and cheer, making it clear that the money will go to them. "I hope everyone can step up," the teacher says, handing out a catalog, order forms, and samples.

Flipping through the wrapping paper catalog, I stare at the colorful prints, mesmerized. My family has celebrated Christmas exactly once, when Mom arranged it with a church. On Christmas morning we awoke to find a tree surrounded by gifts for each of us and all the food for a Christmas feast, already prepared: a turkey, mashed potatoes, green beans, dinner rolls. The thrill of having a tree and a meal and presents lasted until the hunger returned and we were evicted, leaving the toys behind.

Though I'm not motivated to sell for a school fundraiser, I'm sure that I can bring in a lot of sales because as a homeless kid I've developed some sales skills. In the winters, Jessica, Alex, and I go door-to-door offering our snow-shoveling services. We know how to pick customers who won't ask a lot of questions and will just hand us a few bucks and a shovel because we're kids. For the school fundraiser, the first apartment building I walk into has a row of doors on the first floor. One of the doors itself is wrapped like a shiny green-and-red gift. If they're wasting wrapping paper like this, they'll definitely want more. I know a perfect target when I see one.

I knock, and an older woman speaks through the closed door in a squeaky sweet voice. "Can I help you?"

This'll be tough. She can't see how cute I am, and I can't read her face and body language. Nonetheless, I go for it.

"Hi, I'm David. I go to Pittsfield Middle and today we are selling holiday wrapping paper to benefit the school," I say loudly through the door. I hear mechanical noises as she undoes multiple locks. She wears a worn housecoat, but is otherwise clean and tidy, smelling of lavender.

"Well, well. I was just thinking I needed to buy some. I have all these grandkids now, and they don't live near here, so I have to send the gifts early. Their parents used to come home for every holiday. Then they stopped coming for Easter. Then it was every other year for Thanksgiving. Then Thanksgiving stopped. Now, they want me to come to them for Christmas, but I'm old. You don't understand, but it's hard to travel when you're old."

She's a talker and time is money. I have to take control of the situation. "Oh, I would never do that to my mom. My mom is the best.

She chose our neighborhood because it has the best public school in the area. It's not wealthy like some schools, but it's safe and the teachers are really good," I say, steering the conversation back to money and school; her money, my school.

"So, what are you selling, honey?" she asks.

"Wrapping paper, special scissors, fun tape…all sorts of holiday stuff."

"Let's take a look, then." She opens the door wider to let me in.

This woman's apartment is smaller than I expected, but warm. We pass the living room, where a large red Oriental rug stretches across the floor, and the furniture is comfortably worn. The surfaces are cluttered with family photos. I stare at them, fascinated. Here are six people, standing in front of the ocean. Here is a child, opening a present. I think about how we don't have any photos of our family. Sometimes Mom manages to order the school photos, but they've always disappeared by the next move. We don't own a camera, but even if we did, taking pictures is a way of thinking ahead to the moment you'll want to look back on good times. We live in the present.

She offers me a seat at the kitchen counter, which is a putrid yellow Formica. I hand her the catalog and, putting on her readers, she begins to turn pages.

"Ma'am, if you tell me what you like, I can take down the order here." I hold up the official form.

She makes her selections, the order coming to a good amount.

"This is great, thank you. I'll need you to pay half now, and half when I deliver," I say.

She tenses up. Perhaps she can tell that I have no intention of turning in the money to the school or delivering the paper to her.

"I'll prepare the receipt with the school's information on it. That way you can speak with the principal's office if you have any questions," I say.

She relaxes. "Let me get my purse," she says. *Score.* But then she pulls out a rather large rectangular wallet, the sort that holds checkbooks. She thinks she's going to write me a check.

"If you pay cash, I can offer you a discount. The school will pay the tax for you. It saves more than three percent!" I say, improvising.

There is a slight pause. Her features bunch in a little.

"I can note that on the receipt too," I say.

The checkbook goes back into the purse, and she withdraws some cash. As she carefully counts the money, I look over her shoulder into the kitchen. Dirty dishes are stacked on the counters and in the sink. The trash is overflowing. A pantry door, slightly ajar, reveals chaos within. Perhaps she doesn't have much more than we do. For a moment I consider aborting my mission. It doesn't feel right. But she does have her own apartment. The dishes are dirty because she has food. She has a family. We need this money more than she does. The shelter is feeding us for now, but they'll kick us out soon enough, and then what? The poor eat the poor; we have no choice.

"Thank you for making that so easy," she says.

I walk down the stairs of her building and pause on the landing to count the money. Though she carefully counted it out more than once, she gave me far more than the cost of the order. I'm caught off guard by this unexpected grace. Does she know? Should I give her back some of the money? Should I thank her again? But after a moment I continue down the stairs. Walk away. Survive.

I also use my sales experience to help Mom with the part-time job the shelter has found to help her transition to independent living. She's supposed to sell Electrolux vacuums and carpet-cleaning services in the neighborhood. The first challenge is getting her out the door.

"I'll do all the talking, Mom, I promise. Remember what Claire said? It's part of your contribution to the community?"

She grunts and hauls herself out of bed. "Where are my cigarettes?"

I find them for her, and we walk, lugging the vacuum and products to a nicer part of the neighborhood.

On the sidewalk in front of the first house, I try to make her presentable. "Mom, you can't smoke." "Mom, fix your blouse." "Mom, get ready. We're about to sell." I urge her from house to house, helping get homeowners who aren't looking to spend one hundred dollars on carpet cleaning to say yes to this big, disgruntled lady who's huffing and puffing at the door and her adorable son. The shelter's intention is to help Mom get back on her feet, but they've never asked the question that should come first: *Is this person able to work?* Mom can't sell vacuum cleaners, because she's ill. Poverty is traumatizing especially for those with mental illness. The opportunity to change one's circumstances has to begin with mental and physical health.

In addition to helping their resident mothers find work, the shelter also pays the children to do chores, which are posted on a bulletin board. This responsibility and the token pay are meant to instill a work ethic and to make us feel like part of the community. It seems like a worthwhile system, and some of the other families are making the most of it. We do, too, in our own way. Most of the other kids dutifully perform their assigned tasks. I visit the board in quiet moments and move things around so that I never have bathroom duty. We're paid in quarters, which Mom demands we hand over. But we skim some off the top. We have big plans.

While I was selling wrapping paper, Jessica and Alex's class was sell-ing tickets to a raffle to raise money for the school. Now we organize our own raffle, which will benefit our favorite charity: us. At Caldor, we use the quarters we earned at the shelter to buy a roll of raffle tickets. With it tucked in my backpack, we hold up our passes and board a bus headed to a nicer part of town, where the residents have more money to squander on raffle tickets. We sit halfway back and spend the bus ride planning our hustle and what we will do with the gains. How much do we need for household expenses? How much should we allocate for Mom's cigarettes? Should we save any rent money for whenever Mom makes us leave the shelter?

We disembark and walk up a side street. "How about that one?" I say, pointing to a neat two-story clapboard with a square of green grass out front and a stone path to the door. On either side of the front door is a large pot of bright red flowers. How I love these well-kept houses. I like to imagine how the occupants live behind the walls. Fridges full of food that will be cooked in proper pans and served on matching dishes. Closets of warm winter clothes, perhaps an argyle item or two. Parents who drive their children to school and greet them afterward carrying trays of milk and freshly made cookies.

I knock on the door, hoping for a mom because they're the best marks. When it opens, indeed, it is a mom. It's always a mom. In this crucial moment, I have to choose what angle we're going to take. We can pretend to be well-fed churchgoing kids or poor street urchins. If the woman looks beleaguered, we play up our poverty because we know she needs to feel like people have it worse than she does. If there's a fancy car, we work the church angle. If there's a Volvo station wagon, we know we've hit the jackpot. For some reason people with Volvo station wagons are the most generous.

The woman who answers looks put-together and a bit busy, so I don't waste any time.

"Ma'am, our school is doing a raffle to support after-school programs," I say, holding up my bus pass to look official, knowing my siblings are holding theirs up too. "Each entry is two dollars, and one hundred percent goes to support after-school programs."

"Well..." she starts.

I cut her off before she can say no, talking quickly and smiling a lot. "Our school really needs the help. A lot of poor kids go there, and this program helps them."

"It's just that—"

"You can also buy twelve for twenty dollars. That's the best deal." If they won't go for the upsell, they'll come in with a ticket or two to soften the blow.

"I don't think I need twelve, but perhaps—"

"Wow, that's great," I say.

"Okay, cool," Alex says.

"Thank you so much!" Jessica chimes in. We are a powerful force of hope and positivity.

I pull off eight tickets and thrust them at her, along with a pen.

"We just need your name and phone here." I show her.

She dutifully fills them out, then hands the tickets back to me.

Carefully, reverently, I crease and tear them apart. Each one of these is a chance for her to win the grand prize. A prize that I have not specified. She's probably assuming it's a portion of the proceeds.

I give her the stubs she's to keep, and she hands me a twenty-dollar bill. I fake search for change in my backpack, knowing exactly what she'll say next.

"No, that's okay, hon, just keep the change."

"Oh, wow, thank you, that's really nice. We all get to participate in the program after school, so this will really help." With big smiles and a chorus of thank-yous, we turn and head to the next house.

On the bus home Alex counts our earnings. "One hundred and twelve dollars," he says. "Let's go to McDonald's!"

I hesitate. I'm in the habit of considering Mom first: keeping her calm, making sure her needs are met, making sure there are no unpaid bills that could provoke a conflict. My immediate hunger comes second. Alex's hierarchy of needs is different. Hunger first, then basket-ball. He copes differently. But this shelter is so generous that we have a reprieve. McDonald's it is!

___

It doesn't take long for Mom to start showing her true colors at the shelter. "We need more space. There are four of us. Jessica needs her own bed," Mom demands of Claire. We are at "Group," a meeting when some of the residents gather with staff in the dining room to "share." As soon as Mom speaks, I can see the train wreck coming. I avert my eyes, studying traces of a fireplace that's been boarded up and painted the same beige as the room.

"Mary, this is not the venue for that conversation—" Claire starts to say.

"Why not?"

"Mary, we can talk about this another—"

"It is not right. There are four of us and we're sharing two beds," Mom declares. Last week, she called Claire a lesbian in an accusatory tone. Claire calmly told her that she didn't think there was anything wrong with being a lesbian, but that they were not having a conversation about her personal choices.

"Mrs. Ambroz, we can speak to this after the meeting," Claire tries again.

"I know the room across the hall is emptying out. It has three beds, and my family needs it. Jessica is a young woman."

We get the room, but the end is nearer than I realize, and, in spite of all my efforts to keep us stable, I soon become the center of our eviction from the shelter.

In the new room, I wake up one morning head to toe with my brother, who is still asleep. My hand meanders to my penis, almost dreamily. Today I'm itchier than normal. I flip the bedding and fold down the waistband of my white Hanes briefs to get a look. There I discover that, seemingly overnight, bumps have sprouted above my penis.

"Oh my God," I exclaim. "Alex! Alex! Dude, wake up!" I give my brother a slight kick to his chest.

"What the fuck, man, what?!" Alex opens his eyes, but he doesn't raise his head.

"Bro, look at this," I say, gesturing at my exposed crotch.

"I'm not going to look at your dick, man. What the hell is wrong with you?"

"I think I'm sick, Alex. Look!" I plead. "I've got a rash."

"Show Mom if you think..." He trails off, realizing that's not a good idea. "Fine, show me, but be quick." He sits up and I pull down my waistband again, keeping my penis covered but showing the area just above. The skin is covered with a million little red bumps.

"Oh fuck, David," Alex says, too loudly.

"What are you doing? What's wrong?" Mom says, waking up. "Show me, David."

I've had fleas, herpes, and more than my share of rashes, fungi, and parasites. Though the shelter is clean, I naturally assume I have yet another disease. I show the bumps to my mother. As a nurse, she might have realized that her twelve-year-old son was beginning to sprout pubic hair, but Mom takes one look and yells, "What did you do? Who did you let touch you?"

Her voice must be audible throughout the shelter. She grabs me closer, then completely yanks down my briefs. I stare at the graceful windows, the oak floor, anything not to watch my mother examine my genitals.

I don't see the first slap coming, but it connects hard with my face.

"Who touched you?!" Mom roars. "Did he put it in you? Was it Chris? It was Chris."

I don't know who Chris is or what he might have put in me. I stagger a few steps back, my underwear around my ankles. *SLAP.* I try to pull my underwear up. I'm not giving her the answer she wants, so the slapping continues. Left, right, left, right, question, slap, question.

"Who fucked you?" Mom demands. I flash to my circumcision, the blurred invasion of my body. But since then, nobody has touched me, injured me, broken the rules.

"Mom, I—" I begin. *Slap.*

"You liked it." *Slap.*

"No."

Slap.

The pounding is loud and comes out of nowhere. Her head jerks toward the tall oak door.

"What is it?" she asks.

"Mary, we are coming in." The disembodied voice of a savior comes through.

Chris—oh right, *that's* Chris—stands there, and it dawns on me that she thinks this harmless old man is molesting me.

"You pervert, I know you touched him!" Mom yells. By now all of the residents must be hearing the play-by-play. My underpants are up, and I'm seated on the bed, my face smarting.

"Mary, calm down," Chris tries.

"*Get out of my house!*" Mom yells, even though we have only this room, and it's not ours.

"Mary, you cannot hit your children here," Chris says.

"Don't lecture me. I'm a nurse. I know you diddled him. He's got an STD from your filthy cock," Mom hollers.

"What?" Chris is taken aback.

"I knew it. You are disgusting. He's twelve, for God's sake!" Mom continues.

Claire appears. "What the hell is going on here? Chris, what's this about? Mary, sit down. Everybody, calm down," she says.

"Get him the fuck away from my children. He's a molester. Fucking dirty pedophile."

Chris turns and walks away without saying anything. Claire looks from me to Mom and pulls a chair out from a desk. She sits down, as if this were Group.

"Mary, this behavior will not stand. If you have concerns, you need to talk to us. You believe Chris molested David, is that it?" Claire says in a calm, therapy voice. "Mary, Chris is married. He's sixty-five years old—"

"We are leaving. This is a house of perverts. Russian molesters. Perverts," Mom informs her.

Nobody wants to tangle with my mother. And so, at this shelter for abused women, the response to our mother's unhinged behavior is to move us to an apartment where they won't have to witness the abuse. Their work is challenging enough without my mother's accusations to complicate it. They abandon us, but that is likely not the story they tell themselves. Everywhere, we encounter adults who intervene with temporary kindnesses but know, because it is plain to see, that we need more. All of them tell themselves stories to assuage their guilt. They need to believe that their incidental kindnesses make them humane. Maybe the story the shelter workers tell themselves is that being in a group home is stressful for Mom and that if they give her an apartment where she has more independence, she'll stop hitting her children. It's a weak story, but it's the easiest move. This is a pattern that is repeated across the country—children in poverty are given kernels of assistance but are rarely rescued from their circumstances. My family is a car accident on the side of the highway. Passersby slow down long enough to gape but do nothing or very little to provide life-saving aid. America watches its children suffer in poverty, shaking our heads in sadness, and driving onward thinking it's someone else's job to help those poor folks. And so our family moves to an apartment at 81 High Street, where nobody will see our situation go from bad to worse.

Chapter 9

*T*HIS COULD WORK, THIS COULD *finally work*, I think. Our new apartment is on the second floor and it's full of good surprises. First of all, in the living room, next to the sofa where Mom will sleep, is a TV.

"There's a TV!" I yell, even though we all can see it. I turn it on. "It works! We have TV!" The kitchen faces the back of the building, and on the counter are new dishes that the shelter seems to have provided: three plates, three sets of utensils, three clear water glasses, and three white coffee mugs. One of us didn't get counted, but it's a good start.

There's a full-sized bed in the back bedroom, where Jessica will sleep, and two mattresses for me and Alex in the front bedroom. Our room faces the street and has three large windows with closets on either end. I take a few minutes to unpack a collection of rocks I've been carrying around. I arrange it next to a little lamp on the floor by my mattress, making the space my own. Then I open the closet on one end of our room, expecting it to be empty, but it, too, is full of gifts. "There are towels! Sheets! Mom, come here. Blankets!" I report excitedly. Mom does not come—she is on the sofa smoking—but Alex and Jessica are right behind me.

"This is awesome," Alex says.

"Let's make our beds," Jessica says, smiling. The three of us pull out the identical beige linens and gleefully head to our beds. When I'm done making mine, I go into Jessica's room, and Alex follows. Jessica is on her bed, reading a book she brought from the shelter. Alex and I join her, and we sit quietly together. We have beds, other furniture, a few possessions, a decent amount of food coming regularly from a food pantry, and some money from the shelter to help Mom adjust. The rent will be paid by the shelter for a few months. This is more of a runway plan than we've ever had, and I feel a sense of hope.

In the new apartment, Alex and Jessica, who are thirteen and fourteen now, start to spend as much time as they can away from home.

"Mom, I'm going to be at Nicholas's tonight after school. I'll be home by eight thirty," Jessica announces on her way out the door.

"Mmm," Mom replies. Nicholas and Jessica are classmates, and she's increasingly finding excuses to spend time at his house.

Sensing an opportunity, Alex chimes in. "Abby and I are going to hang out at the library and study." We are all old enough now to want less of Mom, to want our freedom, to want friends our age. The difference with me is that I see Mom as my responsibility. I struggle with making friends anyway, so I tell myself that someone needs to make sure she has what she needs. Someone needs to make sure we don't get kicked out. I'm obviously the best one for the job.

"Take your brother, Alex," Mom says.

"Mom, no. He's not even in our classes. We're studying—" Alex begins.

"Take your brother," Mom says again, a harsh undernote to her voice. When I go to their friends' houses with Alex and Jessica, I am most focused on their kitchens. They have big, clean suburban refrigerators filled with food, and they're allowed to eat whatever they want, whenever they want. When we first moved into this apartment, the women's shelter arranged for us to have food delivered to us from a food pantry. After a while, we were supposed to pick it up ourselves. The idea was to wean us off the aid. That didn't work, so they referred us to church pantries, which we visit inconsistently. We therefore take every opportunity to snack at or bring home food from other people's houses.

Mom stations herself on the brown sofa in the living room, watching TV and smoking. Someone, presumably at the shelter, has signed us up for a free trial of cable, and she's getting into Pat Robertson's Christian lifestyle show *The 700 Club*, a troubling development.

"Turn on Pat," Mom instructs me. I watch, wary, as he says, "If God gives you a dollar, it doesn't hurt to give ten cents of it back. You must keep tithing if you want God's blessing."

The last thing I need is someone putting such ideas in Mom's head.

At the shelter, there was structure: a schedule with designated meal-times, TV-watching times, chores, and bedtimes for the children. We had to go to school, and Mom had to work. She couldn't spend all day lying on the sofa wrapped in a makeshift toga watching Pat Robertson. Now, with no other adults around, Mom starts to devolve. She refuses to go out and sell vacuums, even with me along to help. She stays in the apartment, smoking, watching TV, and drinking the same cup of coffee for days. After a few months we stop visiting the church pantries, the cable gets turned off, and she rarely gets dressed.

In the outside world, the Giants have made it to the Super Bowl, the Patriots having failed to make it, and suddenly everyone's a Giants fan. They're wearing Giants hats and shirts, there are Super Bowl signs on the buses, and it's on the front page of the newspaper every day. Everyone is focused on which team will win. They are so invested that they paint their bodies blue. But I don't understand how this grabs their attention and homeless kids don't. Why don't we look at *those* statistics? We need to obsess about their outcomes with the same fanaticism that we devote to a quarterback. My mom is almost catatonic and we'll likely be evicted soon enough, and there are other kids like me, so I can't understand why sports matters and we don't.

While Jessica survives by spending as much time as she can at Nicholas's house, my brother retreats into books and video games when he's not with his girlfriend, except my mother cramps his style by continuing to insist that I chaperone them.

"David, go with your brother," Mom demands.

"Mom, why?" I protest. "I don't want to go. They just ignore me."

"David, I am not asking."

We trudge out of the house, Alex pestering me to hurry up. We pick up his girlfriend, and when we get to the baseball field, Alex says, "Don't be up in my business, okay?" While they playfully touch and make out for hours, I'm at a respectable distance, doing my best to ignore them. For a while, I practice a duck call, manipulating my lips and basically farting out my mouth. Then I pull up blades of grass, one at a time, and examine them. Sometimes I just stare up into the clouds. Alex and his girlfriend try to slip farther away, but I stay on them. I don't want Mom to be pissed.

I watch as his girlfriend's hand slips into his pants and his hand goes up her shirt. *Revolting.*

When I'm not chaperoning, I'm in the house keeping an eye on Mom. I'm too worried to leave her alone. Once, back in New York, when I was around seven years old, Mom was furious that we were being evicted. Nearly naked in the apartment, she thrust a handful of food stamps at me. "Go buy a quart of gas," she ordered. "I'm going to burn down this shitty apartment."

"Mom...I...Mom, I don't..." I stuttered, trying to understand.

"Do as I say," she said, looming over me.

There were people in the building! I had to do what she said or risk being beaten, but I didn't want to hurt anyone else. *Surely they won't sell me gas*, I told myself.

"Eight sixty-five," the convenience store clerk said. I handed over mostly change and some bills for a quart of oil—the closest thing to gas that I could find—and walked away from the gas station in a daze.

You can't do this, I told myself. Hatching a plan, I hid the can of oil under a bush in front of the house, where I could fetch it if she beat me too badly.

"He wouldn't sell me the gasoline, so I brought you these," I told my mother, handing her the cigarettes.

She backhanded me. "Give me those. Did you get matches, at least?"

"Yes, Mom. Here." I handed over the matches and backed out of the room. Outside, I grabbed the quart of oil and threw it out in a neighbor's trash can. I didn't want her finding it.

I don't want to leave 81 High Street, and I definitely don't want her to decide to burn it down. When the landlord starts asking for rent, I tell him we'll have it in a week, and hope for a good day to urge Mom out the door to sell carpet cleaning.

When she is on edge, bringing her cigarettes is still my first resort. That spring, however, the cigarettes aren't enough. Mom is worse than she's ever been, not just in a fugue state, but also violent. She strikes like a bolt of lightning on a sunny day. You're walking, the sky is clear, and suddenly you're knocked to the ground. Jessica is beaten for having knots in her hair. I call my brother a fag, and she lets loose on me, not because being gay shouldn't be an insult, but because there is no insult worse.

Teachers must notice our gashes. But I don't have hope that officials will intervene. Over the years we've been investigated many times without getting help. Mom always fights to keep us, and it's a battle she's mostly won. The most recent time she lost custody of us was in Albany, when she was in court fighting an eviction.

"Ms. Ambroz, you owe four months of rent. You signed the lease. There is nothing I can do for you—you and your children have to vacate," the judge said from high up on his bench. We three sat there, next to Mom, looking earnestly up at him. I burrowed my stare deep into him, willing him to be on our side, willing him to realize that if we vacated, we would be homeless, willing him to decide we needed help.

"Where do you think I'm going to go?" Mom suddenly hollered, startling the courtroom out of silence. Then she bent over, as if to pick up her purse and papers, but instead grabbed my sister's shoe off her foot, a white moccasin with a beaded eagle, and hurled it at the judge. It struck him in the face with a thwap. I half hoped it would wake him up to our situation. The courtroom cop was moving before I could even react, coming right at Mom.

"Jesus, lady," the judge said, tossing the shoe down to the floor.

Mom was taken to the Troy Medical Psychiatric Center for two weeks. The judge had been content to evict us into homelessness, but now that he had taken her away, the city of Albany could no longer ignore us.

"Is there anyone we can call?" a social worker asked.

"Call the Jeremys. I babysit for them," Jessica suggested, both shoes now on her feet.

We stayed with the Jeremys for the two weeks that Mom spent in the psychiatric ward. But when she was released, nobody cared that we were being put in the custody of a homeless woman who'd recently thrown a shoe at a judge in a court of law.

The Jeremys drove us to the hospital to reunite us with her. Mrs. Jeremy walked us into the waiting room. "Your mother is getting out, okay? But we are always here for you," she said.

Then Mom emerged, a too-wide smile on her face. "Did I say thank you?" she asked Mrs. Jeremy.

"Of course, Mary. Do you know where you are going? Do you need a ride?" Mrs. Jeremy asked.

"No, I've arranged an apartment. It's all set, right near the kids' school. We don't need your help anymore," Mom said, her smile frozen on her face.

"Here, Phil wanted to make sure you had some money to get started," Mrs. Jeremy said, and handed Mom some money.

"Did I say thank you? Say thank you, kids," Mom said.

After Mrs. Jeremy left, we sat in the waiting room for a long while, until finally Mom ushered us toward the door. "Let's go," she said.

"Where?" I asked.

"Walk straight."

In the apartment on High Street, I've long given up hope of being rescued, but as a twelve-year-old I'm starting to have a clearer view of our situation. Mom is getting worse, and I now understand the real danger we're in. I also can see how the system is supposed to work. When a parent is violent or negligent and an authority finds out, they are supposed to help the children. Perhaps the mistake I've made over all these years—with the judge, with the Jeremys, with the teachers and school nurses—is not asking for help. Mom has us hide our injuries, and I finally understand that we're hiding them from the people whose job it is to stop her from hurting us. Instead, I want to take action. I want to save us. When a D.A.R.E. officer comes to give my class at Pittsfield Middle School an antidrug seminar, I am desperate enough to try again. "Drugs aren't cool," she says to the class. "If your friend tells you drugs are cool, do you think that person is really your friend? Because drugs will kill you."

We are in the fluorescently lit classroom where I take French. With its polished linoleum floors, posters of the Eiffel Tower, and desks carved with names and penises, it is the safest place I know. It seems absurd to be warned that drugs will kill me. I would have to choose to take drugs in order for them to kill me, and the danger in my life isn't coming from my own bad choices. It's coming from my mother. The officer says she's here as a resource. She cares about us. She wants us to be safe. We can tell her anything. She sounds sincere. I'm desperate for help, and I start to think that maybe this woman could actually do something to help us get away from our mother. What would I say? What would happen if I told her the very real threat I feel: *Drugs aren't going to kill me. My mother is going to kill me.* I know that foster care is a possible solution. It's a fact of life in the communities where we live.

Poverty often leads to neglect, and neglect is the reason 60 percent of children go into the foster care system. Sometimes the kids whom I see leaving for foster care come back home, sometimes I never see them again, and sometimes I never know because we've moved away. We ourselves have been investigated many times, and we've been in the system before, briefly, in Florida and in New York. Both times we were given back to Mom when she convinced the authorities that she was a good mother. If someone were to ask me what foster care is, I couldn't articulate it, but I know that it could save me from Mom.

When class ends, I go into the office the D.A.R.E. officer is using. I sit down to wait for her. The wooden seat of the visitor chair is molded with two butt indentations, but it does nothing to help my ass, which still hurts from yesterday's beating. At gym class today, I pretended to be sick so I wouldn't have to change in front of anyone and expose my bruises.

The officer gives me a friendly smile, but I can't look her in the eyes. Am I really about to tell her? To do so is to break the most sacred rule in my family: We don't tell our secrets. To rat on Mom is a betrayal. After all the effort to keep our family together, I feel like I'm starting a fire that I may not be able to control. I fix my eyes on her neat desk and blurt out, "My mom's hitting me. My mom's hitting us."

"What do you mean?" she asks.

I roll up my sleeves to show her where Mom hit me with a hairbrush. The bruises go all the way up my arms. I feel exposed—I have spent my life hiding bruises. It feels wrong to show them, like I've opened a door that I can't close.

She gives a short gasp, but quickly composes herself and becomes clinical. "Whose class are you in? Where do you live? How long has this been going on?"

For the first time in my life, I give the answers, the real answers, the ones I'm never supposed to give. I feel the potential explosiveness of them. I'm doing it. I'm getting us help. And I'm risking everything

Mom has told us to preserve. I love her, but I want to protect us from her.

The D.A.R.E. officer is in a police uniform. Her head is tilted toward her notepad as she writes down what I am saying. Her black hair is back in a short ponytail. She is listening, but her reaction doesn't seem equal to the secrets that I'm sharing. I've never sought out help before, never walked anyone through my situation. I'm crying out for help, finally, desperately, and she's behaving just like the social workers do when they interview us for food stamps.

"Mom hits us, a lot. She gets mad...at nothing...well, sometimes at something...but really nothing. She hits us. She uses brushes, or hangers, or books, or her fists...or anything."

"When did you last get hit?" she asks calmly.

Didn't she see my arms? How bad does it have to be? I don't understand why she needs more proof and detail, but in frustration and desperation I pull down my T-shirt to expose my clavicle, which has a nasty bruise, changing from purple to yellow.

"I see, honey. Don't worry, you are going to be fine," she says. I find her attempt to reassure me hollow, as if she's just saying what she's supposed to say.

After I answer her questions, she hugs me mechanically and gives me a coupon for McDonald's. I never see her again.

Two weeks later, however, two social workers show up at 81 High Street. The knock reverberates throughout the apartment, and Mom rises from the sofa. "What?" Mom says to the closed door.

"Mrs. Ambroz, we want to talk to you. Please open the door." The voice is muffled but demanding.

Mom lets them in and immediately shifts her demeanor. "Please come into the living room. We just moved in, so we are still shopping for furniture. I'm doing laundry, so..." She gestures toward her toga.

"Mrs. Ambroz—Mary—I'm Margaret." She is a white woman with dark hair and fair skin dressed in monochromatic beige—stirrup pants and a blazer over a sweater—a professional look that I know will garner Mom's respect. Her tone is tough and authoritative. "I'm an investigating social worker, and this is Darrell; he helps me. We need to talk to you and the kids. Can we ask you all some questions?"

"Of course. Please sit. David, get the other chair from your room," Mom says. I retrieve the folding metal chair and give it to Margaret.

"David, please come here and sit," Mom says, pointing toward the end of the sofa. The four of us sit facing the two of them. Margaret reaches into her leather briefcase and pulls out a yellow pad and a pen. Clicking the white pen with indecipherable writing, she looks up and smiles.

"David, does your mother hurt you?" Margaret asks. I can't believe it. Why would she ask me that in front of my mother? It was enough of a risk to ask the D.A.R.E. officer for help, but I can't tell these people the truth in front of her. If she finds out I betrayed her, she really will kill me. They are putting me in a very dangerous situation—and they're supposed to be protecting me.

I steal a glance up at my mother. She's looking at me lovingly. Alex's and Jessica's faces are aghast, and they are looking anywhere but at the social worker.

"No," I say.

"That's not what you told the D.A.R.E. officer," the social worker says.

"I lied. I was mad at Mom."

"I see," Margaret says.

"From my notes, it says she hits you with hangers, brushes..." Margaret starts.

"*That's not true!*" I yell. She has got to stop. I've let an outsider into our family. I've endangered us even more. I look at Mom, trying to gauge where she is in this moment. Few things trigger her as much as government intervention. It doesn't occur to me that if she explodes here and now, we might actually get help. I'm too locked into the need to manage her mood. My cover-up seems to appease her, but there's no telling what will happen when these people leave. I was an idiot to think I could save us. Now we are in a precarious situation, and I don't know what to fear more—that Mom will lash out in front of these people, which might have bad consequences for her, or what she'll do to me if they leave me alone with her.

"How did you get the bruise on your neck, then?" Margaret asks.

"I was . . . wrestling . . . with . . . Alex." I look toward him for affirmation. He's a beat behind, but nods.

Margaret stares at me hard. I look at her as innocently as possible, knowing Mom is watching my every move. The interview goes quickly after that, with similar questions asked of Alex and Jessica. We look directly at this woman and lie. They leave, and nothing comes of it.

———

That spring, Alex endures the worst of Mom's violence. Her obsession with his father, Alex Sr., has risen to new heights. She has always been angry at him for the breakup of their marriage, even though, by her own account, she was the one who left. Her stories about his alleged abuse, which were currency in the women's shelter, spin in her head with increasing velocity. She beats us all, but Alex, his father's namesake, her favorite, who is small for his age, is hit with brushes, belts, and hangers. The more she hits any of us, the quieter we get. I worry that Alex is disappearing. He seems less like my brother and more like a cornered animal. I blame myself. What did I think would happen? The fuse was lit by the investigation that I launched, and now here we are.

One day Mom puts a yellow legal pad in front of Alex and demands that he write down the names of all the men he's had sex with. When I'm given assignments like this, I know to write something down or risk her wrath. But Alex writes a silly poem. Big mistake.

When Mom reads what he wrote, she throws the pad to the ground and yells, "You think this is a fucking joke?" She tears a white metal curtain rod off the wall. I know what's coming, and time slows. Mom bears down on him, barefoot and braless. Everything slows down, and I see her body ripple with movement, her knuckles white with pressure. Worst are her eyes, laser focused and furious, the irises impossibly black.

She raises the curtain rod diagonally behind her, about to swing it down on Alex. As she does this, I notice that a bracket once attaching the rod to the drywall is dangling off one end. The rod will hurt, but that bracket is going to make it worse. Then, as the rod reaches the top of its arc, the bracket falls to the floor. She swings, and an extra screw drops down onto the exhausted carpet.

Alex raises his hands to protect his head and face.

"Noooo, noooo..." he screams.

"You fucking little shit!" Mom roars back. The impact catches his open hands, and they're pushed down, exposing his head.

"Stop! Stop it, Mom. You're going to kill him," I scream, but she's raising the rod again. I leap one step, two steps, a third, and I'm on her, pulling her left arm. Her anger gives her strength, and she hurls me toward Alex. My head strikes the wall, and my vision goes fuzzy. The rod comes down, this time striking hard against my shoulder and cheek. I instantly taste blood in my mouth.

She raises the rod, now bent, back up and over her shoulder. My blood is on it, running down toward her hand. She turns her body back toward Alex.

He holds his devastated hands out. "Mom, stop..." he cries.

She brings the rod down again. She's trying to hit his face, to permanently erase the sly grin that instigated this attack. I want to tell him to lower his hands—if he lets her get at least one solid connection, this might be over. But in moments like these there is no strategy except what position is least vulnerable, what response is least provocative, what will make it stop. Alex instinctively continues to protect his face, and the second hit connects with the same ferocity.

Now he's bleeding. I hope that's enough, but Mom brings the rod down on his head one more time. He's completely defenseless. His scream stops abruptly. His teeth clap together as his mouth is forced closed.

Mom raises the rod to the side. She's trying a different angle.

"Mom..." I grunt. "Mom, *stop*."

Wielding the rod like a tennis racket, she strikes him hard against the side of his head. I'm not sure if he's still conscious when he falls to the floor. He's quiet. She stands above him, panting. The misshapen rod drops from her hand, and she turns and walks out of the room. I'm lying on my left side, looking across at Alex. His feet are closest to me. His white Hanes socks are dirty on the bottom, and above them I see his chest rise and fall. I lift my face, get one hand under me, then the other, and push up. Wooziness overtakes me. Blood is coming down my face from somewhere on my head. I cannot stand, so I crawl.

"Alex, are you okay? Alex..." I whisper, keeping quiet so she doesn't come back. He's on his side, cradling his fingers and hands. Welts are rising on his face; blood gushes from a head wound and a cut above his eyebrow.

Where are the adults? Where is the D.A.R.E. officer? Where are the teachers? The social workers? Where is anyone who can protect us? They have left us here. We are kids suffering in plain sight. Save your prayers, they won't protect us. Over and over again, the three of us were left with a woman who was clearly hurting us by people in positions of authority. I want others to know what it means to be equally neglected by a parent and a society. I want it to be impossible to walk past a child who is begging in the street. Thank you for the Christmas presents collected at your office, but I'd rather you vote for people and policies so children don't suffer from neglect, abuse, hunger, homelessness, violence, and maybe death.

Alex's eyes are open. "Alex, it's over. It's over...It's over..." I whisper. I lower myself so I am facing him, our bodies inches apart. I know he needs ice, but for now all I can do is lie there and stare at my big brother.

At twelve, I have spent my life trying to find a way forward. I thought I could solve my mother's problems by placating the people around her, by making everything perfect. Then I realized that I needed to help myself, and I thought telling someone about the abuse and neglect would save me, transport me to a safe life. But the authorities did nothing. Their visit made her worse. If they aren't going to help me, I'm stuck in this life. I don't know what my next step is going to be. I just know I don't want to die like this, on the floor, unheard and unseen.

Chapter 10

SOME BRUISES LAST LONGER THAN others. Mom keeps Alex home from school the next day, and the days after that, waiting for the marks to fade. The three of us don't talk about what happened, but we see that after all the years of untreated mental illness, constant instability, and the prison of her paranoid delusions, Mom's violence is escalating. All of us, without speaking, come to the same conclusion: She could kill us. Something has to give. One night, while Mom smokes and watches TV, the three of us huddle on Jessica's bed. Alex has a T-shirt on, and the bruises on his arms are beginning to fade into yellows and purples. He leans back against the wall, winces, and sits up straight again. I recognize that feeling of not being able to find a comfortable position.

"We have to get away," I say, quietly enough that Mom can't hear.

"But where can we go?" Alex asks.

"Albany. Maybe Aurora will help," Jessica says. It's been two years since we've seen Aurora, our outspoken and kind neighbor in Albany. We don't even know if she still lives there. But anywhere else would be safer than here.

During school breaks, and on the walks to and from school, we plan. We don't have much money, and I'm afraid of what will happen to Mom if we leave her, so we decide to run away one at a time. Alex, because she beats him the most, has to go first. Jessica will go next, and I'll go last, but I'm planning to go to New York City; I think Cyd Donahue might help me. Maybe he'll adopt me.

On the way home from Alex's girlfriend's house one night, we see a women's ten-speed bike on a porch, unlocked. Which we take. Mom won't notice—she rarely leaves the house now—and this solves the travel problem. Instead of taking a bus to Albany, which would cost money that we don't have, he can ride.

We find a map and figure out that from Western Massachusetts to Albany is almost forty miles, through the Berkshires.

"I can do it in one night," Alex says optimistically. "There won't be traffic, and nobody will see me." This plan makes perfect sense to us, so over the course of a week, we gather forty dollars' worth of food stamps, candy, and snacks.

On Friday night he puts the stamps, the food, and some clothes in a white plastic bag. He pretends he's taking out the trash, but instead Alex rides off, the grocery bag dangling off one handlebar. We're not sure we'll ever see him again, but we can't think of any other option.

Saturday comes and goes, and Mom assumes he's at his girlfriend's house. But on Sunday she notices his absence.

"Where is your brother?" she asks.

"I don't know," I say. It's only a half lie. I don't know if he's made it to Albany, if he got a flat tire or got lost, if he's lying on the side of the highway, if he's been kidnapped. If all went well, he should be at Aurora's by now, but there's no plan for him to check in with us. We don't have a phone.

"Go tell him he has to come home," Mom says, meaning I should go to his girlfriend's house.

I play along, going to his girlfriend's house and asking for him, then coming home and reporting the truth: "She doesn't know where he is. She's worried."

At first, Mom has us walk around town, looking for Alex. Then she must have called the police, because they show up and interview us together. They are skeptical. Mom is already a known presence in this small town. They take the report and promise follow-up that never comes.

Mom gets increasingly frantic. Like any mother with a missing child, she summons all of her resources to try to find him. She picks up Electrolux work again and drags me with her selling carpet cleaning door-to-door, then spends the money she earns on the pay phone at the Wendy's in the middle of town, calling psychics to ask where my brother is. She puts the pay phone number on a missing person flyer, which we tape to lampposts throughout the town.

Jessica evaporates into her boyfriend's house, and I am alone with Mom and her distress. She suspects I know where he is, but "I don't know" is my lie, and I stick to it. Eventually, Mom has me stop going to school so that I can accompany her to Wendy's, where we monitor the pay phone.

"Watch my pocketbook," Mom instructs me, standing up from our small table. She's going out to the pay phone to see if the psychics have any new information for her.

"Mom, I'm really hungry," I say, hoping to divert some of the money she's going to pay them.

"Watch it. Do as I say," she says sternly and heads out. Hours pass this way, with Mom on and off the phone with the psychics and the Pittsfield Police Department. Sometime after lunch she comes inside. "They think they are getting closer."

"That's good, Mom. I'm glad."

"Get a small fries, and refill my coffee," she says.

When I bring back our order, I say, "Eat some with me." I push the order of fries between us.

"No, David, you eat," she says absently, stirring five creamers into her coffee. She is certain Alex has been kidnapped. The specter of his father, Alex Sr., returns to haunt her. "When Alex and Jessica were babies, their grandmother took them to Slovenia," she reminds me. "I had to get the ambassador and State Department to bring them back." We've heard this memory of losing her babies so many times over the years that it may be at least partly true. Now her paranoid theories are electrified with anger and obsession. Daily, she rants about Alex Sr.

"You know he abused you kids, he touched you," Mom declares. She's never provided a reason for me to believe this is true, but I nod along. I do not remind her that he was already gone by the time I was born.

Two weeks become three. We hear nothing from Alex, and Jessica and I begin to worry. The cops are useless, and each time Mom calls they have less and less patience. She is also afraid that I'm next to be kidnapped, so she uses a store-bought hair color kit to dye my hair blond on the logic that whoever came to get Alex now won't recognize me. My hair turns into a brittle mess of orange rust. I drink Frostys and cream packets at Wendy's, miss school, and put on weight. I am afraid. She is so far over the edge, so frenetic, and none of my usual strategies work to calm her. I feel awful about putting her in this situation, until she hits me and I remember why Alex had to go.

At last, the police notify my mother that Alex has been found. He has, miraculously, made it to Albany. He tells me later that after biking all night, past the Massachusetts border, he came to the intersection where the Taconic Parkway led up toward Albany. He wasn't in great shape. The brakes on the bike didn't work, so he'd been using his sneaker in the wheel well to slow himself down when he descended through the Berkshires. One of his sneakers was completely worn out. He stopped at a diner and ordered toast for ninety-nine cents. A kind waitress gave him a full breakfast.

When he left the diner, he faced a steep hill. The gears were no good—or he didn't know how to use them—so to manage the hill he was zigzagging up, tripling the distance he had to travel.

A truck pulled over in front of him and a man stepped out.

"My friend's the waitress down there," he said, gesturing toward the diner. "I heard you were biking up this hill. Where you headed?"

Alex didn't want to reveal too much, so he said he was heading to Troy, New York, which is just across the river from Albany. The guy offered him a ride, so he threw his bike in the back of the truck and climbed into the passenger seat. He fell asleep instantly, and the next thing he knew he was in Troy. He made his way back to our old neighborhood and stopped in front of the apartment building where Aurora and Mom would yell back and forth at each other. Aurora was sitting right there on the front stoop, smoking a cigarette as if no time had passed.

"You ran away, didn't you," she said, not a question in her voice. "You can stay here if you want."

The operators of the Chinese restaurant with the perpetual GRAND OPENING sign told him, Hugo, and David that if they delivered food, they could keep the tips and get one free meal a day. They worked and played all summer, carefree and unsupervised.

Alex eventually made his way uptown, to the nicer neighborhood where the Jeremys lived. This was the kind family from the neighborhood whose kids Jessica babysat. They were the ones who'd taken us in when Mom threw Jessica's shoe at the judge. In the world of the Jeremy family, children weren't abused, and when they were, the government stepped in to help. In one of Alex's check-ins at their house, they surprised him with an in-person visit from police officers, who brought Alex to the station for questioning. There he told them about the years of physical and mental abuse we'd suffered. After contacting the Department of Social Services (DSS) in Massachusetts, the police drove Alex to the Massachusetts–New York border to drop him off with a social worker.

"Are you going to jump out of my car once we get on the highway?" she asked. Alex was now classified as a "runner."

"Can we go to McDonald's?" Alex asked in response.

I don't know any of this when the police arrive at Wendy's to tell my mother that they have Alex, so I'm just glad to hear he's alive.

"Ms. Ambroz, we have your son in custody. He's safe," the officer says. This white man with no chin delivers the news that changes everything. I'm struck to my core with relief, followed by fear. Is he all right? Where is he? Did he make it? Will Mom find out that Jess and I knew?

"I don't understand. Custody? Where is he? What are you doing with him? Who kidnapped him?"

"Ma'am, please calm down," the officer says, and I wonder if telling someone to calm down has ever worked for him.

"I want to see my son," Mom demands, her voice rising.

"Mom. Mom, listen to him," I say gently. She looks at me, then the officer, and then asks again, in a softer tone, "Is my son all right? I just want to see my son."

She sounds like any loving mother, desperate to be reunited with her missing child, but for weeks she has been a land mine, easily triggered by the smallest step in the wrong direction. I'm afraid that they'll give Alex back to her, and she'll succeed in killing him this time. I stare at the officer, trying to telegraph the whole story: why we had to break Mom's heart, why Alex had to run, why I'm at Wendy's every day, why I fear for my life.

"Mary," the officer says, dropping the Ms. Ambroz and "ma'am." His voice is suddenly authoritative. "We need you to go home and wait. We'll answer all your questions, but right now what I can tell you is that he is safe and under supervised care. Please stay home. Stay by your phone—"

Mom cuts him off. "We don't have a phone. Is he all right?" I watch them volley back and forth between the cop's unemotional reasoning and her unhinged mix of fear and relief.

"Like I said, that's all we got. We'll be in touch. We'll come to your home and share the information as we have it. Here is my card. You can call from a pay phone. We'll keep you up to date." The officer turns to leave and starts to walk toward the exit.

Mom stands up abruptly, and her chair hits the wall behind her and crashes to the floor. She grabs my hand and pulls me toward the same door as the officer. But he turns around in a flash.

"Mary. Sit down. Now." Something in his voice says that he's had enough, and Mom rights the chair and sits down. For the first time, the authorities seem to believe Alex. Instead of the quick reunion that would typically happen if a runaway child were found, he's put in foster care with a couple named Mae and Buck, and the authorities turn their attention to me and Jessica.

Once again, in our mostly empty living room, I sit next to my mother on the tired beige sofa. Across from us are a police officer and a social worker in metal folding chairs. They're both white. I know this will matter to my mom, but all it means to me is that she won't say anything racist. Oblivious to the bullet she just dodged, the social worker is reading off what appears to be a script.

"Does your mom love you?"

"Does your mom ever yell?"

"Has your mom ever been physical with you?"

"Are you scared of your mom?"

Again I'm being interviewed in front of my mother. I don't know if those involved simply don't have the means to implement best practices, but it's unlikely that questioning an abused child in front of his abusive parent was the standard protocol. Nonetheless, the situation has potentially profound consequences for me. The sun blares through the windows, hitting my back. Mom lights a new cigarette with the expiring one. I can feel the heat coming off her large body. I wish Jessica were home.

Yes, she loves me. No, she never yells. No, she's never been physical with me. No, I'm not scared of her. All I have is my family. My mother, looking at me with love in her eyes. She's already lost Alex. I can't betray her.

The social worker scribbles notes on her paper without looking down, like a stenographer. Her auburn hair is in a bun so tight that it looks painful.

When my interrogation is over, they turn their attention to my mother.

"Mary, what do you do for work?"

"Mary, how do you buy food?"

"Mary, do the kids have an after-school routine?"

My mother's voice is calm, measured, and controlled, but I know that underneath it all, she's on fire. She gets furious when being challenged. My anger and resentment for these people, for the entire ordeal, returns. I wonder if I'll have to pay the "bill" after they leave.

"I shop once a week, and focus on fresh fruits and veggies, and I make sure the children have plenty of meat. I do what I can, but I know they sneak crap food at the convenience stores," she says.

Look in the fridge, I want to scream. It's empty. I'm hungry right now. I have not eaten in twenty-four hours. I'm drinking water to ease the pain.

"Mary, we spoke to the school, and the kids were in and out last year?"

"We've been settling in here, and I've needed their help."

I look around our sparse apartment. There's no evidence of any "settling in." Isn't this lie clear to these people?

"Mary, we understand your son Alex ran away; do you know why he might have done this?"

"I believe his father, Alex Sr., kidnapped him." Mom is burning through the last of my cigarette stash. *Shit. I'm going to have to replenish,*

I think. "He's done that before. Have you spoken to him? He's a doctor but does nothing for his children."

Normally she can control her crazy in front of authorities, but this time she's letting it show. If the condition of the apartment isn't enough, can't they see it in her behavior? Her head is darting around, she's fidgeting madly, and her stories make no sense. I want them to realize she's lying. I want them to rescue us. But I don't want her shamed.

"Hmmm. Okay. Tell us about Alex Sr.," the social worker says.

Mom launches into a speech I've heard many times. A litany of offenses and crimes against her, with only occasional mentions of us. The room fills with cigarette smoke. The officer sits completely impassive, manspreading, a solid block of blue. The petite red-headed social worker wears a smart navy pantsuit. I let the dark blue of their outfits blur together as my mother rambles.

"I think he touched them..."

Where's this going? Are they going to stop her, or will they let her rant indefinitely? My hands are sweating; my stomach is tight with pain. I am steps away from my freedom yet trapped. It's a sickening, terrible feeling.

"Instead of harassing me, what you should really be doing is dealing with the staff at the shelter. I think they touched David. David, tell them." She turns to me expectantly.

Mortified, I look down at my lap. Do I have to lie for her?

"Actually, Mary, I don't think we need to cover that right now. I think we have what we need. David, is there anything you want to add?"

I look up, first at the officer and then at the social worker. I know better than to hope anything will change. My mom has won this battle for my entire life. If they aren't taking me away now, they never will. This is my last hope. I shake my head. No, nothing to add.

"Okay, I think we are good here. Thanks for accommodating us, Mary," the social worker says. Everyone rises. These are not bad people. Courts move slowly, as they should. Nobody wants to give the state the unrestrained power to break up families. We want them to do it rarely and with caution. After they leave, I stay very still, waiting to see which Mom returns from walking them out.

She comes in and gives me a hug. "What assholes. Do you have more cigarettes?"

———

Thud, thud, thud. I hear her steps, but my eyes are closed. Just a few days after the interview, my mom is descending the flight of stairs she has just thrown me down. Her clogs pound the wooden risers like a drum. Which version of my mom is coming? The crazy mom, who will continue to beat me or walk right past me, detached from what she's done, or a repentant mom who feels bad about it? *Thud, thud, thud.* I open my eyes. Splayed at the bottom of the stairs, motionless, I'm beyond pain. I observe the situation with a detached curiosity. The thuds of her clogs stop when she reaches me. The pause lasts an eternity. She kicks my head. Then everything goes dark.

I don't know how much time has passed when I finally crack my eyes open just enough to see that my mother is still looming over me, loosely wrapped in a white sheet, one breast uncovered. I'm so close to her that I can see blue veins in her breast. She drops to the floor next to me and drags my limp body into her lap. Her skin radiates a musky scent, mixed with that of cigarettes.

"Why, Jesus fucking Christ, why?" she moans in a mix of anger and regret. Unsure if I'm supposed to answer, I let my eyelids flutter closed again. Perhaps she won't notice that I'm regaining consciousness.

I can feel the heat of her body. This woman birthed me. These breasts fed me. In her head she is Mother Mary holding her crucified son, like Michelangelo's *Pietà*. She is devastated at what the universe has done to her son—with no sense of herself as the perpetrator of my suffering.

"David. David. *David!*" she shrieks. I open my eyes, not sure what's coming next.

"You fell, you fell, you fell, you fell…" she chants, invoking a narrative that she can live with.

My head is throbbing. I can taste the blood in my mouth, raw, metallic. I reach up to the tender spot on my head and find where it is bleeding. Whether it's from the kick or the fall, I don't know, but I'm bleeding from there, from my nose, and from the cuts in my mouth.

Now that she knows I'm awake, Mom slides me off her lap to the floor and walks away, pulling up the sheet and tucking the folds so that it stays up. My blood has left blotches on it, like a macabre tie-dye. I look down and notice I am wearing my beloved Tasmanian Devil T-shirt. Irrationally, I try to take it off, but I'm only semiconscious. It's like I'm underwater drowning, and when I get up to the surface for air, I see the blood soaking into the shirt and collapse again. *There is so much blood.* My shirt becomes increasingly unrecognizable each time it appears, and I sink further into my sadness. When I surface again, my mother is sitting on the second step. I can tell that the storm has passed.

"Mom, I need to go to the hospital. Please."

"Yes, yes, okay. You fell, you fell, okay? You fell."

Through the blur of pain, I realize exactly what I have to say. "Yes, Mom," I say. "I fell. And now I need to go to the hospital, okay?"

"You fell," she utters one last time and stands, turns, and walks back upstairs to the apartment.

I focus on my breath, trying to slow it down. *You are not going to die here on the floor, like a broken doll,* I tell myself. *Get up. Move.* I do not want Mom to kill me. I do not want to be here with her. I cannot save her. She has suffered from years of untreated mental illness and the perpetual stress of poverty and deprivation. She lives in the prison of her mental illness and will never wake up from the nightmare. I remind myself of this in order to understand why this is happening. I'm not mad at her. In my heart, I know she isn't culpable.

Get up. Now! I command myself. I put one hand on the first step, and then I reach up to the handrail. I manage to pull myself to my feet. I'm unsteady but I hold the banister and breathe. Inhale, hold, exhale. I must take action. Now. I cannot go upstairs. That is where she is. That way is hell. I cannot get to the hospital; it's too far. I have no money. I walk out the front door. Breathe in, hold, exhale. It's very bright outside, the sun oppressive. I begin to sweat. I walk toward the civic center. I remember there are police there and a courthouse. Surely a cop or a judge can help.

The block stretches, and I walk straight, counting breaths so as not to focus on everything that hurts. At Main Street, I turn left and come to the courthouse. I enter the chilled, air-conditioned space. I have no idea where to go, but I head toward the first pair of wooden doors and push through to a small room. It has pale blue walls and benches like a church. On a barely raised platform, a judge sits. She is the only one facing me, and she sees me immediately.

"What in the hell? Are you okay? Help him," the judge commands the bailiff.

One last step and I collapse. I have nothing left. From the floor, I look up into the face of the bailiff, a kind-looking Black man. He scoops me up in his massive arms, and I can smell his aftershave.

"I got you, honey, I got you..." he says, and I close my eyes. My head lolls to one side against his badge. It digs into my cuts painfully, but he's got me. We are moving, I don't know where. "Who did this to you?" he asks. He's chewing gum, and his breath comes down directly into my face. It's Big Red gum, I just know it...and then I pass out.

For years, I have been starving, bruised from head to toe, surrounded by clouds of filth. Teachers, school nurses, judicial figures, and religious leaders have all been witness to the abuse. When I finally summoned the courage to report my mother, they told her what I'd said, for which she beat me. Yet I try again. Some spark in me simply refuses to be blown out. Broken as I am, a hunger for life courses through me.

I open my eyes. I'm lying on a black pleather sofa. Seated on the same sofa, next to my hip, is the bailiff.

"Hello there, son. I'm cleaning up some of these cuts. I need you to lie still, that's it. Now…who hurt you?" he asks. He's holding white gauze against the gash in my head. His gentle palm is a pale shade of pink, his face dark, his eyes filled with compassion. I see that I've gotten blood on his uniform.

"Take it easy on him," a woman calls out. My head jolts toward the voice, and I gasp in pain. His hand comes down on my chest, softly pressing to let me know he's there.

"It's okay, that's the judge. You came into her courtroom. What's your name, son?" he asks. In this moment, I have a choice.

I do not want this, I decide with every fiber of my being. I can't go back to my mother. I do not want to die. "I'm David Ambroz. My *mother* did this. She beat me…she beats us all the time. We have no food…my brother ran away…I helped him…we had to…my mother…she kicked me…my mother…my mother…" The sobs break through, and I'm weeping for the pain, for my fury, for my brother, for my sister. I am betraying our mother, I know it, and I cry for that too. This gentle giant hugs me, pressing me into his crisp but now bloodied uniform. "I got you, David. I got you," he says, and I know he does.

Things happen quickly then, and I'm forced away from my hero bailiff into an ambulance. Mom is called, or picked up, I don't know. But she's at the hospital soon after I arrive.

"He fell," I can hear from my hospital bed. "I'm a nurse, goddamn it. Who did this to him?" She rants and raves incoherently, but I'm too tired to care. I sleep.

"Well, it's not impossible, but these are pretty extensive injuries for a fall." I hear snippets of adults talking quietly outside the curtain that

surrounds my bed. "The doctor is concerned, and not convinced—"
"Let's talk to him." The blue curtain, suspended from a track, creates a bubble of safety, but it is pulled back unceremoniously. A woman comes in and sits in a chair next to my bed.

"Honey, I'm a social worker here at the hospital," she says. "We need to talk about next steps."

I have no idea what next steps are, but nod okay.

"Your mother is here. She loves you, David, very much, and wants you to know that. Your mother says you fell, and that's how you got hurt. Is that true, honey?" she asks.

"*What?*" I sputter. "Does this fucking look like I fell?!" I cannot let her deceive them again. I cannot go back to her. "*No,* Mom did this. She kicked me. She threw me down the stairs. *Mom* did this to me." I am outraged. What will it take for them to understand?

"Okay, baby. Okay, I need you to calm down. Can you calm down?" she asks.

I cannot calm down. Every muscle in me feels explosive. Her tone is not good. I've heard this before. The disbelief. The cultivated objectivity. The saccharine-sweet "honey" and "baby."

"Well, we need to investigate what happened, do you understand? There is a process. For now we think it's best that you go home with your mom. But we'll be supervising..." She trails off, condemning me to something she can't even begin to understand.

Within hours, I'm in a taxi with Mom, heading home. She is loving, remorseful, affectionate. Kind Mom. Her arm rests heavy on my shoulders, a bludgeon that only a day before had nearly killed me. "They are going to have a lot of questions about your fall, David," Mom says. "I know you'll explain what happened." I am afraid, but I've channeled that fear into resolve. My life matters. Mom is a black hole, pulling me back to her relentlessly. But I won't let her kill me. I don't know how to escape her, but I will.

A week passes slowly as I recover in the apartment. My injuries ache.

The bruises on my arms and legs are vivid purples and yellows. I'm not supposed to be in Jessica's room, but it's a hot summer day, and her room is in the back of the house where there is less direct sun, so it's cooler. She's at her boyfriend's, so I take refuge there. Mom is out in the living room in her regular, semidressed state. She's been volatile, but today she seems muted.

In Jessica's room, I dare to play my favorite song on the one tape that I'm proud to own: "Mama, I'm Coming Home" on Ozzy Osbourne's album *No More Tears*. I carefully climb into Jessica's recliner. We rescued it from the trash, and it is permanently in the reclined position. Music playing, I carefully lean myself back. I find a particular angle, perched on my side, where I can sit without pain, and start to reread *Four Past Midnight*, a collection of Stephen King stories. I've got a book, music, water. If I'm lucky Jessica will bring some food from her boyfriend's house.

Late morning, I'm still in the same place when the apartment rattles with a pounding. My heart races. My wounds are healing, but I have been on edge ever since I came home. I assume the sound is Mom, coming for me, and I leap behind the recliner. Child abuse and neglect have a long shadow that stretches beyond physical pain. For decades I'll flinch when someone goes to hug me—sometimes I still do. It's an irreconcilable contradiction between the love of a caregiver and the damage she does.

The knock comes again, and I realize it's coming from outside the apartment.

"Open the door. This is the Pittsfield Police Department."

A room away, I can hear my mother in motion. Is she looking for a weapon? Is she looking for me? Can she get to me? Will she be mad? Frantically, I look for an escape. There's only the window and we're two stories up.

"Mrs. Ambroz," a stern voice says, "open the door. Now."

From the pounding it sounds like they're going to break down the door.

"You need a warrant," Mom says. "You can't just barge in."

"We have a warrant. You need to open the door. This is the last time."

The voices stop on both sides of the door as Mom unlocks it, the dead bolt echoing in the sudden silence.

Then a woman sticks her head in the doorway where I'm hiding and in a commanding voice says, "David. Jessica. My name is Mel and I work for the Department of Social Services. We are leaving." She has dark, feathered hair and is wearing nice jeans, a button-down shirt, and a cardigan. Her voice is deep and gravelly, and she speaks with authority. She knows she's entering a volatile situation, and leaves no room for argument.

My stomach drops, my hunger vanishes, my bruises heal, my heart lifts. They are going to save me. I stand straight up.

"David, where is Jessica?" Mel asks.

"She's not home."

"David, you need to get dressed and pack." It's so hot that I'm wearing only underwear and a T-shirt. "You are coming with us. Here." She thrusts a black trash bag at me. "You have five minutes."

I give a victorious fist pump. It's finally happening. Mel looks at me with an odd expression. Later she'll tell me she'd never seen a child so excited to be separated from his parent.

I hear my mother yelling, "You cannot take him! He is my son. Who the fuck do you think you are?" Her anguish tugs at me, but I slap it away. *No more.*

"Sit down, ma'am. You need to sit down, or we are going to arrest you."

"Fuck you."

I've stopped to listen, and Mel notices. I'm confused. They're threatening to arrest her for her current behavior, but they hadn't arrested her for beating me. Because, as far as they are concerned, I am her property. Human rights begin only at age eighteen. Adults who hit adults go to jail—but if an adult hits a child, they get therapy and help. Hit him again, they get more therapy and help.

"David, pack. Now."

"My room's that way," I say, pointing past her.

"Fine, let's go."

On the way to my room, I glance in at the scene in the living room. My mother's breast is barely covered by a white bedsheet. Two officers stand right in front of her. She doesn't see me.

In my room, I look around. I have almost nothing, but I shove some clothes and my rock collection in the garbage bag. Still without pants, I go back to Jessica's room and collect some of her things, and my book and tape.

"Okay, I'm ready," I say brightly.

"David, pants. Shoes." Mel's curtness communicates what I already know: Mom is unpredictable and we need to move fast. I pull a pair of shorts out from the bag and slip on sneakers.

"David, David," my mother wails. "You cannot take him! David, I love you. David, don't leave me! He fell."

I'm at the top of the stairs; my mother cries, my bruises throb, and my steps stutter. I know these steps. They are the steps she pushed me down. Two hands firmly grip my shoulders, and I shudder, but it is only the social worker behind me, urging me forward. *David, she's not going to throw you down the steps. Move,* I tell myself.

"You cannot take my children. You fucking assholes. David!" My mother is screaming and yelling and fighting. I am betraying her. But I can't endure this anymore.

I take the first step, haltingly, then the next, and then I run down the steps, trash bag in hand. High Street is deserted. The lights on the cop car are flashing in a circle, but there is no siren. Mel leads me to her two-door maroon car, a Pontiac Firebird. It's parked facing the wrong way on the street. She opens the passenger door. The interior is soft, gray, immaculate.

I look up at the apartment. My mother, my abuser, my burden. She is still nearby, but she can't touch me. Another firm nudge, and I sit down, black trash bag on my lap. The door closes, and I stare up through the window.

"David, belt."

I fasten my seat belt, and the car rolls away. I am driving away from Mom. This is it. I'm free.

PART TWO

Chapter 11

THE BLACK TRASH BAG WITH all my possessions is in my lap, too large for its contents. *You're okay, David. They won't send you back to her*, I tell myself, closing my eyes to pray. The DSS waiting room is barren except for a few toys and books, and just when I'm starting to worry that they've forgotten me, there are two knocks, and the door swings open. I leap to my feet, still in fight-or-flight mode.

"Hi, David, it's okay, just sit and relax. You hungry, honey?" Mel asks. I've seen the vending machines outside, and I ask for a coffee. She brings me one along with some snacks. I realize I haven't eaten for a while—maybe a day—and scarf the food down.

"David, your sister will be joining your brother's foster family, but we're looking for the right placement for you."

"Can I see her? Is she okay?" I ask worriedly.

"Not yet, but soon I hope," she responds.

I haven't spoken to Alex since he left on his bike, and I wonder how he is, but knowing he's in a home with a family is the most I can wish for right now. I'm glad he and Jessica will be together, and I don't question why their foster family won't take me. I know I'm different, and I know that *they* know I'm different. It's woven into the way I talk, the way I groom myself, how I carry myself, and what I care about. The social workers can tell that I'm gay. And it's a big problem. I don't articulate this to myself—the idea is too scary and dangerous— but I am starting to understand it in millions of subtle ways. Foster care is a federally subsidized program, but it is administered locally. In the nineties, there are no standards or protections for LGBTQ youth in foster care. "Gay" is a dirty word, so the problem of where to place me is communicated only in the looks they exchange. It's in their coded language when they tell me they're looking for a place where I'll "fit in." There is something wrong with me, and they know without asking that foster parents won't want me when they realize it, so I am a challenging placement.

Two years ago, when I was in fourth grade, we briefly lived next door to a boy named Jamal. Jamal's building was like mine, with dirty hallways that smelled like garbage, but when I stepped into his apartment for the first time, I noticed how clean and orderly it was. Jamal and his two older brothers had a single mother who worked odd hours, but she somehow managed to make the apartment a cocoon of safety and love. Jamal and his brothers were always dressed nicely in clean clothes. There was a bowl of fruit on the counter. If we played with Legos or made ourselves sandwiches, we knew to clean up after ourselves. His mother was working as hard as she could to give her children a better life, and her efforts to keep the apartment neat felt to me like one of the ways she gave her family attention and love.

Jamal, like me, didn't fit in, and one day when the other kids turned a corner, he and I ducked out of sight, bolted down an alleyway, and went to his apartment. Neither of us liked the thieving and rough games that our friends in the neighborhood got into on the playground and in the streets.

"Let's pretend I'm sick," he said, and lay down on the floor in the room he shared with his brothers. "You're the doctor."

Jamal had dark skin and bright eyes, and he was beautiful. "You need to give me a checkup," he urged me.

"You should be in a gown," I said, catching on to the game. "Here, use this as a gown." I grabbed a bathrobe from the floor. "Tell me what hurts, and I'll figure out what's wrong with you."

"You go out, then come back in, Dr. David."

His brother was home, so we moved the exam room to the closet, pushing clothes to either side. "Okay, I'll count to one hundred and come back," I said. I closed the closet door and waited, too excited to count. After a while I said, "One hundred," and entered the closet. Jamal had a flat white sheet spread over him.

"Hello, um, Lionel. What seems to be the problem?" I asked in my best doctor's voice.

"I don't feel well."

"Is it your stomach?" I asked, crouching next to him. I felt his forehead. "You're a little warm. Let's look at you." The robe wasn't tied and fell to one side as I pulled down the sheet. He was wearing white Hanes briefs.

"I'm going to listen to your heart," I said, leaning over to put my left ear on his chest. Looking down his torso, I saw the small bulge of his penis. I placed my right hand on his stomach. A funny giggle escaped his lips. I raised my head and said, "It's my turn to be the patient."

"Okay, we can be patients sharing a room. You lie that way." He gestured for me to place my feet by his head. I turned away from him and stripped down to my underwear, then I leapt under the sheet.

"Let's close the doors," he suggested. "You do that one." I slid one of the accordion doors closed, and the closet immediately felt smaller. We were pressed body to body under the sheet. I was excited and scared, my breath coming quickly.

"What if your brother finds us? He'll kick our ass."

"Not if we're quiet. We are sleeping patients...okay?"

"Okay." I was quiet, eyes wide open in the dim closet.

Eventually, I sat up, and he did too. He smiled, and I smiled back. He was like me, hiding in the outfield, wondering if there was another way to play or another game altogether. Jamal felt like a brief ray of possibility and comfort, but I didn't give a name to the feelings.

Whatever the term, the adults in the foster care system have one, and it means they can't place me with a "normal" foster family. Because they're having trouble finding a place for me to stay, I sleep in emergency housing in the office that first night. The small room is an unofficial refuge for kids like me, who are stranded while the social workers figure out what to do with us. All that's in the room is a folding cot with a plastic mattress and a plastic-lined pillow that smells like bleach. There is probably a twenty-four-hour guard somewhere in the building, but it feels like I'm alone. I'm nervous but elated to be safe at last.

Early the next afternoon a different social worker brings me to a facility for juvenile delinquents. Like Mel, like every one of the revolving group of social workers I encounter, she is a middle-aged, frazzled woman who is trying to do her best while constantly juggling the messiness of child welfare: the biological parents, the foster parents, the paperwork, the kids that are her cases, and the other kids in the house. She is part of a system that gives her limited options, and she has learned to prioritize the kids who are on fire. She will be fierce, like Mel, if she needs to forcefully remove a child from their parents. Right now, I am a parentless child who can't sleep in the office another night, so I have her full attention until I have a bed, and then she will run to put out another fire.

"This isn't the right place for you," she tells me in the car on the way to the placement. "These boys are here because they broke the law, and you didn't do anything wrong. It's not long term. But you can't keep sleeping in the office, and we don't have a place that can accept your kind."

I have a sense of what "my kind" means. I think of how angry Mom would be to hear this. Mom hates my kind.

"Okay, that's fine," I reply. So long as she doesn't take me back to Mom.

The social worker glances at me in the rearview mirror, then turns her eyes back to the road. "Just be careful," she says. "These boys are—" She stops herself. "Be careful, and we'll figure something out for you as soon as we can. Please try to fit in. You got to tone it down some, okay?"

I want to tone it down. I don't want anyone to know this about me. I agree, let it be a secret. I stay silent. More than anything I want her to stop talking about it.

The facility is based in a big, old Victorian house that's been expanded with a concrete addition, a trailer in the yard, and several sheds. It's isolated on a bare plot of land surrounded by forest. At the edge of the property is a tall chain-link fence, but even if someone made it over the fence, where would he go? We're locked in by the fence and the isolation.

Every change that has been made to the house, including its additions, is institutional. The floors are linoleum. The halls have dropped ceilings with long fluorescent lights, and they smell like disinfectant. The windows are sealed shut, and there is no art on the walls, but there are fire extinguishers at regular intervals. All the furniture is heavy and indestructible. The only sign of humanity is in the boys' bedrooms. As we walk past the open doors, I see items arranged neatly in the space alongside the beds, like little shrines. There are photos of their families and girlfriends and ticket stubs and pictures of basketball players— mementos of their lives outside these walls. In their photos, each boy is smiling, their faces bright, a stark contrast to the suspicious eyes I see staring back at me.

"We need to inspect your belongings," the administrator who admits me says.

I open up my Hefty bag and unload all of my possessions on a bare, gunmetal-gray desk. I have a few items of clothing, a Stephen

King book, the Ozzy Osbourne tape, and the toothbrush they just gave me.

"That's everything?" he says, after logging them into a sheet. I nod. "Okay, now have a seat. I'm going to ask you some questions and then we'll get you oriented."

The social worker and I sit. The right side of my body is still tender, so I lean to the left in the chair as he runs through a list of health-related questions.

"Are you itchy? Does anything hurt? When is the last time you showered? When is the last time you ate?"

I'm always itchy. The pain is near what I think is one of my kidneys. He notes my responses and then calls in a boy who is passing the office.

"David, this is Jordan. Jordan, please show him his room. It's in the old section at the top of the stairs, where Devon was."

Jordan leads me up a wide staircase with an intricately carved banister. For all their attempts to institutionalize the place, they haven't been able to strip the staircase of its designer's original intent—to build a home. Either to protect or to ostracize me, I am given a bedroom separate from the other boys. It's in an isolated section of the second floor, and mine is the only room on that part of the floor.

Jordan has told me that we have to brush our teeth and make our beds before breakfast, but the first morning, when I return from brushing my teeth, there is a counselor waiting for me in my room.

"You didn't make your bed before brushing your teeth. That's a demerit."

Unlike my experience at schools and shelters, the rules here are un-predictable, and I seem to be breaking them no matter what I do. After breakfast, I'm briefed on the rules, but instead of learning rules like "You must make your bed before you brush your teeth," I'm told that the key to avoiding demerits is respect. Whatever the staff says goes. On the wall in the dining room there is a giant demerit whiteboard with a column listing every kid by last name. Across the top are the days of the week, and the chart shows how many points we each have lost or gained every day. At the end of the week is the running total. Each demerit means a week without privileges. No phone, no TV, no recreation time. In place of those privileges are additional chores—the worst ones, like bathroom and dish duty.

When breakfast is done, I am guided to my math and English classes, which will meet every morning in the same room in one of the newer concrete buildings. The windows are narrow and high, with glass that is reinforced with metal mesh. At the front of the room is a dry-erase board, and we are seated at folding tables, three to a table, facing the teacher. The messages and images scratched into the tables are almost all about cocks: cocks to suck, so-and-so is a dick. It's nothing I haven't seen on the walls of bathrooms at Penn Station. The graffiti is at once titillating and offensive, and the slurs remind me that this is the only place the discussion of homosexuality belongs—on bathroom walls.

For the first time in my life, for all the school I've missed, I am in a math class where I already know the concepts. It's an incredible feeling not to be behind. I'm used to feeling like I've been dropped into a foreign country and expected to thrive without speaking the language. Here I'm fluent.

"David, enough. Let someone else answer," Mr. Shawn demands, clearly exhausted by my enthusiasm.

"I'm not answering," I reply. "It's just that I think you're explaining it wrong. You see, if you—"

"David. Demerit." He stops me in my verbal tracks. "One demerit for interrupting and another for insubordination." Later, when the kids are asked to turn in their homework, none of them have it. All of them receive demerits.

I soon understand why they haven't done their homework. We are assigned chores for the afternoon. I mow a portion of the lawn with a manual mower and receive a demerit for my attitude. When I don't finish my dinner, I receive another demerit. I clean the bathrooms until lights go out. There's no time left for me to do my homework. I feel misunderstood and alone—there is no way for me to thrive in this place.

Juvenile detention is currently under reform across the country because it is widely recognized that isolation and punishment don't reform young offenders. Like me, the kids in this center were, through no fault of their own, raised in a variation of hell. They were in some way deprived, abused, assaulted, or missing school, and, like me, had turned to crime as the best or only option. Unlike me, they'd gotten caught.

Detention facilities criminalize poverty. We remove kids from unsafe situations without hope. Then we put them in a system that further destroys them. Many of them will serve time in juvenile prisons and then be sent back into the streets, still deprived, abused, assaulted, and missing school, with a lack of care and adult supervision. They'll return to juvenile detention for the same petty thievery and other crimes, and it will escalate. There's no one to save or stop them, to hug and nurture them. Then we're shocked when, at eighteen, they're in poverty, just like their parents. If we tried, we couldn't design a more perfect system to perpetuate violence, poverty, and racism. This governmental structure functions as a pipeline to prison. When a child comes into the care of the state, they become *our* child. We are responsible for their care. No matter what we might think of the parenting that brought them there, when they are in the government's care, we owe it to them to raise them as children deserve to be raised.

I don't have the perspective on each kid to reflect on how they got here, but I know what we have in common: that, like me, they are only trying to survive.

I've been at the center a few days when I'm on the basketball field for our recreation period, not playing so much as lurking on the periphery, waiting for Group to start. I haven't been to Group yet, but we had Group at the home for abused women in Pittsfield, so I have a sense of what it will be like. The staff therapist, James, comes out to herd us there.

"Let's go everyone, move your asses. Group is in the dining room today," James says. "Enrick, I swear to God, if you don't—" I watch as Enrick weaves around the other players, abruptly stops, and then leaps straight up, toes pointed, and arches the ball perfectly into the net with a swish. He is a tall, lithe boy who handles the basketball like it's an extension of his hand. He walks off the court toward James, who is in awe just like the rest of us. This kid has something. But as Enrick comes off the court, his face closes, his posture shrinks, and he merges into the group. I see the transformation as he moves from a place where he is free and relaxed to a situation where he is nervous and uncomfortable. He puts his chains back on and gets in line with the rest of us.

I hang back so as not to be in the middle of the pack as we enter the dining room. I am new, and I don't want to get hurt. I have no idea who might attack me or why, but there's a constant feeling of tension here. I see the same feeling in Enrick and a lot of the other boys. The need to protect ourselves from each other.

"This is not a runway, Ambroz, let's go," James says. I hustle to catch up with the rest.

In the dining room, we sit down with James in a circle of chairs. The kids all sit next to each other, leaving a few seats on either end between them and James. It feels like I'm the only one without a friend, so once everyone's seated, I take an empty chair at one end of the curved line of kids.

"This is your chance to share what's on your mind. You've all been through this before so let's hear it," James says. "Ms. Ambroz, why don't you start us off?"

"I'm not a 'Ms.,'" I say.

"Excuse me?" James asks.

"You said, 'Ms. Ambroz, why don't you start us off?' and I'm saying, I'm not a 'Ms.,'" I clarify quietly.

Voices ring out from around the circle: "That's debatable." "Fag." "Homo."

Being labeled gay feels riskier here than anywhere I've ever been. The boys are on edge and ready to attack at any sign of weakness, and calling me a Ms. doesn't help my situation. But for some reason, James has it in for me, and it's obvious that it has something to do with the core of who I am.

It's not the first time I'd been called out as queer. The first time was in fifth grade, in the parking lot at PS 22. I jumped in to play a game we called ledgie, which involved bouncing a ball off the ledge of the building and then pushing and shoving the other kids out of the way to be the one to catch it. I saw the ball coming toward me, and bulldozed forward to catch it, but it skimmed past my hand, and hit the ground. One of the guys that I shoved came up and pushed me back hard.

"Fucking fag, can't catch the damn ball with those limp-ass wrists," he yelled so all the kids could hear.

I've been called names, but never in front of an adult as the kids are doing now, in front of James. He is our assigned therapist, but he's been an asshole toward me since we first met. I sense that I remind James of himself, and he's angry because he's gay, too, but wishes he weren't.

"Fag." "Homo," they keep taunting. I look at James. He started this by calling me Ms. Ambroz, but is he really going to let the kids run with it?

"Aren't you going to do anything?" I ask him indignantly.

"Can you skip the drama, and just fucking share something?" James says.

"I'd like to share that I'm not a woman, I'm a man. I have a penis," I say. I have to kill the label before it's too late. "I'd like to share that you are cruel. I'd like to share—"

"Enough. Jesus fucking Christ, Ms. Ambroz! Always with the drama," James responds.

"*You did it again!*" I shout. "I'm not a Ms.!"

"You are losing telephone privileges for talking back," James says, smiling victoriously. "Got anything else to say?"

I have always been a "good" kid. I am, as my social worker told me, the only one who hasn't been sent here as a punishment. But I can't get it right in this place. I give up.

"I have no one to call anyway, so that's fine," I retort, but it's not true. The week after I arrived, I got to talk to Alex for the first time, and we've been speaking once a week. The phone is in the dining area, and there's no privacy, but Alex opens every call with "Hey, bro," and his familiar voice is the only connection I have to who I am and where I came from. Now, James is planning to take that away too.

"I'm giving you ten demerits," he says.

"Ten demerits? Are you kidding?"

"Eleven. Want to keep going?" he threatens.

"You asked me to share *anything*, right?"

"Yes," he says, watching me. We're like two fighters circling in the ring; everyone's eyes go from him back to me. The room is ready for a brawl. I surprise myself by my attitude. I've always gotten myself out of trouble by being smooth and savvy toward adults, but now that I'm away from my mother, I fear nothing.

"I'd like to share that you are a bully who gets off on bossing around powerless kids. I'd like to share that you are petty and cruel, and you probably couldn't get a decent job, which is why you are here picking on kids half your age and twice your intelligence. I'd like to share that this may be the best job you ever have. You can take your demerits—" He suddenly stands up and approaches me, fists at his sides.

"David, you are done. Go to my office" is all he says.

I do as I'm told. I hate Group.

Later, almost two months into my stay, I'm drying off after a shower when I hear the stairs groan with the unwelcome rush of weight. Footsteps thunder up the stairs. Nobody else should be on the second floor. There are never footsteps in this direction at this time of night. I dash into my room.

I'm supposed to be safe here, in the protective custody of the state, but after twelve years of abuse, I can smell violence. I know I'm in serious danger.

I slam the bedroom door shut. None of the doors have locks, so I quickly push a dresser in front of it. Moments later a storm of pounding and hollering rattles the door, the wall, my world.

"What's wrong, fag?" the boys taunt. "Let us in."

The door shakes in its frame.

Still naked, I scan my environment quickly. The dresser won't be enough to hold the door closed. I try to move the brass bed against the dresser, but it's too big and heavy. It won't budge. The dresser tilts backward as the door pushes against it. I flip up the mattress and fling it against the dresser, but it won't last. They are coming in; this is happening. I scan for a weapon, but there is nothing in my room, not even a lamp.

They shout "fag" this, and "cocksucker" that. There are at least four staff members on duty just one flight of stairs below. They've got to come to my rescue.

"*Help! Help! They are going to kill me!*" I yell at full volume. My screams only seem to egg the boys on. The door inches open, the barricade slides, and one kid slips through, then another, then another, and maybe a fourth. One final shove and the mattress flips back and over to the floor. Backed into the corner of the room, I stand to face them, cupping my penis.

"Fucking douche, running away like a pussy," one boy says angrily, striding toward me. It's Enrick, the kid I've watched playing basketball. I don't know a lot about him, but he's usually mellow, and I've never seen him start a fight. I sometimes sat next to him at meals because we're both quiet. I know from Group that he's come from a life a lot like mine. He'd been sent here for breaking into cars. Right now, his natural grace on the court is gone. His movement seems robotic. He punches me right in the stomach. The wind is knocked out of me, and I drop to the ground, instinctively curling into a ball to protect my face and head. Kicks pummel my back and leg.

"Look at her, covering up her twat," another one yells, laughing as he kicks at me. His voice is strained, and his eyes are blank, staring down at me.

"*Help, help me!*" I yell again. I don't understand why the staffers downstairs haven't heard the commotion. Where are they? Why isn't anyone coming?

Peering up, I catch sight of a broom in Enrick's hand. Terror shoots through my body.

Enrick walks past the others and kicks me over onto my back. Sitting on my chest, he uses his knees to pin my arms at my sides. I thrash and squirm, desperate to break free. The broom is in his hand, the rounded handle jabbing toward my mouth.

Facilities like this take a bunch of pubescent boys and isolate us without any meaningful sex ed, without any privacy, unable to masturbate, without any outlet for self-expression, charged up and frustrated by childhoods of neglect and abuse. I don't blame the boys for attacking me. I blame the poverty into which we were born: a poverty of hope, a poverty of opportunity. We are trapped in a cycle of poorly governed public programs, unsafe neighborhoods, failing schools, intergenerational violence, and a societal script primed to tell us that we don't matter.

"Is this what you want, fag?" he sneers. Our faces are so close I can see his pores.

"Please, don't," I say quietly, looking him in the eye. I want him to see me as a person, not a naked fag but as a human being. He falters for a moment. The blank look unlocks, and I see in his eyes a recognition of my terror. Someone hurt this kid; someone taught him to do these things. Now he's doing the same to me. "Please, don't. You don't have to."

The broomstick hovers at my lips, pressing just slightly. My mouth is tightly locked shut. He pauses, his better angel fighting, and possibly winning.

"Enough, guys, enough," commands a calm voice at the door.

Enrick stops, and I catch a glimpse of relief in his eyes that he quickly hides. His eyes drill into me and his mask of power goes right back up. He hitches backward off me and stands straight up. He never unlocks his gaze.

I scramble into a protective crouch, holding myself for dear life. James stands in the doorway with cold eyes and a mild smile, almost as if he sees value in my assault. That should teach me a lesson. Maybe now I won't be so mouthy or different.

The boys file out past him, and he never takes his eyes off me.

"Clean it up, and for fuck's sake, put some clothes on, fatty," he says and walks out.

The door closes, and all hope is gone. I am destroyed. It took everything I had to escape my mother. I thought nothing could be worse, but now, at twelve years old, I feel like this is it. I will get hurt. Fairy tales may have a monster or a witch hidden in the woods, but in my world they are everywhere. They are adults, and they are destroying us with their indifference.

I push the dresser back. My breath is ragged. The mattress is still on the floor, and I lie down and cry. I cry for myself. I cry for my brother and sister, worried that they might be going through the same thing—because of me. I sent my brother away; I put us in foster care. I cry, racked with frustration. Homeless, a mentally ill mother, a fag, and now this.

"What else do you want from me?" I shout to God or whatever force is trying to snuff me out. How much more can I take?

No. Stop. Crying. Now, I command myself, and eventually I do.

Your tears are useless. Tears are going to get you killed. No more tears, I vow. No more emotion. I can dim that part of me to almost nothing. These people can't have that power over me. I take the pain and squeeze it into a tight square. Then I pack it in a box and place it on a shelf next to another box neatly labeled Hugh. I know where it is, and maybe one day I can take it down and feel again. But right now, feeling is a luxury I can't afford, not if I'm going to survive. Whatever is coming, I need to be bulletproof and numb. I'll wear a mask. I don't know this yet, but I won't shed a tear again for twenty-three years.

Chapter 12

I DON'T UNDERSTAND. THEY SAW the blood. They put Alex in foster care," I say, looking over at him outside the courtroom. I've seen Alex and Jessica only a few times in the past year, often before court hearings like this one. In order to stay in foster care rather than be returned to Mom, we've had to testify against her. Slow to start, the bureaucracy of courts, social workers, and lawyers has lurched into motion. The process is very formal, with language that is foreign to me. Social workers bring us to the courthouse. Before each hearing, we sit in an anteroom with our lawyer. This is not a criminal proceeding, so Mom doesn't have a lawyer, but we do. We're offered beverages, and our lawyer tells us the sort of questions the judge will ask. I don't understand why there's even a need. Now that the full truth is known, there have to be consequences. We had hidden our injuries specifically so that the authorities wouldn't take us away. Now that they are no longer hidden, I expect to be protected at last.

"Your mom has rights, David. In the eyes of the law, you belong to and with her," the lawyer responds.

"What about my rights, my right to not die? Won't she be punished?"

"That's not how this works. Your mom is not in trouble for hitting you. She may lose custody, but that is not a punishment, per se."

"She should be arrested for hitting me. That must be a crime," Jessica says.

"Not exactly, Jessica. Family law is different than criminal law."

"So you're saying that my mom owns us, and she can hit us whenever she wants and all that happens is that she *might* lose custody?" I ask, incredulous.

"More or less," our lawyer says.

"Are they going to put us back with her?" Alex asks.

"Could they?" I can't believe it.

"David, we are going to go in there, and each of you is going to tell the truth. The judge will listen and issue a ruling. In all likelihood, they will put you in foster care temporarily, pending a longer investigation. There will be another hearing, and that will consider a more permanent solution."

I'm confounded by this process. "So the goal of foster care is to give us back to her?"

"It's an awesome power that the state has, to break up families," the social worker says. "It's always the goal to reunify if possible. The court will likely put together a plan that your mom will have to follow in order to regain custody."

"She's going to kill us if they put us back with her. I won't go back."

"Let the process play out, David. I'm here for you," my attorney says.

"It's time, let's go." Our social worker opens the door and we enter the courtroom.

"Are you comfortable testifying in open court, David, Alex, Jessica?" the judge asks us in a friendly tone. I don't understand what this means.

"Yes," I say, wondering what closed court is.

From the witness stand, the judge smiles at me and continues. "It's brave of the three of you to be here today. You are completely safe here. You can take a break when you need to. If you don't understand a question, just say so. Now, raise your right hand and repeat after the bailiff." The judge is wearing an enormous black robe, and instead of a human body, all I see is a red tie at his neck.

On the record, in front of these agents of the state, I swear to tell the truth.

"David, why do you think you are here today?" the lawyer asks me.

"My mom can't care for us. She's sick. I don't feel safe with her. She beats us. We have no food; we barely go to school. She's going to kill me if you put me back there." I glance at Alex and Jessica. Both have tears in their eyes but hold their heads high. One by one, each of us is called up to speak.

Finally, the judge rules that all three of us will be placed in the custody of the Commonwealth of Massachusetts.

"We'll reconvene in six months to examine the progress Mary has made toward the plan counsel will establish with the department." And just like that, anticlimactically, we are out of her reach. I don't hear my mother's outburst. I'm in my own world, no longer in hers.

Foster care placements are made based on what is available, and the options are limited. Often kids are thrown into ill-matched families, and that is the case with me. There is a probationary period to see if it's a match, and, with a week's notice, I can be removed for no reason. And moved I am. I quickly cycle through a few placements. In between, I am put in group homes. These facilities, which have since been rebranded as "congregate care," could be big or small, with or without therapy or other support for kids. At the time, and still today, there is not enough thought given to race, religion, or any other cultural or emotional elements that might be good for the kids.

During this bumpy time, I have occasional conversations with Alex and Jess, but there isn't much substance to them. I take the call in the foyer of whichever facility I am in, with no privacy and other kids waiting for the phone.

"Hi. How are you?"

"Good. How are you?"

"What's going on?"

"Not much."

The system recognizes that maintaining a relationship with siblings is important, and it checks the box by allowing phone calls to take place, but siblings are used to living together, eating and playing and connecting in a home environment. Structured phone calls are a difficult way for siblings to love and support each other. We never ask each other the important questions: *Are you safe? Do they hit you? Did they buy you clothes? How much do you get to eat? Do you have toys? Do you have your own room? How's the house? Are they nice? Do you miss me? Do you think about Mom?* Our lives have diverged. Their sudden absence is profound.

On top of that, the temporary placements I am in are restrictive, and I've lost the freedom and agency that I had as a street kid. I wanted to escape Mom, and we had, but I'd forgotten to wish for more. Though I am deeply unhappy, I don't ask Alex or Jess for help. And they don't ask for it from me either. What can we possibly do for each other?

<hr/>

After what feels like a lifetime of separation from my siblings, my social worker and I pull into a cracked black asphalt driveway. In the front yard there is a basketball hoop, a broken-down Mustang, and flower beds veiled in black plastic for the winter. I consider these things as if they might be clues to what is to come, but I don't know how to interpret them. The house is a yellow vinyl A-frame with white plastic windows. A small, blond woman comes to the door to welcome me, but her smile does not reach her eyes.

This is the home where my brother and sister are living. In the car on the way here, the social worker told me that at last their foster parents have agreed to assess whether I'm a "project" they're willing to take on.

It's a split-level home, so in the foyer, I take off my shoes and climb a short set of beige-carpeted stairs. I walk behind my social worker, Jennifer, as we follow the wall-to-wall carpet to the living room. Every wall within view is painted mauve—the entire house looks like a washed-out Barney the dinosaur. Eyes cast down politely, I take a seat on the beige sofa, waiting to be spoken to. Faces peek around the corners of the room—the kids who live here are checking me out. I think I glimpse my sister, but I'm in the middle of an audition, so I do my best to ignore her and the others and to focus on my performance.

"We have one rule, David," the woman says. "Upstairs is off-limits. It's private space for me, my husband, and our kids, Tiffany, Neil, and Sandy. The rest of you kids have the run of the basement."

I nod. I'll do anything this family wants me to do. I'll clean the house, I'll keep my mouth shut, I'll stop being gay. I'll be the perfect boy if they let me live here, with my siblings.

After half an hour, Jennifer stands up. "Well, this is just fantastic. Thank you, Mae. What you're doing for this family is wonderful." She turns to me. "David, please walk me to the door." Only then do I realize I've been accepted. I'm about to live with my siblings again for the first time in more than a year. It is all I want.

I see Jennifer out, and at the threshold she faces me and places her hands on my shoulders. She leans down, her head close to mine, and whispers, "Don't fuck this up." Then she pulls back and pats both my shoulders as a send-off.

"This way, David." Mae ushers me to the dining table. The main floor is a large open plan with rooms delineated by the placement of furniture instead of walls. Only the kitchen is a proper room with a door, which is closed now, and, as I will learn, always. The dining table is blond oak, with glass inserts. The chairs match, and I sit down, marveling that I can see my legs through the glass top. *Stop tapping your foot, David,* I tell myself. *Be a blank slate. Learn who you need to be.*

I try to wait to be spoken to, but I can't help myself. "Can I see Alex and Jess?" I ask. The question hangs there unanswered, as if I did not speak. Mae's husband, Buck, comes in. I stand up to shake his hand. He's a big man with a patchy mustache, and a full head of curly black hair. His belly bulges from underneath a T-shirt. He crushes my hand, chuckling when I grimace. "So you're the third. Your mom was pretty busy, huh?" A flash of anger jolts through me, but I put a smile on my face. Alex and Jess are here. I need this to work.

Buck, a former factory worker, now drives an independent 18-wheeler. Mae has been clerking at a grocery store since graduating from high school. They have three biological kids. The older two, a boy and a girl, are hers from an earlier relationship, and then they share a seven-year-old daughter, Tiffany. They have four foster kids besides me right now, all boys except for my sister.

"Alex, Jessica, come on in," Buck bellows. And instantly, they walk through the kitchen door. I'm on my feet, and in their arms, surrounded by their love. I can smell Jessica's shampoo. It's the one with the kangaroo on the bottle.

"Okay, okay, you can show him around," Mae says. Alex and Jessica are stiff in her presence but smiling. We walk back toward the foyer, and then it's just the three of us.

"So, how is it? Are they nice?" I ask.

"It's…fine, just do what they say. They are big on that. There are a lot of rules. Sometimes they seem to make 'em up as they go, but just do it," Jessica tells me.

"Here, this is my room." Jessica indicates a hallway nook in the high-traffic area between the foyer and the kitchen. There is a love seat and some shelving. I recognize a few of her possessions: a plush pig, some of her drawings. "That pulls out into a bed," she says, motioning to the love seat. "Sit." I have craved this for so long. The three of us, under one roof, without the threat of Mom. I sit on the love seat, and Jessica joins me. Alex is hunched forward in his chair, facing us. When

I parted ways with them, Jessica was taller, but now Alex has caught up to her. They both look really clean.

"Are you okay?" Jess asks. I don't know how to communicate what has happened since we left Mom.

"I'm fine," I say. "Are you in school? Did they buy you clothes?"

"Yeah, they'll take you shopping once they get the check from the social worker. We walk to the high school. You'll be in the middle school, so you'll walk, too, but in a different direction."

"We're in different schools, damn," I say.

"David, get settled in downstairs. Dinner is soon," Mae says from the doorway of the kitchen.

Jessica squeezes my hand. "I love you."

"Come on, bro," Alex says. "We're down here." He leads me through the foyer to a door that goes down to the somewhat finished basement where the boys sleep. The upstairs is light filled, with windows on all sides, but the stairs down to the basement are steep and dark. The air is dank. It feels like we are descending into a cavern. The only windows are thin slits near the ceiling. The felted carpet is the same texture and green of a pool table. The walls are covered with buckling wood paneling. Stopping at the base of the steps, Alex points to a bed in the corner. "That's me." There are four beds and a futon lining the walls of the basement, and two other boys for me to meet: Ben, a thin ten-year-old with a shaved head; and another boy, who will stay with us for only a few weeks. Alex points to the futon. "That's yours, bro."

"Can I sit on your bed sometimes?" Ben asks. Without waiting for an answer, he says, "Let's play basketball in the driveway."

"Not right now, okay?" I say.

"Maybe tomorrow? Are we definitely playing tomorrow? Can I see your stuff?"

Alex gives me a look, and I get the message. I don't answer Ben, hoping that this is the right strategy to shut him up.

We've only just finished introductions when Mae calls us upstairs.

Tonight's dinner is mac and cheese with chopped hot dog and Kool-Aid. Everything is served in Tupperware.

At the end of dinner, Mae says, "David, I know you just got here, but we are going to have you jump in on dishes tonight. Tiffany will get you set up and make sure you know how we do things here."

"When's your birthday? Mine is November first," Tiffany says, leading me into the kitchen. There are stacks of dishes piled on the sink. There are ten of us, but even so I can tell that these can't all be from dinner.

"We have the same birthday!" I tell her, hiding my dismay at the volume of dishes.

"One sink of water, one sponge, one rinse. It's easy. Don't use too much soap, Mom hates that," Tiffany instructs me, then leaves, with a perky "Bye!"

I sort the dishes into piles, putting the pans at the end. Then I fill the sink with soapy water and begin to wash. Lunch appears to have been burgers. The water darkens, so I pull out the stopper to refill the sink.

"What are you doing?" Mae appears behind me.

"I'm sorry, what?"

"Tiffany told you one sink of water, yes?" Mae says.

"Yes, but the water was filthy. Lunch looks like it was good." I try to be charming.

"One sink, David. One." She leaves.

Okay, I got this. The washcloth is thin and worn, so I use my nails to scratch the crusted remains off the pans.

"Are you done yet?" Tiffany reappears without warning.

"Oh shit, you scared me."

"You're not supposed to curse."

"Sorry. You scared me. Yes, I'm done," I say.

"Okay, now I'll inspect."

"Inspect?"

"It's my job, David."

"Okay."

She holds up a pan. "This is not clean. Do it over."

I take the pan and examine it but can't see what she sees. Nonetheless, I put it back in the sink.

"You have to start over. Wash all of them. You can't ask for inspection until you are sure they are *all* clean. You didn't listen, and now you have to do it over."

I look at her, my head cocked to one side. "I have to wash all of them again, because one is still dirty?"

"Yup. Bye!"

I move the items I've already washed back to the other side of the counter and begin to clean the clean dishes.

Later, falling into my futon, I'm exhausted.

"You'll get the hang of it. Tiffany can be an asshole. Butter her up, you'll be fine," Alex tells me. "Good night, bro."

I close my eyes. Alex is only a few feet away in a bed. Jessica is upstairs, safe. We are under one roof. Fuck the dishes. I'll do them as many times as they want.

In the following days, I am introduced to more of our chores. As with the dishes, there are procedures to follow. When hanging the laundry, there is a certain way each type of clothing must be hung so that the clothespin doesn't make a mark. When I vacuum the house, I must leave even lines across the rug, as if it were the lawn at a golf course.

More troubling than the chores are the rules. The first morning, when I wake up, I start to go upstairs to the bathroom.

"Stop. What are you doing?" Ben says. I stop in my tracks.

"I have to pee."

"We're not allowed out of the basement until she opens the door," he tells me, explaining that once we are downstairs for the night, we aren't allowed back up for any reason, not even to use the bathroom, until Mae says so.

Alex fills me in on more of the rules. "Bro, the only shower is on the second floor, but we can't go up there without an escort. That's the family's space. Also, don't go in the kitchen except at mealtimes. There's no snacking. If you're thirsty, drink out of the bathroom tap. You can ask 'em for water, but they get annoyed."

This home has values and behaviors so different from what I'm used to that it feels like I'm contorting myself to fit into the environment. When social workers seek placements for children, there are never enough options, especially for sibling sets. The focus has to be on finding any space at all, not on making a match. I join this rigid household with no capacity to understand what is going on around me, no support for the transition, and no tools to manage the new issues that arise. Instead, I focus on the most important thing: my siblings. We used to dig in the garbage for food. We used to sleep outside. Our lives were in constant danger. I am uncomfortable and wary, but with Alex and Jess I feel whole again.

Still, I don't tell them what happened at the juvenile delinquent group home.

Every day, after school, I go about my chores while in the back of my head I am tracking whether Alex and Jessica have arrived home. They're in ninth grade together. They share teachers and friends and a walk to school. I'm still in middle school, on a different schedule, and feel increasingly isolated from them. One day, I'm hanging out the laundry, and I see them walking up the road together. They are talking with broad hand gestures and animated expressions. The three of us, who survived our childhood by the strength of our bond, have been divided physically and psychically. I can see the two of them on a parallel path, but I can't seem to find my way back to them. They are still connected, but not to me.

Mae and Buck never sit me down and say, *You are gay and we're going to fix you*, but, like the counselors at the juvenile home, they find something wrong with everything I do: how I speak, dress, and act. Buck makes fun of the way I talk, parroting my words and adding a lisp. If I use a multisyllabic word, he repeats it with derision. He doesn't like me to sound "smart." I'm not allowed to sit with my legs crossed. If I do, Buck says I have no balls. The DSS puts me through a battery of tests to assess my issues and needs. Nobody tells me my diagnosis, but I am put in therapy. We rarely talk about the abuse I experienced. Instead the focus is on how I present, or whom I like. The unspoken goal is to make a hetero man of me.

My therapist, Karen, pulls up to the house in a hot-pink Suzuki SUV that smells like cigarettes. She'll be one in a string of therapists that come and go, all committed to repairing that thing in me that they don't like. The therapists reinforce my mother's message that being gay is wrong. If I ever want to get out of this life, I can't be gay. Gay people don't achieve. They don't thrive. They suffer. It is drilled into me that homosexuality is wrong and disgusting, and means a short, sad life followed by a lonely, miserable death from AIDS. I dread these sessions. After each one, I feel fragile, like glass. The damage that is done in those hours will stay with me long into adult life. I tell nobody. Not Alex. Not Jessica. I would never tell them. I would never talk to anybody about this subject.

Mae and Buck—possibly under the direction of the therapist—have their own strategies for making me straight. My mom had been obsessively worried about our being molested. Here the concerns are different. One day I come out of the bathroom and Buck is standing there with his arms crossed.

"Taking your time in there, weren't you, missy?"

I don't know the right answer, so I don't answer.

"I won't have any perverts in my house. New rule. Door stays open."

From then on, I am never allowed to close the door to the bathroom all the way, not when I shower, not even when I shit. After I have my first accidental ejaculation in the shower, I think I finally understand why. I might do something sexual if left alone, and every sexual thought

I have is wrong. The authorities I encounter are united in their efforts to set me straight. Being gay is a mental illness, and trying to fix it is the status quo.

Mae and Buck also design special manly chores for me, to help me "butch up." One Saturday, after I've been at the house for a couple of months, Buck yells down to the basement, "David, I want your help."

He shows me a shallow hole in the yard and hands me a shovel. "We're making a swimming pool," he tells me. "I want you to move dirt from here, over to here." He leads me forty yards away to a gully. "This'll toughen you up." He smacks me on the back, hard, and I stumble a couple of steps forward. He chuckles. "Like I said."

Back and forth across the yard, day after day, I endure this Sisyphean task. Sometimes other kids are sent out to help, but it's short-lived aid. With a shovel and a five-gallon bucket, I begin to dig out a pool.

"Alex, this is killing me. I've barely made a dent. I'm going to be digging this pool for a fucking decade," I tell him.

"You just gotta do it, bro. This ain't a democracy."

When spring comes, the pool project stalls out, and Mae and Buck decide to reclaim a swamp at the back of their property. They send me out with a handheld Weedwacker to take down the swamp weed, which smells like skunk. After days of work, my body is covered with poison ivy. The rash forms bubbles on my hands, and when the blisters rub against the Weedwacker, they begin to bleed. Finally, I go to Mae.

"Mae, I can't...I can't hold the Weedwacker—" I start. I hold out my hands as evidence.

"It's not that bad, David. Don't be so dramatic," she says, turning away from me.

I won't go back down there, up to my shins in muck, swinging a dull tool to take out fast-growing swamp plants. In the area where I started, the plants are already beginning to grow back.

"I can't do this, Mae," I say again.

Turning back around, she looks at me, raises her hand, and in one smooth move backhands me across my face so hard that I fall. I'd rather be hit and call it a day than continue with this project, but she says, "Shut the fuck up and do what I say." All at once I realize her goal. It isn't to clear the swamp. Nor is she trying to teach me to take responsibility or to lend a helping hand. "Shut the fuck up and do what I say" is the goal.

"Shut the fuck up and do what I say" is why, in the middle of winter, without mittens, I am sent to hang wet clothes on the laundry line, where they don't dry, they freeze, like my hands. Then I have to take them down and rehang them in the laundry room. In the beginning at least, digging a pool and clearing a swamp seemed like tasks that might have reasons behind them. Maybe Mae and Buck even told themselves that they wanted to make the backyard better for the kids. But there is no logic to hanging wet clothes outside to freeze in the winter night. The only reason is to break my spirit.

I begin to understand that the only way to stay out of trouble is to hide not just my sexuality but all of who I am. I practice at Washington Middle School, where I am in eighth grade. For some reason the school was built at the bottom of a large hill, in a swamp. Each year, the structure unevenly sinks a few inches. There are dramatic cracks in the walls, and the pipes burst at the first freeze. I feel the same—that I've been stationed in a swamp where I am slowly sinking.

"David? Do you have anything to add?" Mrs. White asks in English class.

"No," I reply. I'm exploding with thoughts about *Lord of the Flies*, but I'm supposed to tone down my enthusiasm, my love for school, my ideas. The others aren't raising their hands, eager to share. I imitate this apathy. Bit by bit, I downshift in all my classes. I do the minimum on my assignments. I don't speak unless addressed. I'm compliant, a robot, a ghost of myself.

And yet, underneath this increasingly shut-down exterior, I am alive. I am thirteen years old. I know that I am attracted to boys, although I don't yet know that I'm not attracted to girls. In an ongoing negotiation with God and myself, I allow myself to dream. I can do *this*, but I'll never do *that*. I can lust, but I'll never act on it. Lucky for me, there is fodder for my dreams right there in the basement with me. I read *Sports Illustrated*...for the underwear ads. There is a picture of Michael Jordan from the magazine taped above my bed. Someone probably put it there to encourage me to be interested in sports, but I don't care about basketball. I take in the details of his muscles, the line of the compression shorts he wears under his uniform shorts. Malcolm, a tall, well-built fourteen-year-old, is the newest foster kid. He is oblivious to the role he plays in my fantasies. He smells like Drakkar Noir cologne and wears a gold chain with a swagger. When we aren't doing chores, we are sent down to the basement. Five of us boys spend whole days with nothing to do but pass the time. Malcolm steps in as our leader. His games are different from anything we've ever come up with.

"Put your head down between your legs," Malcolm says. So I do.

"Now breathe in and out quickly, pushing out all the air," he says. So I do.

"Come up," Malcolm says. So I do. *Anything you want, Malcolm.*

Standing right in front of me, he gently puts his hands on either side of my throat. With just the right amount of pressure, the world goes black. I wake up in his arms.

I can play this game all day just to wake up in those dark bronze, muscular arms.

Alex is there, playing the same game, but he's on a completely different planet. "Everything went black!" he exclaims, and I know he hasn't noticed how soft Malcom's hands are or what cologne he wears. He just wants to know what it's like to pass out, or to make someone else pass out. This makes my fantasies safe—because there is a group, because it is just boys being boys, nobody will notice the secret joy I'm taking in my crush.

Malcolm, like the rest of us, wears Hanes briefs. But his are a slimmer cut—bikini briefs. He strides around in them, and I avert my eyes, sort of. At night we all sleep in our underwear, and his bed is just feet away. After he falls asleep, I watch his sheets rise and fall with his breath. I can't stop watching. Sometimes I stay up late into the night just to watch him breathe. I start to masturbate for the first time. I know I'll be punished if I get caught, so I do it into a sock that I hide.

One day, before school, Mae calls me over.

"We need to talk after school," she says, holding my sock up between two fingertips with her nose wrinkled in disgust. All day at school I feel like a dead man walking. I don't know what awaits me: mortification, punishment, violence.

When I get home Mae and Buck sit me down in the living room. "You're disgusting," Mae says. "Disgusting people do this." We're the only ones in the living room, but I know all the kids can hear every word they say. I wait for it to end, head bent in shame. I promise to stop. From then on, I do a much better job at hiding or burying the evidence.

My sexuality isn't the only part of me that Mae wants to change. I have been at the house in Holyoke for about six months when she tells me that I'm on a diet. "You are fat, David. You're soft and girlie. You need to stop eating so much." We already don't have access to the kitchen, and there are no snacks, but now Mae keeps a vigilant eye on what I eat.

"This is your plate," she says. The other kids are eating mac and cheese, but I am given only carrots and a cup of Kool-Aid. Sometimes Tiffany will slip me a few Doritos. If I do anything Mae doesn't like— studying when her kids are trying to watch TV; asking to shower when she doesn't want me to shower—she takes dinner away from me as a punishment. I've been hungry out of poverty, and now I'm hungry out of restriction, so one thing hasn't changed: I'm still hungry all the time.

Without thinking, I pull out my old strategies for feeding myself.

School has always been the most stable food source I have, and Washington Middle School is no different. At school the poor children are given coupons, like food stamps, that we present to the woman at the cafeteria in exchange for lunch. Some kids find this embarrassing, but I don't care at all.

Another source of food is a convenience store on the way home from school called Common Variety. Holyoke is a once-thriving former mill town still clinging to its industrial past. Empty brick factories cluster around the river and pond, crisscrossed by abandoned rail lines that have been crudely paved over. Churches of various denominations still anchor major intersections, although they remain mostly empty on Sundays. The most prominent store in downtown, other than the grocery store, is the 7-Eleven. Common Variety is a funny name for a store that has very little variety—the standard candy, sodas, packaged snacks, and the same Saran-wrapped sandwiches every day. After school, when kids flood the place, I join the chaos and steal untold quantities of sweets.

One day a kid named Timothy follows me home from school. He's a big redheaded kid who has been bumping into me in the halls and elbowing me out of his way. I walk faster, but he catches up to me.

"Fag," he says, and shoves me. I stumble forward but don't fall. He has no idea what he's gotten himself into. I'm still a New York street kid. I turn to face him.

"Your mother and father are brother and sister," I spit out. I've been in countless fights, and I know that fists are a waste of energy. I bite, poke, yank, and beat the shit out of him. But the next week his brother comes over from the high school with a few friends and attacks me on the long walk up the hill from school.

The boys have me down on the sidewalk when a car screeches to a halt at the curb, and a tiny woman jumps out. She starts screaming in Taiwanese. The kids run away, and the woman throws me into the back of her car, into the lap of her daughter, Su-Hui.

DAVID AMBROZ

"Why'd they do that?" Su-Hui asks. "They are trash." Before I can answer, she continues. "We're from New York City, well, Queens anyway." The pride of Holyoke has shrunk with its prospects, and with the discontent came a resistance to outsiders. Being one of the only Asian Americans in town, Su-Hui understands what it's like to be different. Her mom drives us to their home, which turns out to be a small apartment above Common Variety. I had no idea anyone lived above it or that the Cheng family ran it all.

We park behind the store and climb the wooden stairs up to the second floor. The family's apartment is immaculate, and at the dining table, Mrs. Cheng plies me with food. She is kind, gentle, and firm, and I feel safe and welcomed. I eat until I realize I'm expected at home.

"I can't be here, my foster parents will be mad," I say.

"Why mad?" Mrs. Cheng asks.

"It's just that...I mean, it's, I can't...I'm not supposed to be here," I stammer, unsure what I'm allowed to reveal. I stand up to leave. "Thank you, thank you, Mother Cheng." I hurry toward the door and bend over to put my shoes back on.

"You don't have to go. You can stay for dinner," Su-Hui suggests.

"I have to go," I insist, pulling the door open, throwing my backpack over my shoulder and racing down the steps.

After meeting the Chengs, I try not to steal from their store, but it's my only resource when the hunger gets to be too much. Only days after Mrs. Cheng saved me from the bullies, I pick up a small Charleston Chew and make my way to the counter register.

"Hello, Mother Cheng. Just this, thank you," I say.

"Okay, David. Are the kids leaving you alone?" she asks.

"It's fine, they're fine, thank you," I say, and make my way out. As I leave, I catch a glimpse of her watching me go. She knows that I am stealing from her. I can tell. Like the woman I sold wrapping paper, she understands my situation better than she lets on. I'm angry at myself for stealing from this family, but I need to get through another hungry

194

night. I feel like I have no other options, but Mrs. Cheng does have a choice, and she chooses to help me survive.

I'm red in the face, and I pick up my pace as I leave, veering off the street to walk along an old, abandoned rail line that cuts through the woods. I sit down on a rusting iron bridge that crosses a creek and dangle my legs off the side. Opening my black JanSport backpack, I pull out a premade, plastic-wrapped turkey sandwich. After I eat, I gather my trash and press it into a tight Saran-wrapped ball. I carefully place the ball under a pile of dead leaves and stand up. Now that my stomach is full, I resolve to find a different place to steal from and hurry home to do my chores.

Chapter 13

ONE WEEK AFTER I FINISH eighth grade, a rusty gray Cadillac rolls up in front of 10 Christopher Lane. The driver, Bobbie, is a high school friend of my brother and sister, with a suspected crush on Alex.

"Ambroz, let's go," Bobbie hollers, but I'm already walking out, backpack slung over one shoulder. The car's exhaust is a thick white cloud that sits unmoving in the early summer morning. Everything is electric—the grass is super green, the sky, super blue.

Bobbie talks as she drives. "So...cool. Day one is pretty relaxed. I'm going to be working with the older kids, but you'll be a junior counselor in Camp Ibits, with the younger kids. You'll like Ibits, the kids are adorable. My cousin, Holly—the woman that I got to hire you—she runs the camps. She's super nice and super busy. She'll love ya but expect the world from you at the same time." I'm just thrilled to be out of the house and getting paid.

The day camp is one town over from Holyoke, and we pass a stretch of farm country between the two towns. As we approach Northampton, the houses get nicer, larger, and better-maintained. The retail along the streets is quaint, with none of the vacant storefronts I've seen in Holyoke. We jackknife into the upper parking lot at the YMCA.

"Okay, let's do this!" Bobbie says, and she puts her arm through mine as we walk toward the front door. The YMCA is a low-slung brick building. Inside, I am hit by the smell of a chlorine pool. Bobbie steers me to the right, into the larger of the building's two rooms. "The campers get here later," she explains as we join the rest of the counselors and junior counselors. We take our seats in a circle of chairs.

"Hello, counselors!" Holly says, walking into the center of the circle. It's my first look at her, and she is beaming. She has long, curly brown hair and bright eyes. She's fit, wearing high-waisted jeans and a tucked-in camp shirt. But what stands out most is her radiant smile.

After introductions, I'm sent over to Camp Ibits to prepare for the campers' arrival. The room is festooned with brightly colored images of happy children, streamers, and designated activity areas. There's a paint station, a dress-up area, a train set, and a reading nook.

"Hi. Hi. Who are you? I'm Brianna, but you can call me Bri. Lots of people call me Bri." A small girl, maybe five years old, comes right up to me as the other campers are still saying goodbye to their parents.

"Well, hello, Bri. I'm David. Where is your backpack?" I ask. I'm supposed to help the kids put their backpacks in cubbies.

"In Mom's office," she says, and without further explanation she grabs my hand and says, "Let's read." She leads me over to the reading corner. "Sit here." She points to the floor, and I sit. She walks over to the bookshelf to make her selection. Her chestnut hair is cut in an adorable bob, and she's wearing a summer dress patterned with water-melons. After a pause, she comes back with a book. "Here," she says, plopping into my lap.

"*The Giving Tree*," I begin to read. Bri snuggles into me. "Once there was a tree..." Children are arriving and beginning to play. The noise level is high and increasing, but Bri and I are in our own little world, the sun coming in through a window and making shapes on the carpet around us.

There are five other junior counselors, an adult counselor, Caroline, and twelve children under our supervision. Once the kids have had time to explore the space, Caroline attempts to marshal them into a parachute game.

"Let go of hers, Joshy, hold yours; Cindy, I see you hiding over there, come on, you can have red. There ya go. David, you are here—green. Come on, everyone, grab a color."

The silk parachute is divided by color into pie-shaped wedges. When we are all organized in a circle around it, tightly gripping the edges, Caroline calls, "Ready? One...two...three...*up!*"

We raise our hands, lift the parachute high into the air, and then let it fall slowly. The rainbow of colors floats down, the kids' laughs are infectious, and I find myself laughing at the simplicity of it.

"Okay, you ready for these?" Caroline asks as she tosses rainbow beach balls onto the top of the moving parachute. We shake the parachute, trying to keep the beach balls in play.

Then Michelle prompts the grand finale: "On the count of three, raise your arms above your head, and we are all going to go underneath the parachute. One, two, three!" We lift the parachute high in the air, beyond the outstretched fingertips of the little kids, and then all of us duck underneath, sitting on the floor as the parachute forms a bubble over us. In that bubble, the sun's beams filtering through the rainbow cloth and warming the bunch of us, I realize that this is what might have been for me, Alex, and Jessica: eyes of wonder looking up at a candy-colored world. Gentle nudges of guidance. Snacks and nap times. Laughter and parachute games. This is what childhood is meant to offer. Pure joy.

The day that follows is a blur of construction paper, glitter and glue, and more games. After the kids leave, I help the other junior counselors clean up the room. I'm exhausted, but it isn't the same exhaustion I feel when I do manual labor for Buck. This exhaustion comes from giving all of my attention and care to children. They'll take all you can give, and I want to give so much. All the junior counselors look as worn out as me, and we're punch-drunk with the success of our first day as we clean up and start to get to know each other.

"Holyoke, gross," Amy teases me with a smile.

"I'm not from there, just live there now," I say, avoiding all mention of foster care. Just then Holly comes in.

"Great day!" she says. Bri is in her arms, her head nestled into her neck. And then it clicks: Holly is Bri's mom. Holly turns to me and says, "Bri tells me she has a new friend that loves to read. Thank you, David." She smiles at me, and I smile back.

"Bri is a delight," I say, and I mean it.

All summer my days are hours of running after kids that have endless energy except when they collapse at nap time. The group of junior counselors—Amy, Jennifer, Tanya, Lyndsey, and Bryan—seem to become friends. I think they make plans together after work. I like them, but I wouldn't want to hang out or go to their homes—that might mean I'd have to invite them to mine. When people find out I'm in foster care, they immediately assume there's a problem with my parents and therefore me. They want to know what went wrong. To explain, I'd have to share painful truths. I just want to be normal and fit in. My particular foster situation doesn't help—how will I explain that we're not allowed to have snacks? Will I invite them to hang out in the basement where there is no light? I'm happy to keep our friendships safely confined to the day camp.

Each morning, Bri finds me and folds her small hand into mine. "Read to me." It becomes our routine, and I love it. I love her. We read a new book each day, and our daily routine is bookended with an afternoon goodbye.

"David, I'll see you on Monday, okay?"

"Yes, Bri. Monday! You wore me out—" And before I finish, she launches herself right at me for a bear hug. "Okay, girl. Go to your mom, see you Monday."

I dread weekends, when I won't be at the YMCA with this crew, with the kids, under the sunshine of Holly. One Monday, I come in to work after Mae and Buck have spent the weekend relentlessly focused on my weight. They have withheld food, and except for a cookie that Alex snuck me, I have had very little to eat. I'm thinner than I've ever been, my pants sliding down on my hips. In the morning, before lunch is served, I play four square in the playground with the kids but I keep losing track of where we are in the game. Holly sees me and calls me into her semiprivate office area.

"David, what's up? You seem...not like yourself."

"I'm just tired." I stare just past her face, out the vertical windows. I can't look her in the eyes and lie, but what am I supposed to say? I'm not just tired. I'm wrung out, my head hurts, and I'm trying to power through a stomach-churning hunger.

"David, look at me," Holly says.

"I have to go back. Amy is covering for me."

Holly waits for a moment, peering at me. She knows that I'm in foster care. She had to talk to my foster mom and social worker to arrange for me to have the job. But if Holly finds out what's going on at home, she'll take action. She cares about kids, and she's a fixer. She would probably storm the foster home and demand that they treat me better. Which would only make things worse for me. It would definitely be the end of this idyllic summer job. Five days a week I find peace and joy at the camp, and I don't want anyone messing with it.

I avoid Holly's gaze, and she finally just says, "We'll talk more, okay?" I nod and dart out of her office as fast as possible. Then I do my best to throw myself into the day of small victories with a roomful of Ibits. While we play, I can almost forget that I'll have to go home at the end of the day.

But Holly has her eye on me, and all summer she watches me closely, with a care I haven't felt before. One afternoon, Bri and I are reading in our usual window spot. Bri is in the same watermelon summer dress that she wears on top of another outfit every single day. It's ridiculously endearing.

"Bri, I think that's enough, honey. Let's get packed up," Holly says, walking up to us with a smile across her face.

Bri leans back into me in protest, but I put the book to the side and scoop her up onto her feet as we've done a million times. She laughs and runs off. Holly reaches out her hand to help me up.

"You are so good with her, David. Are your siblings younger?" Holly asks.

"No, I'm the youngest. Jessica is one year older than Alex, who is one year older than me. But I am the 'mom' in all this," I say, basking in her attention.

"I can tell, David. And do you all get along with your foster parents?"

I cannot think of the safe answer. The pause stretches on too long, until finally I say, "I guess so." Holly keeps her gaze on me, and I feel gentle pressure to say more. This woman is kind, but I can't rock the boat.

"Bri is an amazing kid," I blurt out, changing the subject.

"She really cares for you. You have a way with these kids, David. You must have grown up with a lot of younger kids around? Where did you grow up?" Holly pivots back to me like a pro.

"New York, mostly. But we moved around a lot." I turn my body, implying that I need to go, but Holly, in her benevolent way, is still trying to engage me.

"That's hard, moving around. I've lived in Northampton my whole life. My whole family is here too. I married my high school boyfriend."

"That's cool," I say, but Holly waits. It's my turn. "I like Northampton, at least the part I've seen. Holyoke is run-down, and the school is literally sinking."

Holly laughs. "I know. That's what happens when you build on swampland. Do you like school?"

"I love it. Especially English. Mrs. White is hard, but I love that. She walks around with a yardstick that she slaps down on the table when you are talking out of turn. But she's really good at explaining the stories," I gush. "But I don't always get to do the homework, and she calls on you even if your hand isn't up."

"Why can't you do the homework?" Holly asks.

I've said too much. "Um...because...well, I have a lot of chores, and sometimes I stay home from school to finish them. Everyone in the house has to contribute."

"They keep you home?" Holly asks.

"Um...no...sort of...I don't know," I stammer.

"Okay, David, it's fine. Pack up, and we'll see you tomorrow. We'll talk more, okay?" Holly puts her hands on my shoulders, looking at me directly.

I avert my gaze. "Yeah, um, okay. Sounds good. Bye." I look up briefly, pull back, and pivot away.

The summer slips by, faster than I want. At the end of August, the days are long and humid, and when we have the kids outside, it's sweltering. But I don't want it to end. Neither, apparently, does Holly. She gathers the junior counselors and tells us that when camp is over, she wants to take us on a beach trip together.

"Each of you need to have your parents sign the permission slip. We'll be gone three days and two nights. All the information is on the slip, but we'll be camping just outside Provincetown. I'll bring everything we need—tents and sleeping bags. But you should bring clothes, swimsuits, and some pocket money for shopping in Provincetown."

"Provincetown is awesome!" Bryan exclaims. "I've been out there with my family. It's past Boston, at the very tip of Cape Cod. It's basically a town built on a sandbar in the ocean. It's adorable."

I want to go. I want to drag out this experience with Holly for as long as possible. But there is no way Mae and Buck are going to let me go on this trip. Not a chance. Holly must see the hopelessness on my face when she says, "David, let's talk."

"I can't go, Holly. I can't ask. I'm sorry."

"Slow down. Why not? Do you need me to talk to your foster parents? Your social worker?"

"No. Don't. They'll be mad."

"Mad? David…" Holly is confused. She can't fathom why they would deny me this opportunity. "I'm going to try, okay? You and the others earned this trip. I'm driving; there is no cost. I'll be glad to pitch your social worker too."

I haven't wanted her to engage with them all summer, but now that my job is ending, I have nothing to lose. And I want this so badly. I don't care where we go or what we do. I just want to be with this group of friends, going on an adventure with this woman.

"Okay."

Fixer that she is, Holly somehow makes it happen. She even somehow knows to give me a duffel bag in which to pack my things. On the day of the trip, I wait in the foyer for her to pull up in her red Dodge Caravan. Duffel bag in hand, I run out and jump into the van with the others. I'm the last to be picked up, and the six of us talk and laugh and sing for the five-hour drive to Provincetown. This is the first time I've been in a group of peers where I don't stand out. I came out of a house and got into the car, just like everyone else. I have a duffel bag, just like everyone else. I've had months with this group in an environment where I knew exactly what was expected of me, and I loved doing it. I like these kids. I feel included and wanted and like I belong. And yet they know nothing about me, and I don't want them to.

"We're here!" Holly announces. Our campsite is at Race Point Beach, just outside of Provincetown. I've never seen anything like this place. Massive sand dunes covered in seagrass buffer the ocean. The sky is a vibrant blue. I can feel the ocean in the breeze.

"Let's set up camp," Holly says, but we pile out of the van and completely ignore her, running over the pathway carved through the dune to get to the beach. There is almost nobody here, and the sand stretches endlessly in either direction. And then—the ocean. I've never seen the ocean in person before, but it looks just like a photo from a magazine. It's breathtaking. The mist of the waves coats my skin, cooling me as it evaporates. This ocean has been here all along—and it will be here long after I'm gone. It doesn't care if I'm rich or poor, hungry or full, young or old. It's here for anyone and everyone. Immense, and accessible. I wiggle my toes. The sand is warm, with fine particles that feel like silk.

Meandering back, we unload umbrellas, towels, coolers, and sunblock. There is plenty of room on the beach, but we spread our towels close to each other so we can talk.

"Ambroz! Sunblock!" Holly calls, tossing me the bottle. The lotion is warm and has a chemical but not unpleasant smell. I squeeze some out and start to spread it across my skin like the others are doing. I have never applied sunblock before. It feels thick.

"Oh, wow. That's enough for all of us!" Bryan says. "Give me some." He holds up his forearms so I can wipe some off on him. I rub the extra across his sun-warmed skin. Our eyes meet for a brief moment, and he grins.

The day spreads out. I can't remember a time when I was in a situation where all I was supposed to do was sit and relax. It's an unfamiliar and wonderful feeling.

When the sun starts to inch toward the horizon, we go to our tents, get dressed, and head into town. Provincetown, located at the tip of a spit of land jutting out into the Atlantic, is the first place the Pilgrims landed in the New World. It's a lively former fishing village that gets taken over every summer by tourists.

"Listen, guys, I want you to stay on Commercial Street. We'll meet back here, at town hall, at seven. I made reservations for dinner. Okay,

y'all?" Holly asks our crew. We wander the endless retail of Commercial, breaking into groups of two or three as we're drawn to different
stores. Bryan and I stay near Holly, strolling and talking.

"Let's go in here. I need at least one thing that says Provincetown,"
Bryan says.

"They've put Provincetown on literally everything," I chuckle.

Bryan ducks in, and I wait outside with Holly. "Go in, get something," she suggests.

"I don't have money for that," I tell her.

"It's fine. Let's pick out a shirt for you. It doesn't have to say
Provincetown." Holly grabs my hand and leads me into the store. It's
a sea of soft shades of blue and beige, with a heavy nautical theme.
I've never been in a nice store where I'm allowed to buy something
for myself. I close in on a section of nicer, less touristy clothes toward
the back, and immediately spot the shirt I want. It's long-sleeved with
narrow purple and orange horizontal stripes. I find my size, and head
to the dressing room. When I try the shirt on, I think it looks amazing.
I step out of the room to show Holly and Bryan.

"It looks great! I love it," Holly exclaims.

"Bryan?"

"*Yess!*" Bryan says, snapping his fingers.

The clerk takes the shirt, folds it carefully, wraps it in tissue paper,
and then places it inside a thick, glossy paper bag—the kind that is so
much sturdier than brown bags. Holly hands over a credit card, and I
realize I never even looked at the price. I take the bag and walk toward
the door with Bryan, feeling proud. I shopped, just like everyone else
in this town. I belong.

Back on the street, Holly points out something I've been trying to
pretend I haven't noticed—there are many gay male couples walking
together down the street.

"It's nice to see these guys out here, just loving each other." Holly
nods toward a group of men who are clearly gay. Among them are

couples holding hands. The men are gorgeous, well-groomed, their muscles stretching their T-shirts. They are talking and laughing—having the time of their lives. Holly grew up in Northampton, which is more liberal than Holyoke, but also Holly herself is a person who naturally loves people and accepts them for who they are. So she acknowledges these men, subtly and gently telling me and the other gay teens in her care that being gay is perfectly acceptable, that it doesn't mean suffering an early death from AIDS, that being gay is beautiful. Her message contradicts everything I've ever been told. I am not fully ready to hear her.

But I'm paying attention, and everywhere I look I see gay men, having fun, walking about as if it's normal. I love it and am mortified at the same time. Bryan, on the other hand, has no inhibitions at all. "Woof," he says with a grin.

"Down, boy!" Holly says, laughing.

"They are hot, but I'm certain I'm not what they are looking for," Bryan says. I clutch my bag and try to become smaller. How can there be a town full of gay men, just living their lives, and how can Holly and Bryan be so casual about it? I've heard from foster parents, therapists, and my country that it's mostly illegal to be gay. How can these two realities exist?

Holly throws an arm around each of us, on either side of her, and we walk among this happy, healthy crowd of gays. Her arm is pleasantly heavy. It rests on my shoulder, pulling me in and pressing me forward toward the future. It comes with no obligations, no negotiation, no chores, just a gift of love.

Chapter 14

THE FOLLOWING SPRING, I COME home from school to find a maroon Pontiac Firebird parked in the driveway, its dents familiar to me. I recognize it as Mel's car—the one that took me away from my mother—and an unexpected visit can't be good. The moment I walk in the door I can feel that something is wrong.

"Come up to the living room," Mae says. I quietly follow her up the stairs. Our social worker is sitting in the living room. She looks at me expectantly.

"Where are they?" Mae demands.

"Who?" I ask.

"We don't have time for your games," Mae says, her tone frigid but controlled. We have company.

Mel says, "David, this is very serious. When did you last see your siblings?"

"I don't know...I mean, this morning, getting ready for school?" *What has happened to Alex and Jessica?* My mind is reeling, trying to figure out what's going on.

"Did Alex say anything to you last night?" Mae asks. She lets her dentures drop down in her mouth and clicks them back into place. A nervous habit. She's only in her midthirties, but she already has a full set of dentures.

"Where might they go? New York?" Mel asks.

"What do you mean? What's going on?" I ask.

"Do you know where they might have gotten money?" Mae asks, accusation in her voice.

I don't know the answers to any of these questions, and maybe it's clear from my distress that I really don't know, because Mel finally reveals that my brother and sister didn't show up at school today. They have disappeared.

"We're all you have, you know," Mae says to me that night during dinner. We are seated across from each other. I feel more alone than ever. "Jessica and Alex don't love you. Your mother doesn't love you. But we do. We won't abandon you." She hugs me, I think for the first time. My body is rigid; her hug is confusing to me. And then, to add to the confusion, her tone shifts from cloying to threatening.

"David, it's important that you tell us if you know where they are." She leans forward, and her face comes in closer to mine over the table.

"Mae, I really don't—" I start, but she slaps my face.

"Don't lie to me. You need to think about the consequences here, David. No school. You're staying home sick tomorrow. Go downstairs."

The slap isn't as bad as the fear that I might be sent back to a group home. If these people are my only refuge, I don't know which is worse. I just don't know. Why did Alex and Jessica leave me here?

Several days later, I meet with Mel in her office in downtown Northampton.

"David, they are fine. We found 'em. Well, actually they called us."

"Can I see them? Where are they?"

"Somehow they put together enough money for two bus tickets to Boston."

"Boston? Why Boston?"

"Honestly, David, I don't know, and I'm not sure I care at the moment. What's important is that they are back. We have placed them at a foster home in Amherst, just a few miles away. They are adamant that they won't go back to your current foster home. They are making some serious claims about abuse there, which we are looking into." She pauses. "Do you understand?"

"Can I move in with them, there?"

"We are going to keep you where you are. You seem to be doing fine. Mae tells me you've adjusted really well and that they love you. We don't want to disrupt that. Plus, unfortunately, the placement where they are can't have any more kids."

"Can I see them?"

"Soon. For now, let's get you back home."

My home is with Alex and Jessica. When Alex ran away, we had all plotted his escape together, but this time the two of them have left without me. They planned and executed it without even telling me. I have always been the one to keep the family together, and now they've abandoned me. Buck and Mae had done their best to separate us physically and emotionally, but now my brother and sister, who had been the only constants in my life, are gone. And I'm still here, surrounded by strangers, and completely alone.

Everything I loved kept leaving.

After my summer working at the YMCA ended, Holly had come to take me out once in a while. At first, this arrangement was fine with Mae and Buck, and I was allowed to go over to Holly's once a week. Then, one day, Holly stopped coming. For months, I looked out the window, watching for Holly's red Dodge Caravan, even just to wave. Now my brother and sister have left without a word, closed the door on me that morning after breakfast without reaching back to take me with them. We were all just kids trying to survive, but I needed them, and it felt like something profound and precious had been snatched from me.

While it takes some time, the authorities take Alex's and Jessica's claims of abuse seriously enough that they are not returned to our home. Mae and Buck are furious at this blemish on their record and incensed by a newly imposed restriction that they no longer foster any older children other than the ones that are currently in their care. That restriction signals that the abuse is real, and it directly affects their income. I am not told much about the claims, but I know that Mae and Buck are not found to be *abusive*, but they have to do additional training on working with adolescents. I don't understand how two teenagers running away and putting forward legitimate claims of abuse doesn't result in the loss of Mae and Buck's certification. I don't know why I am never asked if I want to leave. I'm not even asked if I'm okay.

Things with my mother had gotten worse for me when Alex ran away, and now that he and Jessica are gone, the same thing happens in my foster home.

"David, we've got to work on your weight. It's just out of control. You have to agree, look at yourself," Mae says at the dining table.

I don't know what she's talking about. I'm already underweight. All of my ribs are visible.

"It'll help with your weight, and you acting out. Do you understand?"

I don't. But I sense that I'm not the first child she has done this to. When you're hungry, you can't misbehave. You can't talk back. You can't think. Then, with sudden clarity, I see her—this brittle, heartless woman. I see her standing in the way of everything that's good and meaningful in my life. She's on her second or third marriage, having had a child during high school. She works at her parents' grocery store. She is married to an ill-tempered man-child, living in a sad town that she has no means to leave. Her life hasn't been easy, and the supplemental income she gets from a herd of foster youth is the difference between keeping the house or not. The clothes allowance she gets for the foster kids means her own biological kids get new clothes. She's a sad, beat-down figure who yearns to have power over some part of her life, and that turns out to be us. Today, it's me.

After this conversation, Mae restricts my food more than ever. My portions are further reduced, and often I am made to skip meals. I suck down water in the bathroom to kill the pain in my stomach.

I look forward to returning to school during the week, where I know there will be food, but when I start ninth grade, Mae often keeps me out of school to work at her family's grocery store. I stock the freezer shelves and clean the bathrooms. No one at the school notices my absences—and when they do, Mae explains them away. I have a rotating cast of social workers, who don't have the bandwidth to pay attention to anything but immediate and obvious problems. It's hard for me to concentrate on anything but my hunger. I'm constantly tired. I'm being erased from the inside, calorie by calorie.

One day at school I'm in line at the cafeteria—and next thing I know I wake up on the floor.

"David, David Ambroz. Can you hear me, buddy?" a teacher asks. He is kneeling above me. "Derek, go and get the nurse. Now. Please, don't run."

"I'm okay," I say, and try to sit up. But I've cut my head on the way down.

"Come on, can you walk? Let's head over to the nurse's office." The teacher helps me up, and I walk leaning on him. I look back at the buffet as we walk past it. I came so close.

"Do you feel sick?" the nurse asks. I don't explain that I'm starving. I know better than to get my foster parents in trouble, so I just say I feel a bit ill. The nurse gives me a few crackers to settle my stomach. "I'm gonna go ahead and call your parents. You probably need a good night's rest. Maybe you just overexerted yourself."

The next day, instead of letting me return to school, Buck drops me off at the Carmichaels'. Carmichael Contractors is a general contractor specializing in plumbing. Mae and Buck seem to have an ongoing relationship with the Carmichaels—they are paid to provide foster children for labor, child labor laws be damned. Before she left, Jessica occasionally worked as a maid for them. Last summer, I scraped and painted an entire house for them, working six days a week. Since then, I've worked here on weekends and when Mae keeps me home from school as a punishment. They call it "good male work." Climbing into a cargo area behind the driver's seat of his truck, I accompany Mr. Carmichael and his regular helper to homes all over Western Massachusetts. Mr. Carmichael is not a patient teacher. He doesn't seem to know my name—he simply says, "Hey, asshole," to get my attention. But I watch and mirror their work. I assist with plumbing work, learning to install copper pipe, and I figure out on my own how to solder new pipe installations.

The day after my fainting spell, I walk up to the large garage and knock on the door. Carmichael's helper lets me in without a greeting. It's a cold November day, and the cavernous garage is poorly insulated. I pull my sleeves up over my fingers to keep them warm. Lit by skylights, the place smells like gas. There is a layer of grime over everything, but it is well organized. Tools hang neatly on pegboards; whole walls are filled with red Sears metal tool cabinets. Every tool has a place and a purpose. I appreciate the order.

Ordinarily we'd go out on jobs, but today the helper weaves between vehicles, leading me to the far corner of the warehouse. He thrusts a white bucket at my chest.

"He wants us to clean all the trucks today. And by us, I mean you," he says.

I don't argue. I never talk back anymore. At least these guys leave me alone. And I don't really mind the work. I sing Sheryl Crow's song "All I Wanna Do" to entertain myself and add some humor to my situation. But I've never washed a vehicle before. Unsure of where to start, I look into the bucket. It's full of sponges and other materials. "Do I use everything in here?" I ask.

"Figure it out, asshole." He walks out of the garage.

Taking that as a yes, I get to work. There are three vehicles lined up in front of me: the large pickup that Mr. Carmichael usually uses, a van similar to a UPS brown van, and a small Dodge Ram. I run my hand along the body of the van. Salt and mud from the snowy streets are baked into the paint; it feels like sandpaper.

I dump the contents of the bucket onto a bench. There's a pair of yellow cleaning gloves with small flower designs. They're big for me, but on they go. I run hot water into the bucket, adding the Palmolive dish soap that was in the bucket. I lather up a large yellow sponge and wet the embedded mud.

To keep my mind occupied when I work, I sing a song I learned at the camp that United Methodist church sent me to years ago.

Oh, sinner man, where you gonna run to? I belt out the lyrics, appreciating the echo in the garage. Circling the van, I soap as close to the roof as I can reach.

Run to the rock, rock was a melting
All on that day

The mud isn't coming off. Round and round I go, scrubbing until my forearm aches. Returning to the bench, I consider the other supplies in the bucket. I find a yellow box of steel wool scouring pads. S.O.S. pads will save the day.

Run to the sea, the sea was a boiling
All on that day

Doing a little test patch on the van, I wet the area above the driver's-side wheel, then rub it with the steel wool. The muck comes off easily. It worked! After a first pass on that side, I move around to the passenger side.

My stomach aches with hunger. *I miss my siblings; I wish I were at school*, I think as I scrub. I write with the S.O.S. pad on the side of the van. In big, looping, cursive letters, I clean off the word "Love." Standing back, I'm proud of the effect. I go back around to the other side of the van to finish my work there. What I see devastates me.

The pad has not just cleaned away the mud. Now that the water has dried, I see that there is a dense thicket of scratches across the whole side of the van. My whole body tenses in fear. I instantly grab the S.O.S. pads and hide them in a red tool chest. Then I rewet the truck, temporarily hiding the damage.

When are they coming back? Can I run? Will they tell my foster parents? What will happen to me?

Run to the sea. Sea, won't you hide me?

All on that day

My heart is pounding. I have to hide. I open the passenger door to the pickup and crawl beneath the steering wheel. It's freezing and filthy, but I'll hide here forever if need be. That's my best and only plan.

I'll run to you Lord; oh Lord won't you hide me?

All on that day

I'm there for what seems like an hour when I hear the door to the garage open. The van must be dry now and the scratches fully visible to whoever just came in.

"What the fuck?" It's Mr. Carmichael. "Jesus fucking Christ! What the fuck?" I've heard him yell many times, but never like this.

"David!" he roars, using my name for the first time. From beneath the steering wheel, I see him peering through the driver's window of the truck. As he throws open the door, I scramble across to the passenger side. He grabs both my feet and drags me out. I cling to the truck for as long as I can, and when I let go, I fall to the concrete floor. I look up and see what Mr. Carmichael has seen. There, in three-foot cursive letters scratched into the side of the van, it reads "LOVE."

Then the helper comes in. "Oh, shit!" he says.

Mr. Carmichael leans over me, his face red. "What the fuck did you do?" I scramble to my feet. His open palm hits my face so hard that I spin before sprawling on the floor some feet away.

"Bob, stop it, he's a kid," the helper ventures.

I run for the door and almost make it, but Mr. Carmichael catches me by the back of my sweater and swings me back into the room. That's when he sees the other side of the van. Mr. Carmichael's helper grabs him by the shoulders, and I twist away.

"Get the *fuck* out of here, kid."

I run.

Run to the devil, the devil is a-waiting

All on that day

Oh, sinner man, you shoulda been a-praying

Before that day...

Afraid to go home, I duck into a cemetery between the Carmichaels' and the house on Christopher Lane. I huddle there while night falls, too scared to go home.

Oh, sinner man, where you gonna run to? I'm in trouble. I'm the one running. But am I the sinner? How can I be the sinner when my whole life all I have done is try to obey the people who find new ways to hurt me? When will it be their turn to run?

I curl up against a gravestone, hiding from the inevitable reckoning that awaits me at home. In the quiet night, I am briefly safe.

Eventually, however, the cold and darkness force my hand, and I trudge home to face my punishment. My hunger, for once, has abated. I am full of dread.

Turning onto Christopher Lane, I see straight down the cul-de-sac toward the house. The street is dark except for evenly spaced pools of light beneath each streetlight. I walk down the middle of the street, counting my steps, and as I get closer, I can see that all the lights of the house are on. I quietly enter the foyer. I'm shivering, but I'm not sure if it's from the cold or my fear. Up the half flight of stairs to my left, I can hear the TV in the living room. I head toward the basement stairs but freeze when I hear Mae's voice.

"Come up here, David," she says.

I enter the room with my head down. Maybe seeing my remorse will lessen whatever is about to come my way. My face feels tender where Carmichael hit me. Maybe he's left a mark that will mitigate their anger.

"How fucking stupid are you?" Buck demands. I'm watching his body, tracking his movements to see if he's coming for me. He doesn't rise from his recliner, but he's leaning forward with both feet on the ground. I don't know him as well as I knew my mother and have no strategies for appeasing him. Should I answer him, or is it a rhetorical question? Will he be angrier if I explain myself? I choose silence.

"I asked you a question. Answer me. How fucking stupid are you?"

I'm not sure what to say. *I'm very stupid?* After a careful pause I say, "I'm sorry."

"You're sorry? You're sorry? *You're fucking sorry?*" Buck stands up and backhands me across the face. It is the same way Mr. Carmichael struck me, in exactly the same place. I lurch backward. Regaining my footing, I face him. In my mouth is the familiar metallic taste of blood. I've been here before. I can take this. Instead of listening to him, I focus on the knot of my hunger, awakening it so I can use it now. When hunger is constant, it becomes its own world, a place of familiar pain where I can travel when the world in front of me is unbearable. And now I escape into my hunger, a complex landscape with mountains and valleys and plains. From there, Buck's voice sounds far away. If another blow comes, I will barely feel it. "What were you thinking? You used a Brillo pad to clean a car?"

"I didn't know. He said I could use anything in the bucket..."

Buck turns to Mae, "And the little *fag* didn't just scratch up a car. He wrote *Love* on the side." Turning back to me, Buck walks two steps and grabs my shirt.

Without thinking, I raise both hands above me and strike down, knocking his hand from my shirt. Mistake. Somewhere in me is a growing desire to defend myself, but it's not time yet. I cannot win this one. Buck has seventy-five pounds on me. His eyes widen with outrage at my insubordination. His nostrils flare. I instinctively calculate the best, least painful way forward and through. I need to give him what he needs: control, power, and an outlet for all the many frustrations in his life. *Go ahead, asshole*, I think. Maybe one hit will be enough to get me out of here.

"David, go to your room. Now." Mae steps between us. I'm not sure if she's saving me or protecting their foster business. They've already been investigated, and any visible injury he inflicts on me is a risk to their certification.

"You are going to earn every *goddamn* cent that I am paying that asshole to fix his truck. *Every goddamn cent*, do you understand?" Buck shouts as I retreat, giving him a wide berth as I pass. When I reach the foyer, he yells again. "Look at me when I'm talking!"

I turn to look up at this weak man, with his scraggly mustache and sad, flat face. My brother and sister have fought back, and I want to too. "Yes," I spit out, full of fury. "I understand perfectly." I meet his eyes directly, then turn and go down the second flight of steps into the dark basement.

"Are you okay?" Ben asks in the dark.

"I'm fine, Ben. Go back to sleep." I lie down fully clothed on my futon, eyes staring up into the black. I can hear Buck's heavy footsteps on the floor above. I can't sleep. My mind turns over and over. The worst of it is over, I think. And as I calm down, I start to see what has taken place in a different light. I scratched *Love* into the paint of Mr. Carmichael's truck. The absurdity of it makes me smile, there in the dark. Where had that come from? *Mom would love this*, I think to myself. She'd appreciate the dark humor of it, but also the justice in my destroying his truck. *Every cent*. What was he thinking? He's been renting me out for labor. The jerk is already taking any money I'm earning. Now he's going to have me pay it back with more work that he would have made me do for free anyway. I picture Mr. Carmichael driving around town with *Love* on his van. Ha! It's a small victory over every person who has denied me the nurture, safety, and everything else that adults owe the children in their care. There, on his van, is an expression of the longing I carry. A longing for my siblings, for family, for someone to see me, understand me, want me, maybe even to truly love me. *Love.* I haven't given up on it yet.

Chapter 15

Buck and Mae's Christmas tree stands in the middle of the living room. It's huge—nine feet tall—and heavy with ornaments. From the street you can see it glowing through a wall of windows. It went up early, and from November to January it will falsely advertise a wholesome, cheerful family sharing the holiday spirit. Close up, the tree is plastic, lifeless, smelling more like a new garbage bin than fresh pine.

For weeks, wrapped presents accumulate under the tree. There are no cards or labels on the presents, but Ben tells me that the wrapping paper is coded: Each of us will find out our designated pattern on Christmas morning. In the weeks before Christmas Day, I take every chance I can get to study the neatly arranged piles and wonder which will turn out to be mine. Maybe it's the pile with the *Peanuts* wrapping paper, showing the gang gathered around the sad little Christmas tree from *A Charlie Brown Christmas*. That pile has only straight-edged boxes, nothing soft or round. By Christmas eve, the *Nightmare Before Christmas* wrapping paper has started to look promising. Its geometric pattern covers the presents in the smallest pile. The flat, square gifts might be CDs, and I really want to own one. I don't have a CD player—but it would be a first step on the path to cool.

"David, we can't make the Christmas visit happen with your siblings tonight. I have to work, so it'll have to be a call," Mae says, walking into the room. She doesn't say their names anymore.

"When can I see them?"

"I don't know, we'll figure it out soon," she says, and walks out through the other side of the room.

If you mean "never," just say it, I think.

From my perch on the living room couch, I study the whole tableau: tree, decorations, stockings, even seasonal blankets draped on the furniture. I've always wanted this—a Christmas with gifts and a tree. But now that it's happening, it seems contrived. My Christmases past meant much better meals at shelters and soup kitchens than an average day, and they were shared with my brother and sister. I always envied the presents I knew other kids were receiving, but now I'd rather be with Alex and Jessica than get presents.

Visits have been infrequent, and instead we once again have awkward phone calls, which I have to take in the living room, where there is no privacy. Jessica and Alex know where I am and what they can't ask because I can't answer. Mom is gone, and now Alex and Jessica are receding.

Christmas morning arrives. We boys have already been awake for hours, waiting in our basement cage. Mae opens the door and calls down.

"All right, come up, but walk," she says, releasing us. We run-walk to gather in the living room. Despite my newfound cynicism, I'm still eager to know what I got.

"We are not going to do this like animals. Everyone sit down," Mae orders. The seven of us kids gather in a semicircle on the beige carpet in front of the tree, quiet except for William, the toddler. William arrived a few months after I did. He's not expected to follow the rules. He's a special-needs baby—all we were told is that his mother shook him too hard, and that's why he's in foster care. As soon as he arrived, I knew that I would be his caretaker. Mae wasn't giving him the breathing treatments that I saw his social worker demonstrate. He hates them, and she was impatient and rough. But I've figured out that if I talk to him and rub his belly, he squirms less. He's cranky, but he laughs and smells like a baby. When he wants to be held, he nuzzles his blond head into my shoulder, and I love him.

I lift him into my lap. "It's Christmas, William," I say quietly into the top of his head.

Mae reaches under the tree and picks up a small box wrapped in *Peanuts* paper. She pauses, then hands the gift to Ben.

"Thank you, Mae," Ben says. His body is in constant motion, talking, shifting, feet tapping, a likely case of undiagnosed, untreated ADHD. I know he's gone through sexual, physical, and mental abuse. Even at its worst, I have to think this place is better than wherever he came from. He's not allowed to open it yet, but Ben's entire world becomes the wrapped gift. He shakes it, turns it, feels the edges, and stares hard at the wrapping paper as if hoping it will open itself.

Mae reaches back under the tree and pulls out a present for her older biological daughter, Sandy. Sandy isn't nice or cruel. To her, we're just more kids passing through. Sandy has a blondish perm and tube socks, and her secret sensitivity that I keep in the arsenal but never use is that she thinks she has cankles—ankles so wide they blend into her calves. Today, she's wearing bleach-washed jeans tucked into white socks and an oversized maroon sweater. Her perm is pulled back into a scrunchy.

Turns out I was right about *Nightmare Before Christmas*. My first gift is soft, lightweight, and rectangular. I hold it politely, imitating what the other kids are doing. When each kid has been handed their first gift, we're allowed to open them. I look over at Ben to make sure I do it the way they want us to. His hair is buzz-cut, and I see the crown of his head as he looks down to methodically unwrap the gift. There are numerous scars where no hair grows on his scalp. His forearms also have scars that look to be from cigarettes. He's maybe eleven, and in this moment all that trauma falls away because he is holding a gift. I understand him completely. It's all very strange and enthralling. Ben, who is always in motion, moves slowly now. Turning his present one way, then the other, he finds the tape and slowly peels it back so the paper does not tear. It's a book. I see him freeze for a moment, blinking to contain his disappointment, and then he says, "Thank you, Mae," in a polite, humble voice.

I follow his lead and open the gift as carefully as I can. The cartoon character Jack looks up at me as I tear open the paper. In a white JCPenney box is an extra-large pair of synthetic boxers with characters from *The Nightmare Before Christmas* on them. "Thank you, Mae," I say, hiding my confusion just like Ben. But I've never had boxers before, so that's a win.

My next gift is a bundle of cooking tools: a spatula, a whisk, and some things I don't recognize. This is odd because I don't know how to cook, and I'm not allowed in the kitchen other than to clean. But I love them, nonetheless. I'd like to learn to cook. I'm also given the board game Operation, which I've seen advertised on TV, and I'm excited to try it.

When all the presents have been opened, there is only one item left under the tree—an envelope.

"This one is for all of us," Mae announces.

William is in his favorite blue onesie. His diaper is full—I can smell the poop, and his squirming is changing from excited to uncomfortable. But this is Mae's big moment; he'll have to wait. I hold him more firmly and whisper in his ear, "Okay, sweet boy, just a minute and I'll change you."

Mae opens up the business-sized envelope and holds up a white piece of paper with two words written on it in bold black Sharpie: Disney World.

"We're going to Disney World!" Mae exclaims. Could she mean all of us? Even me? She looks around the room and smiles proudly. It's too good to be true. There's going to be a catch, and we all know it. But we thank her as we did for the presents.

"Oh my gosh, you're so generous!" Malcolm says.

"Thank you so much," Ben murmurs.

"That's amazing!" I say.

Mae clicks her dentures. "Let's eat," she says, and everyone files into the dining area.

Details about Disney World emerge over breakfast.

"We're going to drive, and we'll have an adventure on the way," Mae says. I don't have a firm grasp on how far Florida is or how long the drive will be. I'm not even completely clear on what Disney World has to offer, but I don't care. I know it's the best trip a kid could ever want.

The family has a small camper van with a TV. It's white, with fierce blue stripes, and is the pride of the family. The seats are luxurious—the back seats are captain's chairs. Behind that is a third row that seats three. So in total the van fits seven people. If Mae and Buck both go, then there is room for only five kids. But right now in the house there are three boys in the basement (me, Ben, and Malcolm) and her three biological children (Tiffany, Sandy, and Neil). William will probably stay with a babysitter, but even so, one of the kids won't fit in the van. Mae doesn't share which one of us won't be making this trip, and nobody asks. We're afraid of the answer, afraid that it's a secret test and whoever asks will be eliminated from the running.

A few days later, on the morning we're supposed to leave, Mae sits us down.

"Unfortunately, we cannot bring everyone on the trip. I don't want a lot of hysterics, do you understand? Everyone got a lot of great gifts. My sister will come over, and whoever stays with her and William will have a good time," Mae says, convincing no one.

"Buck and I will be doing the driving. Neil, Sandy, and Tiffany will obviously be joining us. So we only have room for two foster kids."

Ben, Malcolm, and I, seated together on the beige sofa, lean forward, each of us hoping to be picked.

"David and Ben, you get to come," Mae says. "I need you guys to pack and bring your stuff to the foyer."

Malcolm, who is on my right, is trying to hide his tears.

"You are new, Malcolm, the newest. So it's only fair the others get to go," Mae explains. "All right, start packing."

"I'm sorry, bro," I say to Malcolm as we go down to the basement.

"It's whatever. Have fun." Malcolm's tears are gone already, displaced by anger.

On the drive down the van is full of joyful energy—even Mae and Buck are in good spirits. To save money, we sleep in the car while Mae and Buck take turns driving. We have four cassette tapes that we play over and over, starting with REO Speedwagon. I'm in my silky boxers, and I have to admit, I love them. They make me feel like I'm in water.

Two days later, we arrive at the biggest parking lot I've ever seen. We take the long shuttle ride into the park, all of us levitating in excitement. At the gate, we are each given a blue ticket. I make an internal vow to keep mine forever. This is going to be a day to remember.

We walk down Main Street, wearing our winter jackets. In this family there are rules about clothing that are tied to the season, not to the weather. It is seventy degrees out, but it is December, so we must wear jackets. I don't mind. I'm too distracted to worry about comfort. This place is magical. Pluto waves at me and I wave back. The smell of fried dough wafts through the air. On each side of the street are olden-times-styled storefronts. People spill out of the doors; families negotiate maps; kid scream with joy or tears. Many people are wearing Mickey Mouse ears—even the adults. My head swivels back and forth in wonder.

"Listen," Mae says. "Stay with us. If you get lost, meet right back here. Do you understand? I need a yes from each of you." Buck and Mae seem to have a game plan, and they lead us straight to the Pirates of the

Caribbean ride. From outside the arcaded building, we can see that the line is ridiculously long, but who cares? "Yo Ho a Pirate's Life for Me" is painted on a ribbon above the entrance, and thematic music plays. But just before we enter the line, Mae directs us over to the side of the path, beneath a massive old tree that shades us from the morning sun.

"David, wait for us here," she says, then turns to the other kids. "Give him your coats and bags. He'll hang on to them."

I stand in mute shock as the family and Ben pile their belongings onto me. It sinks in. I'm not going on the ride. They walk off toward the entrance, and I am left leaning against a railing. For an hour, I watch armies of families walking in all directions. She told me to stand, so I don't sit.

"Oh my God, that was amazing. The cannons…the waterfalls…did you see the pig?" When they return, their exclamations overlap. I've been here before, watching opportunity and fun and family happen to other kids right in front of me. A knot rises from my stomach up into my throat, and I realize I'm near tears. I swallow hard and hand off possessions to their owners.

Mae looks directly at me. "Good job," she says.

Bitch, I think, and look directly at her without replying.

"Okay, let's go," Mae says, turning away from me and taking a quick look at the map. She's planned every moment of this experience. We walk on toward Tomorrowland. I see the characters, the rides, and the families. I imagine joining any one of them, being part of a family where I am included, cared for, loved.

Space Mountain looms over us, a white UFO. Again, Mae pulls us to the side before we get in line for the ride. Is it going to be someone else's turn to stand and wait with the stuff?

"David, wait here," she says again, looking pointedly at me. Maybe this was her plan all along. But maybe she saw the hatred in my eyes and is punishing me for it. They walk away. My foster sister Sandy looks over her shoulder at me and mouths, "I'm sorry."

A lump returns to my throat. I'm outside again, looking in. Time passes; the temperature rises; I guard the jackets and sweaters that none of us need. *You can't break me,* I think. *The more you hurt me, the stronger I get.* I look at the people around me—babies, children, teenagers, adults—and it occurs to me that no matter what happens, I'm going to grow up. I'm going to finish school, leave this family, get a job, and build a life. This misery is not forever. And when I'm older, when I have my own money and freedom, I'm going to find my way back here. First chance I get, I'm coming to Disney World.

Before they get in line for the first ride after lunch, Mae thrusts her disposable camera into my hands.

"Take a photo of us, and don't drop the damn thing," she says.

They line up, smile, and I point and click.

"Aww, would you like one of *all* of you?" The heavyset woman who offers is wearing a pink T-shirt with Minnie Mouse on it, her frost-blond hair cropped short. She takes the camera out of my hands and enthusiastically shoves me toward the others. I feel like Cinderella, awkwardly forced to pose with her stepfamily. Standing to the far right, I stare into the camera, focusing on a thought that only I will recognize if I ever get to see the picture: *Fuck you Mae and Buck.* I think, *Fuck you. I'm going to come back here when I'm older. I'm going to bring my real family.*

The woman returns the camera to Mae. "You have a beautiful family," she says.

"Those two are not my kids. They're foster kids," Mae clarifies, pointing at me and Ben.

The woman looks taken aback, more by Mae's tone than the information. "Okay, well, have fun," she says, turning to leave. I watch her walk away. When she looked at this hodgepodge of people, she saw a family. I wish it were true.

On the way out of the park that day, Mae cheerily asks, "Did everyone have fun?" She peers at me, looking for a reaction. She wanted me to have hope and to be punished for that hope. Why? I can't say. Perhaps flexing her strength with me made up for insecurity in her own life. But at least she took us in—possibly the only kids who could be grateful for her roof are the ones who know what it's like to have no roof at all.

When we get home, I squirrel away the park ticket and later, the photo, and keep them forever. This is a moment that defines my pain, proves to myself that I didn't imagine the cruelty, and I need to remember it. Over and over, as the years go by, I vow to myself and the boy that I was that I will make it up to myself. I will return one day, with my real family, a family that I make, and I will enjoy that park for all it's worth. And though I can't possibly imagine it then, one day in the future, that vow will come true, and this framed ticket will adorn my office wall at the Burbank headquarters of the Walt Disney Company. When I look up each morning from my desk and see it, I'll remember how far I've come.

Chapter 16

I FEEL THE WARMTH SPREAD down my right side before I smell the urine. "Oh, William, honey. Ugh," I say, bouncing him gently. It's my own fault. I should have put him back in his diaper immediately, but I wanted his rash to air out a bit. I kiss the top of his head, and he makes a soft coo that I've come to know means he's ready for bed. I lay him back, wipe him down with a cotton cloth, and slip the disposable diaper under his small body. "Hush, little baby, don't say a word. Grandma's gonna buy you a mockingbird. If that mockingbird don't sing, Grandma's gonna buy you a diamond ring..." I sing quietly and rub his exposed belly. His breathing is soft and regular, and his eyes droop as I carry him upstairs to his crib.

Caring for him is hard; he's three and easily frustrated. The person who was supposed to love him the most in the world almost broke him entirely. Once he's asleep, I leave his room and head toward the shower, but I hear Mae climbing the stairs, and freeze. When she sees me, she is immediately suspicious. "Where are you going?"

"William had an accident. It's my fault—I didn't get the diaper on fast enough. So I need to rinse off," I explain, pointing to the wet stain on my shirt.

There is a lengthy pause while Mae takes me in, head to toe. "Well, you have some options. Do you want to shower, eat dinner, or talk to your brother and sister?"

I'm struck dumb. She's serious. Alex and Jessica have been gone for almost a year now. They live with a kind woman in Amherst. The DSS requires that we have a weekly phone call and monthly in-person visits. I'm always happy to see them. No matter how hurt I am that they left or what Mae tells me, I love my brother and sister. We meet in Pulaski Park, a small park next to the DSS. From there, Alex and Jessica and I walk down Main Street, making sure to stop in at Faces, a novelty store, and Thornes, a department store that's been subdivided into many small stores.

Jessica and Alex are happy and well-fed, and they don't get hit. They are going to a new school, which they love. We don't talk about why they left me. I try to understand. We're all just trying to survive. I'm happy for them, and our time is short. When we are together, I just want to be in that moment forever.

Mae is still pissed off that they left. She can't do anything about our in-person meetings, but when it comes to our weekly phone calls, she makes it hard. Right now, with urine on me, she's making me choose them over a shower and a meal.

"I want to call them, but can I change first?"

"No."

"I'm so sorry. William has a rash, and I was letting him dry out. I put Desitin on him."

"You made your decision."

So, covered in urine, I speak to Alex and Jessica, and then I head down to bed. I'm not even allowed to go to the bathroom first. Going to bed without being allowed to go to the bathroom is a form of torture. I have to pee. I can't sleep. I can only focus on not pissing myself. Should I pee into a sock? Into the washing machine, or the utility sink? If they notice, that could make things worse for me. When I'm sure they're up on the second floor, I tiptoe into the laundry room and use a rag to clean myself off at the sink. I stare at the laundry sink, and decide, without any other option, to piss into it. I empty my bladder and lean forward against the wall in orgasmic relief.

As the months go on, my foster parents treat me with increasing animosity, punishing me, perhaps, for what Alex and Jessica did. During this time, it's school that sustains me. School is warm. School is food. School is words. School is how I will create a life where I am in control. But a few months after the trip to Disney, in early spring of 1995, Mae summons us up from the basement for school and says, "Except for you, David. You're staying home today." This usually happens when they have me rented out, but on this particular day, I have an exam first thing in the morning. All ninth grade, I've been struggling with math. The concepts we are learning are built on skills I missed in the gaps when I didn't attend school. My teacher has been working with me, and I am hoping to get a decent grade on this test so I can pull up my average. Mae knows I have an exam, because she gave me permission to study last night. Allowed me, as if it were an unreasonable request, because she doesn't believe in education, especially not for a worthless foster kid like me. She wants me to get that idea out of my head, and she takes every opportunity to help me do so by keeping me home from school. Mae knows that I don't mind being slapped around or yelled at, or doing endless dishes, and that missing school is a worse punishment for me—and it doesn't leave marks. She also knows that as long as I pass my courses, the DSS won't take notice.

I rise from the bed. I'm not going to take it anymore. My stomach churns in anticipation of the punishment I'm risking. The other boys are getting ready, going through the normal motions of putting on clothes, and making their beds. One by one, with sympathetic nods in my direction, they head upstairs. When they are gone, the room is silent and still. Then I stand up. I'm not going to let this happen. I'm going to school, and I'm going to take that test. I start to get dressed. Just like at Disney World, regardless of the weather, Mae requires all of us, even her biological kids, to wear winter clothes to school until the end of April. I can tell from the basement that the early spring morning is warm and dry, but I put full winter gear on top of my clothes: hat, scarf, gloves, boots. I don't want to break too many rules all at once. I climb the stairs in darkness. On the final step, I crack the door open, and a shaft of daylight streams from the hallway. The other kids are moving about, getting ready to leave for the walk to school.

"What are you doing, David? She told you to stay downstairs. She's gonna be pissed," Ben whispers as he zips his backpack.

"Dude," Brian, a new kid, chimes in, echoing Ben's sentiment.

I creep into the bathroom, and even though no one from upstairs is nearby, I follow the rules and don't close the door. I use the bathroom, then return to the top of the basement steps, sitting quietly and hoping she'll return to release me from the basement, having changed her mind. Then she suddenly appears above me, a livid, looming shadow.

"Get your damn faggot ass downstairs," she says. "What the fuck is wrong with you? You're going to pay for this."

I hurry back down the basement stairs. When I'm halfway down, she closes the door. I hear her begin to walk away. That's it, then. She's definitely not going to let me go to school today.

I have worked hard all year; I studied to catch up, and I refuse to miss my test. I know what I want, and it is *not this*. I turn around, come back up the stairs, and open the door. Tiffany, Ben, Brian, and Neil are in the hallway, putting on their coats. They turn to look at me, eyes wide. I walk straight past them to the front door. Mae is overseeing the production. When she notices me, she is shocked and instantly angry. She starts slapping at me clumsily, yelling, "You get back down there. Where the hell do you think you're going?"

She cannot withhold my freedom. I own my freedom. I don't stop moving. A surge of adrenaline hits me. She cannot control me unless I give her control. I embody an intelligence and curiosity that she wants to snuff out. My defiance makes her feel powerless. She wants to hurt me, to erase me. But I will not be erased by her, by my mother, by this fucked-up system. I feel strong and sure. Nothing can stop me, not here this morning—not ever. The revelation hits like lightning—I can simply walk away—and that is what I do.

When I reach the street, she yells from the doorstep: "If you leave here, you're not coming back!" I pause. I've lived here longer than I've ever lived in one place. This is the closest to a home I've ever had. But I'm done. I stop and turn to face her. She looks smaller now, almost frail, and I won't let her hurt me anymore. Taking off my snow boot, I throw it at her with all the fury in me. It strikes her in the middle of her abdomen. She grunts and is finally silent, more out of shock than pain.

Mae and Buck were not the right people for the job of foster parents. For some reason, they took out their anger and unhappiness on us. But at least they opened their home and offered shelter to kids who needed it. So many people, good, decent people who are capable of loving kids who are not their own, never consider fostering. Or if they do, they have lists of reasons they can't do it—the timing is wrong, or they don't have space, or they don't want to disrupt the lives of their biological children. It is easy for these people to condemn the likes of Mae and Buck, but until they step up, they don't get to cast stones. I believe many people foster for what we would call the "right reasons." Sometimes their spirit and skills may not be up to the task, but only when the rest of us open our homes can we hope to do better.

As I walk toward school, I tear off the hat, the scarf, and the mittens and leave them on the side of the road. I am wearing only pants, a shirt, one boot, and socks as I head down the street, but I have never felt more free. For the first time, I know for sure that no one will ever hurt me again.

I'm still wearing only one boot when I walk into school. I march into the guidance counselor's office and say, "I'm not going home." I'm riding on adrenaline, hysterically happy, frightened, and unstrung. I know from reporting my mother to the authorities that nothing moves quickly. There will be investigations, I'll most likely be sent back to Mae and Buck's while they're pending, and there will be repercussions. But I also know that what I've done is not just a moment of defiance. I have declared my freedom.

Mel seems to be the social worker who always appears when I am on fire. She picks me up at school in her Pontiac Firebird and brings me to the DSS office in Northampton. It's housed in a beautiful brick veterans' memorial building next to city hall. Someone there finds me a pair of shoes. I sit in an office, waiting while they figure out what to do with me. Waiting just as I did when I was finally taken away from my mother. In times like this, guidance counselors and social workers are not focused on comfort and reassurance. They have legal processes to follow, work to do. I have no faith in this system, no reason to believe they will know what's best for me, or even want what's best for me. A roof and food. Those are their first priorities and I see the value. Yet I know what can go on under a roof, and this time I want to choose who takes care of me. I ask them to call Holly, the nicest adult I know. It's been more than a year since I last saw her, and I can only hope that she still cares about me. She is the only one who might rescue me.

After some time, tired of waiting for the DSS to reach her, I decide to walk to the YMCA and see if I can find her myself. Nobody notices when I walk out of the DSS office. The YMCA is only about three miles away. I reach her office, pop my head in, and say, "Boo." I try to smile, but I also choke up.

To my surprise she has a three-month-old baby, Ruth, in a sling inside her jacket. I pause, looking at this baby. If I leave Mae and Buck's, I'll be leaving William behind—just like Alex and Jessica left me behind. Who will take care of him? It hurts. But I have to save myself. I have to leave him. And that is how I learn to forgive Alex and Jessica. Sometimes, to survive, you must let your loved ones drown. Shyly, tentatively, I croak, "Can I come and live with you?"

Holly stands up and pulls me into a hug, saying, "Let me figure out what's going on." All I hear is that she doesn't say no. We drive back to the DSS office in her red Dodge Caravan.

In the car she says, "I don't know how much they told you. Do you know why I had to stop visiting you?" I shake my head no, thinking of all the times I looked out the window, hoping to see her car.

"We went shopping, remember?"

After the summer at the YMCA, Holly had visited me weekly. One time she had noticed I was wearing the same outfit every time she came, and she took me to buy some new clothes. That was the last time I'd seen her.

"When I brought you home with the new clothes, Mae was furious. She told me not to buy you anything ever again. I thought that was nuts, so I called your social worker—Mel—and asked if Steve and I could become your foster parents. While she was working on getting us approved, she told me not to do anything to piss off Mae."

This was all news to me. This kind woman, the woman I hoped would save me, had already tried. "Why wouldn't they let you take me?"

Holly continued, "Your foster parents insisted it was better for you to be kept with your siblings. I hired lawyers, but they said the same thing."

"They're gone," I whisper. "They ran away, and they got new foster parents."

Holly gasps. "They never told me. Mae told me I couldn't see you anymore. And then I got pregnant, and your social worker told me it was hopeless."

It's too much for me to process. My emotions are torn between gratitude and defeat—it hadn't worked out, but it gives me hope.

Ruth is asleep in her car seat, so I run into the office and bring Mel out to the car. Despite the history here, Mel seems rather amazed that someone actually cares about me. "It's wonderful that this family is interested in you, but they're not certified foster parents. We're going to see if we can accelerate the process by qualifying them as an emergency placement."

Mel takes both Holly's and Steve's social security numbers to do a background check, and I stay with the baby while Holly goes inside to call Steve. Holly and Steve have a newborn, Bri is seven, and Steve's father is dying in Florida. Regardless of all that is going on in their lives, he says yes to bringing me home. I get in the minivan with Holly and go to her house.

The background check takes too long. The emergency placement with Holly and Steve allows me a few days with them, but when Sunday night comes, Mel says that I need to be taken to an emergency shelter in Amherst. I am sure this will be like the detention hall I went to when I was taken away from my mother. All of those places are the same. I feel my insides clench. I become very quiet, anticipating the worst. But at the last minute, an emergency foster placement is found. Steve drives me there while Holly stays home with the girls.

"I love you, David. It's gonna be all right," Holly says at the door. I don't believe her.

The temporary foster parent is a young single woman who lives in a cabin in the woods. She is well-meaning, and she takes in only one youth at a time. She is vegan, the home has no electronics, and there is a pack of rescued pit bulls. My "room" is a loft only big enough for a bed at the top of a small ladder off the living room.

"David, you cannot get out of bed unless I'm up, okay? The dogs are rescues, and they need to get used to you before you're alone with them," my new foster mom instructs. I again need permission to go to the bathroom.

"I'm sorry," Steve says, shaking his head. "This won't be for long…I hope." When the door closes behind him, the dogs snarl and surround me. She talks to them as if they're human: "Guys, David is a friend. Be nice to him. Guys, David is like you—no one wants him."

Finally, within weeks, Mel comes to pick me up. Holly and Steve have been approved to foster me. I have a garbage bag of clothes, rags, and, randomly, a small television that I found on the side of the road. Though Mae and Buck were paid by the system to care for me for more than two years, they haven't tended to my basic needs (although they received money to do so). I have only a few pairs of underwear and trashy clothes, and my sneakers are too small. Holly and Steve have no extra money, and the money they'll get from the state to pay for my basics won't kick in for months. Nonetheless, the night I arrive, Steve takes me to JCPenney, where he buys me underwear, socks, some T-shirts, and jeans. The gesture is instinctive to them—a child in their care has needs, and they immediately feel a responsibility to fulfill them.

Holly is still a counselor at the YMCA, and she is also very active in school and town committees. Steve is a general contractor, hardworking and quiet. They live in a two-bedroom house, and with the birth of Ruth and addition of me, their family of three has jumped to five in the space of a few months. They offer me a beautiful room in the finished attic, but it's right above their bedroom.

"You don't like it?" Holly asks. I haven't said a word, but she's used to working with children. She can tell.

"I'm worried I'll disturb you, walking around."

She insists it's fine, but when she sees that I'm uncomfortable, she asks if I'd like to try the basement. I'm happier there, below them. Their basement is nothing like the prison of Mae and Buck's. Holly does everything she can to make me comfortable there.

"What kind of furniture would you like? We're going to get you a bed," Holly says.

I am at a loss. "I had a futon before—that would be great," I tell them, figuring if that's what Mae and Buck gave me, it must be the cheapest.

Steve, as a contractor, wants to make the basement nice for me and, in a kindhearted way, badgers me into painting murals with him on the wall. It's like carving "love" into the side of a car, except that now I'm being encouraged to do it. I decide to paint an enormous sun.

Not only am I allowed to freely roam upstairs—I am also allowed to eat whatever I want, whenever I want. I discover this when Holly catches me standing at the entryway to the kitchen, looking in. She has just returned from grocery shopping. Loaves of bread are stacked on the counter. Boxes of cereal are lined up haphazardly. Cans of every variety of beans, vegetables, and soup are sorted but not yet shelved. A gallon of milk is sweating on the counter, and fruits and a twelve-pack of muffins are just sitting there, unmonitored.

"David, honey, what are you doing?" Holly has appeared beside me. She places her hand on my shoulder. She is shorter than I am yet exudes strength. I turn slightly and see her dark curly hair and her smile. "You've been standing there for a bit. You okay? Did you want something to eat? I haven't put it all away yet. I love Costco, but I always buy too much."

"No...I, well, maybe...yes. I'm hungry," I stammer.

"Just help yourself. And if there is anything you want me to pick up at the store, please write it on that pad on the fridge. What do you like to eat?"

"I'm not sure," I whisper.

"David, are you all right? Come here, sit down." Holly gently guides me by the elbow to the adjacent dining area. We sit down at the table. On top of the china chest is a crowd of family photos with mismatched frames. Behind the photos is a large mirror. I can see myself in it. My head is shaved, which was cheaper for my last foster parents to maintain. It's just starting to grow out. My cheekbones stand out sharply.

"David, what's wrong? What are you thinking about right now?" Holly leans across the table and takes my hands in hers. I'm not sure when I was last touched like this, so kindly.

"I was thinking about my brother and sister, Alex and Jessica. Once a month, when they visited, they'd sneak me food. I was always so hungry. It was mostly junk food, but I needed it." I know it's safe to tell Holly, but I don't know exactly what I'm feeling or how to express it. "They snuck me food," I repeat.

"You don't have to sneak food here, David, you can have as much as you want. Everything in there is for you too. You don't have to ask permission." Holly's hand turns my face gently away from the mirror toward her.

"They said I was fat, that I never shut up. They put me on a diet there." I'm staring through her as I say this. "My last therapist would take me to McDonald's for our meetings. She'd eat in front of me, and sometimes buy me something. She said terrible things to me, and she'd eat in front of me."

"David, David, look at me. That's over. This is your home. This is your kitchen. This is your food," Holly declares.

But it isn't over. I still hear my foster parents' words, my therapists' words. *You are sick, David. You like other boys. You deserve what you're getting. You are too fat, David, too soft, too girlie. You have to toughen up.*

Hunger is a constant companion. I have learned to let it fill my mind, displacing unwanted thoughts, as a form of meditation. When their fists raged, or their words screamed, hunger was there to distract from the pain. When they called me a fag and tried to erase me, hunger was a refuge. Focusing on the texture of hunger, its needs and wants, what is absent—helps me escape the places that are too painful to face with all of my mind. Hunger is one of the few safe places I know, and this woman wants me to leave it behind. I'm not certain I can or even want to.

"Stand up, David. Now. Stand up." Holly pulls me up. "Walk in here with me, David. What do you want to eat? Right now, I'll make you anything you want. Do you want a cake? Do you want a sandwich? Chili? What, David?"

I look at her, I see her, I feel her hand grasping mine. I have new clothes, but I've unconsciously continued to wear the outfit I arrived in a few weeks prior. The clothes hang off my body. They hide my ribs. They hide the scars. They hide my secret. When I wear these clothes, people only notice how old and ill-fitting they are. They can't see me. But Holly leads me to the fridge and opens it. Inside is a jigsaw of stacked items. She pulls out mayonnaise, turkey, and sliced cheese.

"Let's make you a sandwich." Holly makes room on the counter and puts the sandwich ingredients down. "What kind of bread, honey? White? Wheat? I think I even got rye—it was on sale, I figured why not? That doesn't matter, I guess. Do you like rye?" Holly asks, but she's already opening the bread.

"I've never had rye," I reply. "We used to get big jugs of mayonnaise at food pantries. We'd pass it around. I love mayo."

"Mayo it is! You like pickles, too, right? I know we have some here. Do you like butter pickles? Dill?" I stare at her blankly. "Well, never mind—let's do some of each! Chips? Maybe some chips too? And a glass of milk." All this she says while assembling a plate for me. The plate is clear crystal, etched with an ivy pattern. She fills a matching glass with milk. Carrying everything, she leads me back to the table.

"David, you have to eat." Holly's voice cracks on the last word.

Looking at the food and then at her, I know this is about more than a meal. If I'm hungry, I don't have to think. I don't have to remember the past. I don't have to imagine how I will ever find a way to a better life.

I look up at her, then down at my hands and my forearms. My

knuckles are prominent, my forearms bony. Inches from food, my hands won't move. Food was a weapon in Mae's hands. How is it to be used here? What is the trick? What does she want? I look at Holly again. I picked her, and she said yes. Then it occurs to me, an irrefutable truth. She wanted me even before I picked her. She took me into her home, gave me my own room, bought me clothes. She hasn't hit me. Holly will be my companion now, a friend and a mother; I don't need to hide in the hunger. I decide to trust her.

"Holly," I say.

"Yes." She's quiet and steady.

"I don't want milk. I want a coffee," I say. We both smile, and I eat.

Chapter 17

I walk into the empty house, put on Alanis Morissette's *Jagged Little Pill*, and get to work. No one has asked me to clean every single day, but I've learned that foster kids are valued as workers, so at the LeBeaus' I set out to make myself indispensable. Holly has finished her maternity leave and is back at work, Bri and Ruth are in day care, and Steve usually gets home around dinnertime, so every day after school I'm home alone for a couple of hours. Singing along to the pleasantly rageful songs that I know by heart, I open the cabinet under the kitchen sink where the cleaning supplies are stored. *Don't use an S.O.S. pad,* I think, and chuckle to myself. I lay out my supplies: lemon-scented wood polish, blue glass cleaner, and soft terry cloth squares to buff and polish. I roll up my sleeves and begin.

Holly's home and family are the placement I dreamed of when I first escaped my mother. I am safe and loved. But the survival strategies a child develops in an unsafe or inadequate home often aren't appropriate in a foster home or in adulthood. Some children act out because fighting is all they know. When this happens, they're placed in a group home or a care facility—this is one reason foster kids move around so much. My response is to do what I've always done—to try to create stability.

First, I tidy the kitchen, making sure all the dishes are cleaned and put away. Then I take all the toys upstairs where they belong. I fold the laundry—I love shaping clothes into neat squares and putting them away. I finish by vacuuming, creating those perfect lines in the carpet that Mae demanded. I find comfort in the order I've created and in my belief that it will help me stay in this home.

When Holly walks through the door with Ruth, I lift the baby out of her arms and take her upstairs to change her diaper. I miss William, and I'm glad to have another baby to love. William liked to be in motion, and so does Ruth, so I feed her in a rocking chair that her grandfather made. After she eats, I'm bouncing her lightly, singing a Christian song I learned at camp, "Love, love, the Lord your God with all your heart and mind and all your soul, as you love mankind. We've got Christian lives to live..." I pause when Holly comes to stand next to me.

"I appreciate the help, honey, but I want you to know you don't have to do this. It isn't your job. You can just be a kid." She touches my cheek softly and lifts Ruth out of my arms.

"I like cleaning," I tell her. I don't want to stop. To me, being a kid has always meant surviving, and right now surviving means securing my place in this family.

One night, I relax just enough to make an epic mistake. In the pictures of men in magazines like *GQ*, *Sports Illustrated*, muscle magazines, and Calvin Klein ads that I see at the library, all the men are smooth, hairless, like real-life Ken dolls. Hair is sprouting all over me, especially on my chest, but even on my back. I'm appalled, and I decide to take matters into my own hands. In the drugstore, I buy a women's waxing kit. The box shows an image of poreless skin on a woman's disembodied leg.

Late at night, after everyone's asleep, I sneak upstairs into the kitchen. I put the block of wax in a pan, which I heat on the electric stove. When it's soft, I apply it to my chest and then smooth a cotton strip on top of it. Counting to ten, I rip it off with all the force I can muster from my awkward angle. I scream as the wax tears off not just the hair but the skin.

Holly flies into the kitchen in her pajamas, hair flattened on one side of her head. "What happened?" she exclaims, eyeing my exposed chest. The pan is ruined. I'm afraid I've fucked up this placement. I've never seen Holly angry, but surely this will push her over the edge. I've destroyed something; I've risked everything. Holly comes closer.

"I'm so sorry," I say, tensing in anticipation of being hit.

Holly takes in the scene and just says with a loving chuckle, "Oh, David." Then she helps me clean up. I wait for more of a reaction, but that's the end of it. She isn't angry; she doesn't hurt or insult me. To Holly, *being a kid* means that I am allowed to make mistakes and allowed to be myself. I can understand this, but I can't get used to it.

Steve, in his own way, reinforces the same message. When I finish ninth grade, he brings me along with him to job sites. We build a deck together, and I help him paint. Painting was one of my specialties at the Carmichaels'. The difference is that Steve doesn't use me for slave labor. He doesn't pull me out of school to work. He doesn't curse at me. He teaches me how to use a spray gun and praises my work. On the weekends, Steve tinkers with his Nova, explaining to me what he's doing as he changes the brake pads or installs trim.

I've never had a decent father figure before, and in my imagination I never got past the snapshots I witnessed on TV and those I registered in real life: fathers carrying Christmas presents for their children, helping their Cub Scouts launch homemade race cars, waiting next to their sons on line for Pirates of the Caribbean ride at Disney World. But in Steve, I see a father who simply devotes all of his energy to his family. I watch carefully as every morning he rises at four thirty to drive to job sites. He works six days a week, intense, physical labor, but he never complains. When he comes home, he or Holly cooks dinner, and as we eat, he engages Brianna, asking her questions beyond "What did you learn in school today?" He'll ask her if she thinks schools should be open seven days or whether she thinks kids should get allowances for helping around the house. When she says what she thinks, he challenges her and makes her defend her position. He married a strong woman and clearly wants his daughters to speak their minds. When I get in a fight with Bri over the globs of toothpaste she leaves all over the sink, Steve sits back, crosses his arms, takes a sip of his Budweiser, and laughs, enjoying the spectacle as I try to play his role. The father figure I've imagined pales in comparison to Steve's quiet, consistent presence.

Steve is the one who takes me to get my learner's permit. His truck is a thirty-year-old first-generation Toyota truck, a hunk of junk with manual steering. The driver's-side floor is rotted out, so Steve drops his cigarette butts through the hole as he's driving to the DMV. It took some work to convince him and Holly that I should learn to drive— their children are so young they're still in the mode of making sure nobody drowns in the bathtub. But when I told Holly that the other kids my age were all learning, and some of them even had their own cars, she relented. My social worker was another hurdle—she said it was atypical for foster kids to learn to drive. The state didn't want us to do anything that might cause damage or get us hurt, as my mother might object. That was why we weren't allowed to go on sleepovers or to participate in contact sports without judicial permission. It won't be until 2014 that the Strengthening Families Act will include a provision supporting normalcy for children in foster care. Foster parents are now supposed to let a child have normal experiences and activities in line with what their peers are doing.

I had taken a driver's ed class and studied the paper booklet from the DMV hard. Steve waits for me outside, a cigarette dangling from his lip, and gives his understated half smile when I tell him I passed.

"I'll drive home, and then it's your turn," he says. When we get home, he jumps out of the truck, walks over to the passenger door, and opens it, nodding his head to tell me that I should drive. I hurry over to the driver's side, but once I'm behind the wheel, I freeze. What if I mess up? I want to keep him happy with me. Steve waits patiently, taking a drag of his cigarette and blowing it out the window. As always, he's wearing a white tank top and Lee jeans. In a deadpan, he finally says, "Anytime, David. Engine's on. Clutch, then shift to first, then ease off the clutch and give her a little gas."

I do as he says, the engine revs, and we leap forward. I slam on the brakes and we jerk to a stop. I look at him apologetically, but he just says, "That's it. You'll get the hang of it."

And I do. The manual steering is no joke. The wheel is hard to turn, as if I'm operating a cruise ship. I stare at the road, gripping the wheel, and I break a sweat as I heave us around a curve at a full two miles per hour, but I am driving. The feeling is powerful in a way I haven't anticipated. I grew up using public transportation, and I have felt trapped ever since moving to suburbia. I can't visit my brother and sister without asking for a ride. I can't drive myself to get a haircut if I need one. Now that I am behind the wheel, I feel free. I can go anywhere I want. There is a future I've always imagined for myself, a future in which I am in control of my own destiny. Being able to drive moves me closer to that future.

A few days later, Steve decides I'm ready to practice driving in circles around our cul-de-sac all by myself.

"Remember this isn't a luxury vehicle. It doesn't have power steering, so just go easy. You got it?"

"Yes, thank you. I'll be careful."

Alone in the truck for the first time, I begin to inch down the curving asphalt driveway. There is a camper shell over the pickup bed that blocks the rearview mirror, so I have to rely on the side mirrors. Halfway down, the driveway merges with the neighbor's, coming to a curving flourish at the street. On either side of the driveway are mailboxes—one for the neighbor, and one for us—each mounted on a post. My plan is to go right down the middle, but the curve throws me off. Suddenly it looks like I'm heading straight for the neighbor's mailbox. Panicking, I give the wheel a strong pull and hit the gas.

"Fuck!" I holler as the truck jumps backward, right into our mailbox. Not gently. I knock it over, then plow over it, hearing it crunch against the bottom of the truck. By the time I finally manage to slam on the brakes, the truck is mostly on the road, partially blocking the street. Everything is quiet. I sit frozen in the driver's seat, my heart thumping. I want to bolt, remembering what happened when I destroyed the paint job on Mr. Carmichael's truck. Then I see Steve running out of the house. Here it comes.

"Jesus, David!"

I stare straight ahead. It's okay if he hits me. I deserve it. So long as he lets me stay.

He runs up to the truck and circles it, assessing the damage. Then he opens my door. "You okay?"

There are no fists yet, no immediate hits.

"I'm sorry. I'm sorry," I say hurriedly. My body is tight, waiting.

"Well, I hated that mailbox anyway," Steve says. I don't say anything. There is a long pause, but the impact I'm anticipating doesn't come.

"Why don't you pull in and park? That's probably enough driving for today," Steve says with a chuckle.

Steve and Holly are the first people who don't punish me; they are the first ones who seem to be on my side. They want to help me to be like other kids, to be normal. This gives me the courage to ask for something I've wanted for a long time.

"Holly, I need braces. We need braces."

"Okay," she says without hesitation. "Is 'we' you, Alex, and Jessica?" Holly has met my siblings many times now. Once every two weeks, I take a bus to meet them between our towns at the mall in Hadley.

Now I explain to her that all three of us were supposed to get braces but never did. "We had to get it approved by a judge—that's how it works in foster care. The orthodontist said that they're a medical necessity, so that means the state will pay for them. Our social worker even helped us find an orthodontist who would do it for the approved amount. But we never got them."

"Why not?" she asks.

"Mae refused to take us to appointments. She said that if her kids couldn't have braces, then why should we?"

I've felt ashamed of my teeth for years. At school I see kids in all stages of getting their teeth straightened, but mine stand out—a jumbled mess in the middle of my face that makes me self-conscious, and I feel sure they make other kids think that I am poor, that I'm not cared for. I want to smile with my mouth open and to stop covering my mouth when I laugh.

"David, you have a very handsome smile, but sure, let's get you those braces!" Holly declares. And she gets to work, as is her way, and coordinates everything, finding the orthodontist, reaffirming the approvals needed from the social worker, talking to Alex and Jessica's foster mother, and arranging all the necessary appointments for the three of us.

"B-Day!" I say as Alex, Jessica, and I go into the orthodontist Holly has found.

"B-Day?" Alex asks.

"*Braces Day!* We are getting braces!" We've already had multiple visits for cleanings, fillings, and pullings, and the big day has finally arrived.

"I've never seen kids so excited about braces," Holly says.

One by one we are called into the office, and getting the braces on is surprisingly quick.

"We always do a 'Day One Polaroid.' You guys okay with that?" the receptionist asks me when I come out.

"Absolutely," I say. She directs me where to stand, and I give the biggest grin I can. It's a photo that I'll treasure, years later seeing my enormous smile at the moment I started to straighten the crooked parts of my upbringing.

I am excited to show off my braces to my mother. I don't see her often, but we have a visit coming up at Barts ice cream in Northampton. These state-mandated visits would occur monthly if Mom weren't impossible to track down, drifting in and out of shelters. Instead, it's dependent on when she manages to get herself to the area and calls the DSS to arrange a time with us. The social workers coordinate with Holly, officially serving as an intermediary buffer for the sometimes-hostile relationship between foster and biological parents. My siblings are encouraged but not required to attend these visits, and most of the time they refuse to see our mother.

"Hugh John David," Mom says as she comes into the restaurant. I give her a huge smile and wait for her reaction. It's irrational to hope for a good reaction from her—she doesn't want to see any evidence that I'm better off without her—but I can't help myself.

She hugs me hard, then looks closely at my face. I see her register the braces, but all she says is "I took you to church. I sent you to summer camp. You got straight As." This is the refrain she uses to convince herself that she was a good mother, she's been wronged, and we were taken away from her through a conspiracy. Later, she will stop resenting the braces and will instead take credit for them, insisting that she called President Clinton and made it happen. She isn't consciously lying. She so wants to be the one who helps me that she lives in that invented world.

We find a booth and sit across from each other. Mel is accompanying me today, and she says, "I'll be right over here." She takes a seat in another booth—far enough to give us privacy, but close enough to monitor us. Our visits have to be supervised, and Mel always keeps a watchful eye. She knows Mom. The smell of waffle cones mixes with Mom's body odor, and I take in this strange combination. She reaches across the table and takes my hands in hers. I notice that her fingernail polish is chipped. Across her broad bosom are crumbs and stains and an arch of cigarette ash. Her hair is greasy, and her large tortoiseshell glasses are so filthy that I wonder if she can see. I recognize the signs of her mental state deteriorating, and the urge to help her is another obstacle between me and the carefree life Holly wants me to enjoy.

"Mom, let me see your glasses for a second." I take her glasses and see her as I rarely do. Without them, her eyes are squinty, and her face is less structured. She looks more like my sister. She looks vulnerable. I take an unbleached brown paper napkin from the dispenser and fog the glasses before I start to clean. She smiles, and her teeth are filthy, but I smile back. I don't miss her anymore. Living with Holly has cured me of longing for Mom, but I don't want her to be homeless, in pain, or to die, all of which are very real possibilities. All my life I have been focused on making sure Mom is okay, and that hasn't changed. I understand why Alex and Jessica want her out of their lives. They preserved themselves by getting away from her. But I survived for a long time by believing that if I tried hard enough, I could keep our little family together. And woven into that effort was the conscious decision not to hold her accountable for her disease. It was hard to keep this conviction sometimes. When she put herself and others in danger, I had to remind myself that it wasn't her fault. Knowing that allowed me to understand her, forgive her, love her, and accept the love that she was able to offer. If I blamed her for all of it, I would have lost myself in that hatred. To this day, I have to remind myself that she wronged me, but she's not culpable. I wanted and still pray, more than anything, to be able to reach into her mind and quiet the voices, to meet and love the woman that they destroyed. Mental illness is a thief, robbing the victims and their families relentlessly and without remorse.

She squeezes my hands. When I look up at her, she says, "David, what is with this D on your report card?" Mom is entitled to updates on my health, education, and other basic information. She is given this access based on the fundamental principle that a child is the property of the parent. This idea permeates the system: It is why, in practice, abusive parents are rarely prosecuted and are often reunited with their children. It's bewildering that my mother has access to reports on my mental health when her abuse of me is a contributing factor.

Sometimes Mom has an address or has our records sent to her care of a church, but usually she picks them up from the DSS. The grade she is criticizing is from last year—I got the D when I was moving from Mae's house to Holly's in my second semester of ninth grade. Now that I have regular food and am not kept home from school, I have straight As. But I don't explain. I just say, "Don't worry, Mom—my grades are much better now."

"You never got Ds with me," she says. "These people are trash. Don't let them bring you to their level. You can be a Supreme Court justice, do you understand? I'll be watching these grades."

She shifts gears. "Why won't your brother and sister see me? How are they?"

I'm not sure how to respond. "Mom, do you want coffee?"

"Yes, yes." She gives a regal wave to my social worker. "Get me coffee."

To her credit, Mel doesn't complain. "David, can I get you something too?"

"Coffee too, please. Just cream."

"Tell me, what's up with Alex and Jessica? Are they okay? Are they in school? Why didn't they come?"

I don't tell her the truth. "They're just busy. Alex is playing sports; Jessica is writing poetry. They are doing really well in school. I'll remind them to prioritize visits."

She smiles at me, but her eyes dart around the restaurant. "This place is not right, Hugh John David. You have to watch out, do you understand?"

Ignoring her, I ask, "Mom, where are you staying now? Do you have a place?"

"I'm fine," she says. She's lying.

I make sure Mel isn't watching, then pull some money out of my pocket. "Mom, take this. It's not much, but I get an allowance now, and I want you to have it." I hand her forty dollars in ones. Every time I interact with her, I give her anything I have. The line of her mouth turns down, but she then takes the money and tucks it into her pocket before Mel comes back with our hot drinks. I'm not supposed to give Mom anything.

"I need cream and sugars. Did I say thank you?" Mom says in one stream of words. Mel looks from her to me, raising one eyebrow to ask if I'm still okay alone with Mom. I give the slightest of nods, and the social worker returns to the counter for the condiments.

After an hour, Mel turns to me and says, "It's time, David."

"I have to get to a meeting," Mom blurts defensively. "I love you, Hugh John David. No more Ds." We stand up. She folds me into her soft warm mass. She smells familiar in a way that triggers a complex mix of emotions. Leaving her to survive on her own feels like a betrayal. This woman is my curse, my burden, and my blood. I will never stop loving her. When I leave Barts, I don't turn back to see which direction she is heading. I can't. Every time I walk away from this woman, it's the worst day of my life.

And yet, I am learning what it's like to give and receive a less complicated love. In my new home, on the night before Christmas Eve, Holly hosts a party for all of her and Steve's family, about seventy-five people. I've never had any extended family, and now, all at once, I'm in the middle of one, surrounded by cousins and nieces and nephews. There are people called Gram and Gramp who are actually a kind of relative I hadn't heard of before: *great*-grandparents. There are in-laws who are connected in ways I only sort of understand. There is food everywhere. The house is overflowing. People are on every floor, out in the back, and smoking on the chilly porch. There is laughter and debate, board games and eggnog, kids chasing each other and dishes getting broken, and people I've never met bringing gifts for me too.

I'm in the kitchen, humming Christmas carols, trying to keep things orderly, when Holly puts a hand on my shoulder.

"Please go out there and enjoy yourself. You don't have to clean up."

"I'm just getting a head start on the dishes."

"It's Christmas, my son. The mess is part of the fun. You don't have to clean. Be a child. Go. Enjoy. Yourself. Out, get out of the kitchen," she says, with laughter in her voice.

She called me her son. Holly's simple word choice holds an entire library of meaning to me. A foster child is a child of the state, placed in the temporary care of a responsible adult who filled out paperwork and met the requirements. The government believes we are entitled to food, clothing, shelter, and sometimes braces, but the system makes no promise of love. When Holly calls me her son, she is calling herself a mother and is opening her family to me, her home. It is a place where I am welcome, where the adults are making decisions out of care, where the only way I am encouraged to change myself is to be more of a kid. A place where I belong. This storm of thought and emotion must be playing out on my face because Holly asks, "David, you okay?" her smile warm on her tilted face. She always sees me, even in my inner world.

"Where's the soda?" a cousin asks as he barrels into the kitchen, and I'm pulled out of my reverie. "I'm good," I tell Holly, my smile genuine, and then I dive into the warm mayhem that is family. I have one foot in my mother's world, anchoring me to a past, and one foot stepping into this one, with Holly's outstretched hand reaching from the shore of a loving present and a better future. I've only got to lift my anchor, but I can't, not yet. Holly is offering me the life I have always wanted, if I can just find my way there.

Chapter 18

WHEN I WALK IN THE door of Ken's family's late 1800s Victorian house, I immediately see kids holding cans of Budweiser beer, the same kind Steve likes. They are scattered throughout the foyer and back into the kitchen; they are coming up and down the grand wooden staircase that twists to the floor above with a hand-carved rail. There is no sign of Ken's parents.

"Broz!" Ken, who is on the track team with me, tosses me a Budweiser. I hold it like it's a ticking bomb. We're all underage, but I'm the one who could lose my placement, maybe even be sent back to a facility. Also, at school I've been hiding that I'm gay using the only surefire technique I know—having no real conversations or friendships. I know that beer loosens inhibitions, and I can't risk that.

"We're outside," Ken says, and goes past me toward the back of the house. I don't know who "we" is.

I want to ditch the beer, but every kid is holding one—that, or a red Solo cup of something else illicit. I walk casually over to the sink and pour out the Budweiser. It froths and goes down smoothly, just like the ad says it will. I turn on the tap, make sure nobody is watching, and furtively fill my can with water.

Out in the yard the party has devolved into a Western Massachusetts high school version of Woodstock. Kids are lounging across the lawn, couples are making out on the trampoline, and there's a group floating in a semi-in-ground pool. I sit down on a lawn chair, near but not quite in a circle of guys, a couple of whom I recognize from the track team.

"You did the same thing last year, bro!"

"I know, I know," a kid from the track team says. I think his name is Kyle.

"You don't have a chance with her, bro. When will you get that through your thick skull?" Another kid thumps Kyle's head with his fist, and Kyle play punches him.

I shake my head and chime in as if I know what they're talking about. "No way, man." Someone talks over me, and the conversation shifts to a football game they all seem to have watched together. I nod along as if I saw it too.

"Should we throw Cassie in the pool?" someone suggests.

Suddenly they are all up, running toward a girl with straight blond hair who squeals, "Don't throw me in the pool! I'm wearing a watch! I mean it! Take off my watch!" A moment later she's in the pool, fully clothed, laughing and pretending to be furious. I stand up, acting like I have a purpose, and do a lap around the yard, pausing on the periphery of each cluster, hoping someone will start a conversation with me, but I am invisible. If this were a street game, I'd know how to join in, but while I have been busy trying to survive, kids my age have developed a new language, one I don't speak or understand. If I do approach any of them, I'll be expected to engage in all the heterosexual high school behavior that makes me uncomfortable. They'll ask questions like *Where are you from? Do you have a crush?* It's difficult to make friends if you are hiding most of who you are. I make another loop, then slip out the front door. I'm already some distance away when I realize I'm still holding my water-filled beer can. I chuck it into the bushes. I'm relieved to be out of there, but also sad. I finally have the freedom to be normal, but I don't know how.

I can't function among my peers, but I have always been confident speaking up in structured contexts: selling door-to-door, pushing my social workers to get approval for braces, charming my teachers, and after being temporarily silenced by Mae, I am now speaking up again. I'm a vocal member of student council, and, through my social worker, I join a new group called the National Foster Youth Advisory Council, sponsored by the Child Welfare League of America. The goal of the council is to give foster kids a voice in the decisions that affect our lives. Only weeks after Ken's gathering I am on a plane to DC to speak my mind to members of Congress. Somehow this is less daunting than a yard party.

I've watched planes crisscrossing the sky my whole life, but I've never even considered the possibility of being on one. No one I know travels beyond the range of the bus or train systems. I have no idea what to expect. I walk down the ramp, feeling it bounce a bit, and the plane I board is much smaller than the ones I've seen in movies. I overhear one of the flight attendants referring to it as a "puddle jumper." It feels flimsy—in no way substantial enough to carry my body up into the sky and to keep it there. I have a window seat, from which I can see one of the propellers.

"It's fine, I'm fine, everything is fine," I chant to myself, eyes closed.

"In the event of an emergency, oxygen masks will drop from the panel above your head." The flight attendant is issuing life-and-death instructions, but I seem to be the only one paying attention. *What kind of emergency?* I wonder, my fear mounting.

"In the event of a water landing, your seat cushion can be used as a flotation device."

Water landing? Why would we land in the water? I don't know anything about planes, but it's clear to me that this plane is not designed to land in water. I close the window shade and my eyes and do my best to ignore the next couple of hours.

Because of my involvement in the NFYAC, I've been asked to help lobby for a bill to reform foster care. Senator Chafee of Rhode Island has sponsored the bill, which is called the Foster Care Independence Act, to help kids transition out of foster care at the age of eighteen. The Child Welfare League of America has brought me and other foster kids from across the country to tell our stories to senators and congresspeople and help get the bill across the finish line.

When I land in DC, a staffer meets my plane and leads me to a van full of other young people who come from a host of different sponsoring nonprofits. We're brought straight to the Hyatt on Capitol Hill, where we'll be given a couple of full days of media and lobbying training to help us understand what the bill is and how to push for it.

The conference rooms are named after battles: Concord, Lexington, and Bunker Hill. Our group gathers in Bunker Hill, and I take a seat at a table near the speaker's podium. In front of me, I spread out a notepad and pen from the hotel.

"I'm Nick, hey," says a kid who sits down across from me.

"David, from Massachusetts...New York and Massachusetts."

"Cool." Nick flips over his water glass and pours from one of the pitchers in the center of the table. "Want some?"

"Sure, thanks."

"Grab a seat wherever, let's fill up the front," Fran, the trainer, says. "First, I want to make sure you understand the pending legislation. As it currently stands, when a foster child reaches their eighteenth birthday, the funding ends. They're shown the door of their foster homes and expected to fend for themselves with nowhere to live, no money, no prospects, and shaky family connections, if any. After eighteen, there is no 'family' in 'foster family.'"

"It's worse than getting out of prison," Nick says under his breath.

"Without any support or guidance, a shocking number of foster children end up homeless or in prison. A high percentage of the girls are pregnant within one year of leaving their foster families. This isn't just because they don't have access to sex ed or birth control."

"That's a stereotype," one of the foster girls says. Her nameplate reads Nicole.

"Yeah, but it's true." One of the CWLA executives speaks up. "The abuse that put them in the system in the first place makes them vulnerable and likely to engage in risky behaviors. And sometimes they become pregnant as a way of creating the family they never had."

Fran continues, "The Chafee program—the new law—would provide funding for states to establish programs helping foster kids transition out of foster care, giving them help with housing, health, education, and employment."

"I think girls get pregnant or hijacked into sex trafficking because the system is messed up. No one really talks to you about sex. Group homes are single sex, which is only fine for the homos. My foster parents don't let me date," Nick says. He's leaning all the way forward in his seat. His shoulders are broad, and he's wearing a cool oversized T-shirt. He's definitely got game.

I cringe inwardly when he gives his take on "homos" in group homes, but he is right about there being an educational void.

Fran ignores the interruption. "The bill is stuck in Congress, and we hope that hearing your stories will help push it through."

"Every time I tell any part of my story, it's like people are slowing down to stare at a car accident on the side of the road. They feel sorry for me and are curious to the point of rudeness, but then they drive on and do nothing. We want them to get out. Do something. How can we get them to stop their 'cars'?" I ask.

"That's a great segue for some videos I want to show you." Fran asks someone to roll a TV to the front of the room, and she inserts a VHS tape. It begins by giving us basic guidance on how to behave in an interview, like making eye contact, sitting up straight, and re-peating the interviewer's point back to them to demonstrate that we understand. Then it shows multiple scenes of people being interviewed about a specific topic. In the first scene, the interviewer drives the discussion, but then it presents an alternate version, where the person being interviewed steers the questions in order to make the points they want to make.

"What did you notice?" Fran asks as she brings the lights back up.

"People are rude. They need to mind their own business," Nicole says. Her arms are crossed on her chest, her lips pursed.

"Say more," Fran prompts.

"If you give 'em an inch, they take a damn mile." She pauses in thought, then adds, "But in the later ones, the person got better at controlling the conversation." She uncrosses her arms and picks up a pen. "Like, you don't just answer the question. You take charge." She's clearly excited by what she's figuring out.

"Very good, Nicole," Fran says. "You're not just here to share your story. The story is a tool, not a destination. Remember that. Part of your story should include the obstacles you and kids like you face. And then you explain how the bill is the solution to those obstacles. Story. Obstacle. Solution. The trick is, and you'll see this with practice, you can give them just a little bit of your story, and then get right back to what *you* want to talk about. *You* are driving the agenda.

"Okay, so now we are going to break into teams of three, I want you to role-play according to these scripts." She hands out a few pages. "One will be the interviewer, asking you questions about your life. The second person will answer, filling in the blanks where it gives you a chance to redirect the dialogue. And the third person will observe and take notes. Then we'll rotate. Any questions?" Fran doesn't pause for an answer—everyone is already studying the scripts anyway. "I'll walk around and observe," she finishes.

I love this game. Every time I've gone into a new home, or to court, or to therapy, or to my first meeting with a guidance counselor in a new school—in every scenario, people around me have drawn conclusions about me based on what has happened to me. I relish the opportunity not just to tell my story, but to decide how much of it matters and why.

The next day, the organizations assign us to meet with various members of Congress. They send most of the kids who are Black and Latino to meet with the Congressional Black Caucus and other liberals. Then they pull me aside. "We're going to set you up with slightly more conservative congresspeople," a staffer says. "You're articulate and presentable, they'll understand you." I recognize these adjectives to be euphemisms. I am white, and when they say "presentable," they mean I sound white when I speak. They may not even realize that they are picking the white boy to talk to the white, Southern congresspeople who are on the fence about the bill. The system is a dirty cloud of racial dynamics.

Poverty traps lots of people, and in New York State the homeless kids around me were disproportionately people of color. Society had all of us poor people on the bottom rung, but somewhere in me I knew that I had an advantage because I was white, and they knew it too. We were all competing for the scraps, all stayed at the same shelters, and waited in the same lines for meals, but racism in America gave me an up in the competition for resources. The men in DC saw that, the Black kids I ran with saw it, and so did I. All around us, it seemed like the people in power looked like me. Our presidents, our teachers, and the rich movie stars we envied on TV for their money. And now the lobbyists were assuming that I'd have more success pitching to the lawmakers because I looked like them. What they didn't know was that I planned to pitch for us *all*.

On our third day in DC, after training is completed, we walk up the street to an edifice that reads CANNON HOUSE OFFICE BUILDING in brass next to the door. We enter a soaring rotunda, three stories high. I am ushered into a foyer. The ceilings are vast, and there are too many desks crammed into the space. "Break a leg, David. You got this," my chaperone says, and she's gone. I take a deep breath and go into the meeting.

"Hi, I'm David Ambroz, and I have an appointment with the congressman," I say. On the wall above the intern are posters, paintings, and paraphernalia from the home state. "Buffalo?" I ask, gesturing toward a landscape painting of the Great Plains.

"Bison," the intern says with a half smile. "I don't know the difference either." He opens a door that I hadn't noticed. The congressman stands and comes around his desk to greet me. His hands grip both of mine.

"Sit, sit. I'm so glad to talk with you, David. Now, tell me. Why are you in foster care? What happened?" The congressman is wearing a tailored pale blue suit. Every hair is in place, and his teeth are too white and perfect to be natural. He places his clasped hands on the desk in front of him and furrows his brow with concern, but I can tell it's a role he's played for so long he doesn't even realize he's doing it.

"Well, sir, my mom is mentally ill, and we were homeless—"

"That's just tragic. Was there violence, David?" he asks.

This is exactly what I've been trained for. From Fran, I have learned that receiving empathy feels good; it can be addictive. Someone is listening to you and validating your pain. But it is also a trap. I have to manage this conversation so that sharing what happened to me is more than just a sorry tale. If I can use my story to inspire change, then what I went through won't have been for nothing. He's intrigued by the details of my abuse, and I am conscious to keep it brief so that I can pivot to the reason I'm in the room, which is not to have him pity the damage, as if the day's job is done because he listened, but to get him to help.

"Sir, there was violence both at home and sometimes in foster care too. It's our country's most consistent inheritance: poverty and violence. I'm here hoping we can end that with the bill." Then I stop and wait for his response.

"David, I'm going to tell you—I have a hard time with this idea of supporting adults…at eighteen we are adults."

"Do you have kids, sir?"

"Yes, I do," he says, smiling. "I have a beautiful, brilliant daughter. She'd be perfect for you but she's too old. She's thirty." I throw him a small smile, which is what he wants, because in his mind we're two straight men who speak the same language. He wants to talk to an intelligent, fellow white American who feels like a son, with whom he can make jokes about dating his daughter. I go along with it, knowing that I'm nothing like what he wants for a son-in-law. We both pretend that I haven't just told him I'd been homeless most of my life.

"Well, sir," I say with a chuckle, "then you must know from your daughter that no kid is independent, even at thirty!"

"Ha, point taken." He claps his hands and throws his head back. The performance continues. It's not so different from selling holiday wrapping paper or vacuum cleaners. I assess my target, determine what is meaningful to them, and sell them a reality that fits into their ideals. I am a natural at politics. I'll do what I need to get what I want, which is more than being in-laws with this man. I've been criticized as mouthy, a smart-ass, conniving, but in this context, I am seen as articulate and persuasive. It feels wonderful to discover that these qualities are transferrable and can be used to good purpose, especially to help other kids.

A couple of nights later I am invited to dinner at the home of one of the congress members who seems to support the bill. She's delayed, and so I arrive first to the home—a tall but narrow brick town house. Awkwardly, I am guided through a narrow hallway with personal photos covering both walls. The silver-framed photos reveal her pedigree and that of her husband, with generations posing in front of landmark homes, taking vacations, celebrating graduations, and posing next to dignitaries stretching back at least three administrations.

We pass a formal parlor and the dining room, traditional-looking rooms full of antiques and upholstered furniture that looks uncomfortable. The narrow, modern kitchen is at the back of the house. There are glass doors to the backyard, and light beams off the shiny white marble counters. A young woman, the babysitter, is scrambling about, preparing dinner. She's wearing trendy beige corduroys and a light blue sweater. She eyes me with mild irritation when I take a seat on a stool at the island.

"How long have you been working for the family?" I ask to break the ice.

"A while." Her reply is clipped. She is busy chopping, grating, tasting, and adjusting spices.

"Wow, I've never seen homemade mac 'n' cheese before." The mac and cheese I've had always came out of a box with a bag of dehydrated cheese product. I watch her for a moment and ask her a few more questions before she tries to stop me.

"David, if you don't mind, I have to focus on getting the kids their dinner. To answer some of your questions: I've worked here for two years. I am studying child development and want to work in public policy. I have a boyfriend, back in Georgia. Was there anything else that you'd like to know?"

"Ah, cool. Do you like your job?" I ask.

"David—" she starts, but the representative's husband, Robert, walks into the kitchen. He is tall and narrowly built, with a mostly bald head shaved close on the sides. He stands ramrod straight, crisp and confident.

"Bit behind on dinner, huh?" he says to the babysitter. Then, without waiting for an answer from her, he leans against the wall and asks me what I've been up to today.

"Just getting ready for tomorrow," I jump in, perky and smiling. "Child Welfare League and Children's Defense Fund have us going office to office on the Hill. Talking to senators, mostly, and their staffs about—"

Robert cuts me off. "Yeah, kind of inappropriate if you ask me," he says, "sending kids on a lobbying trip."

"About the Chafee Independence Act," I continue, despite his interruption. "It's really going to help foster kids when they emancipate at eighteen."

"Should we really support kids after eighteen? They're adults at that age. If they're old enough to buy a gun, join the military..." Robert trails off with a self-assured shrug. "Tell me this: When is enough welfare, enough welfare, eh?"

He loosens his wide red tie and wrangles the top button on his starched white shirt open. This giraffe of a man, whom I already know comes from generations of wealth, has the audacity to tell me, a sixteen-year-old foster youth, that I've gotten enough support from the government. DC is impressive.

"You have no idea what you are talking about," I retort. I'm off script. Fran definitely wouldn't approve. I'm not using the tools she gave me. But his inherited polish and dismissal are too much for me.

"Excuse me? I most certainly do," he retorts. "Handouts don't do anything but perpetuate a welfare mentality. The only thing that cures poverty is hard work. Foster youth should be encouraged to get a job. College is not for everyone."

"I want to go to college, and I'm a foster youth."

"Exactly. That's my point. You don't need government help. You study, and you get good grades. At public schools paid for by taxpayers like me. And look at you now."

"Where am I now, Robert? I can't pay for college. I could still use help." He is really starting to irritate me. He has absolutely no idea how hard it is to get through without aid. This man has never been hungry or slept outdoors in his life unless it was by choice. He cannot fathom what it's like to need the state for your survival. I scoot a little closer to him, look him dead in the eyes; I want to help him understand.

"When do the handouts end? Eighteen years old? Twenty-one?

Thirty? Never? Welfare reform is the best thing Clinton's done," he says, stepping back to take off his pin-striped suit jacket and fold it over a kitchen stool with care. Above him is a large oil painting of a stunning horse. It's part of a tasteful gallery wall. The room screams of wealth and power. I'm playing on his court, but I don't care.

"The Chafee Independence Act will cost the government less than half the cost of one single F-21, but it will help twenty-two thousand foster kids every year until they turn twenty-one, not thirty years old. Twenty-two thousand foster kids!" I exclaim.

"Son, the F-21 protects us—all of us, including those kids," Robert says. He begins to roll up his sleeves. He's such a privileged cliché, his conversation, his hands that have never seen real labor. His nails have a subtle sheen. I think of Steve, who labors every day and whose fingers are permanently stained.

"What good is protecting those twenty-two thousand foster kids if they end up homeless, in jail, having babies at eighteen, just like their parents?" I ask. I'm reducing their experience to make a point even though I know that no matter how dramatic I make it, nothing will get through to this guy. He doesn't care because he has no idea what real financial struggle is like.

Robert looks blank for a moment, and for a second I think that I've broken through and cracked the shell, but then he pivots sternly. "My family has served in the military for generations, and you are in the house of a United States representative. Have some respect."

I'm thrown and pause to take him in. He engaged me in this debate, and now that he's discovering he doesn't have the facts and figures to make an argument, he's pulling rank to silence me. He's saying, *Your personal experience doesn't matter in my home. I'm right because I'm older and richer and more educated.*

At this point, I don't care about offending him. "Sir, the state yanked me between foster homes, and I was abused at most of them. I've changed schools so many times I lost count. This whole system is absurd," I say, throwing my hands up. "If the state is going to take kids away from their parents, then the state should make sure it sets them up for success."

"David, you shouldn't use personal detail in debate. It's subjective and anecdotal," he says, issuing instructions on debate tactics as if this were some sort of game, and to him, it is. He isn't really trying to hear what I'm saying. He's probably never talked to someone who grew up homeless, but he doesn't care. This is just a kind of verbal tug-of-war that he has most likely played all his life. I am wasting my time. But I take his bait.

"Ah, so your family's military service is fair game, but my 'service' and experience in the foster care industrial complex are not."

"Listen, the world is unfair. It'd be better if these kids learned that earlier rather than later, with endless government handouts," Robert says, taking a step closer to me. *Does he hear himself?* I wonder. Being raised in wealth is the ultimate unearned handout.

"I'm quite clear on how unfair the world is. Trust me, that's one lesson no foster youth has missed. It's cheaper to send foster youth to college, provide a down payment for first month's rent, or offer health care than to supplement the lives they end up with when they don't have a chance to break out of poverty. Help them get an education, and we won't end up subsidizing their children. Society can either invest a little in them now or pay more later. It's the fiscally smart thing to do." I've lost my temper, but I don't cry or get frustrated. I unload with full force.

"You just don't understand taxes, young man," he says, his voice rising. "Your family never paid them. Where is the personal responsibility? Maybe these women should think about their ability to care for their kids, before having more and more and more—and putting that on me to pay for."

"Robert, my mom is mentally ill," I reply, and my voice rises to just shy of yelling. I don't like his way of arguing. He keeps moving the goalpost. "I'm not sure she made very rational decisions, ever. And even if parents do make dumb decisions, as most adults do, why should the state leverage the kids—the future of these kids—to punish or push the parents toward something they may not be capable of achieving?"

"Good point, David, well said," the representative says, appearing in the kitchen at last. She is as impeccable as her husband, but in her own way: She is wearing a red pantsuit and is perfectly coiffed, every blond hair firmly in place. On her lapel is an abstract brooch, with just the right gemstones to offset the color of her suit.

When she passes her husband, she pauses to kiss his cheek. "Hon, David is a guest in this house, and he's here to get this legislation passed, which I'm leaning toward supporting, as you well know." Then she turns to me. "David, if you want to convince my husband, or the people like him on the Hill, you are not going to win by hitting them with a two-by-four. Stay cool, make your point in a way that speaks to their interests, and leave them thinking."

"Well, that was invigorating," the representative's husband says dismissively. "Thank you, David." He turns and leaves the kitchen.

"How is dinner coming along for the kids?" the representative asks the babysitter, casually but with an undertone of annoyance.

"About ten minutes, ma'am," the babysitter replies.

"Got it, okay. Well, let me summon them," the representative says as she heads down the hall.

In the coming weeks, this woman will vote on a bill that will alter the future for all foster kids. I feel the pressure of knowing that I am one of the very few foster kids who will have a chance to persuade her to support the bill. She might disagree with her husband. Or she might be undecided and looking for a reason to support the bill. I might be that reason. She doesn't need me to explain the economics of poverty. She needs to see me, hear my story, realize that we could have a lot more success stories, and think about me when she makes her decision.

"That was something," the babysitter says. "You held your own. Not sure you changed his mind, though."

"Thanks," I say. "What's your actual name?" Her bosses don't seem to notice her as a person because she's the help, but I do. Her face softens and she smiles. "Diane, my name is Diane."

"In my experience there are some minds you can't change, Diane. But I damn well am not going to be their doormat."

"As a professional doormat for a few families now, I've learned that you can be right, or you can win, rarely both."

"The only way to win is to have more people like me than people like her husband," I say with conviction. "It's a numbers game."

She carries two plates to the table. "It's fine to have opinions, David. It's better to have a vote, to have power." I intend to have both.

We need representatives who will help kids in poverty. People talk about family or values or what it means to be an American, but in order to make all that come true, we have to invest in the kids who need us most. The condition of schools, access to health care, all the key indicators prove we're not doing right by these kids. No wonder nearly half of children who spend some of their childhood in poverty end up poor.

We can start by centering this issue in our hearts, minds, and votes. We can ask candidates and representatives what they are doing about kids in poverty. What plan do they have for homeless kids? How will they fix the schools? We need to make this as important as the other issues we fervently debate every day in our society.

Robert had unwittingly given me a lesson in politics and power. The only way people in poverty will get the opportunities we deserve is by running and winning, by writing our own laws to lift ourselves up. The first step is to get people to vote for this bill—to implement changes that, long term, will help my people be in a position to run for office.

There is hope. In DC my voice and the voices of the other foster kids who can't vote are heard, and every single foster child will benefit—the bill eventually passes.

I go from the vibrant swirl of politics that are deeply important to me back to the everyday of high school in Western Massachusetts. I still haven't managed to make many of my own friends, but I meet up with Jessica and Alex to walk around downtown Amherst with theirs—Sam, Lahn, Marianna, and Anne. Marianna has dark curly hair and a full figure. She is not particularly interesting to me, but she loves to talk, and I'm willing to listen. Then one day she decides to take things to another level.

"David, cariño," Marianna says, taking both of my hands in hers.

I'm seated across from her in Herrell's Ice Cream. Alex and Jessica are up at the counter, and Jessica's boyfriend is next to Marianna.

"Yes?" I ask, confused about why she is holding my hands.

"I know you like me…" I'm not sure how she got this impression because I don't, at least not romantically. "And I think you are cute," she continues.

"Sweet!" Jessica's boyfriend, Sam, chimes in.

Marianna misreads my stunned silence and flaming cheeks. "Don't be shy!" She laughs.

I can only wait, mystified, to see where she is going with this.

"So, we should date!" she concludes.

People are constantly asking me if I have a girlfriend: kids at school, the orthodontist, social workers, even Steve and Holly (although it's clear Holly thinks I'm gay). I know that being gay is an obstacle to escaping poverty and achieving normalcy. Gay people lose their jobs. They risk contracting AIDS. Gay sex is illegal in most states. I'm committed to leading a heterosexual life. I'm going to date, marry, have kids, and hide who I am until the day I die. Marianna is sweet and harmless, a good start. I look into Marianna's eyes.

"Okay. Yeah, okay," I agree to be her boyfriend.

"What's up?" Alex has returned to the table. Jessica is right behind him, both of them carrying cups of ice cream.

"We are boyfriend and girlfriend now," Marianna declares triumphantly.

"Dope, bro!" Alex crows.

Jessica just smiles. And like that, I have a girlfriend.

I rarely have to see Marianna because she goes to school in Amherst with Alex and Jessica, so it's easy to be her boyfriend. In our daily phone calls, I usually just listen. She never asks me about my living situation, why I don't live with my siblings, or anything about my past. And that's great.

The minute I turn sixteen, after dating Marianna for a few months, I get a job at Iris Photo. I earn money to go to movies, buy CDs, and get ice cream with Alex and Jessica and my girlfriend. One day, I'm standing behind the counter when a guy comes into the store. He's older than I am, maybe eighteen. Our eyes connect, flit apart, and reconnect, like a pair of butterflies circling each other. He looks around, smiles again at me, and then leaves. I ask my coworker to cover for me, and I run out the door and catch up to him at the ATM outside Fleet Bank.

"Hi," I say, at a loss for what to say next.

"Hi. Do you follow all your customers out onto the street?" he asks, smiling.

"No." *Say something longer than a syllable*, I want to scream at myself. "You didn't find what you wanted there?" I ask stupidly.

"Well, sort of," he says, a Cheshire cat grin on his face. He puts one hand on my shoulder, and smiles. I can feel it through my shirt immediately. I think it might be on fire.

Pulling back, I say, "I have to go back to work."

"Okay. Hold on. Take this." He grabs one of the deposit envelopes and writes down his number.

"Hope you use it. Nice to meet you..." He taps my name badge. "David."

"You too," I say. I fold the envelope as small as possible and put it in my pocket, stunned that it is in my possession. I have a girlfriend and

I'm supposed to be straight. That night, I take the phone down into the basement, dial his number, and then hang up. I can't do this.

My head is still swirling the next day, when Marianna decides we are going to go see Leonardo DiCaprio in *Romeo + Juliet* at the Hampshire mall. Because the mall sits in the middle of the farmland between Hadley and Northampton, at certain times of the year you smell the manure that has been laid down to fertilize the fields. Neither rolled-up windows nor air-conditioned dark theaters can keep out the odor. But at *Romeo + Juliet*, it mingles pleasantly with the smell of buttered popcorn. The matinee is packed with kids our age.

The space is muffled by thick carpet, padded walls, and acoustic tile. The previews begin. The theater is nearly full, and people are going all the way up to the screen in search of seats, then coming back up the aisle. It's then that I see him. The guy from yesterday at Iris Photo is walking right toward me. He sees me, too, and our eyes connect and hold for an instant. He sees Marianna and keeps walking.

Turning, I watch him take a seat a few rows behind us.

"Do you know that guy?" Marianna asks.

"Uh...from work, just from work. He's a customer," I say. I reach to take one of her hands. Our eyes meet briefly. Then I release her hand. A few feet away from me in the movie theater is someone whose hand I do want to hold. He is right there, and he is a world away.

Chapter 19

THE YELLING CARRIES DOWN TO my room in the basement.

"Don't worry, honey. It's almost over," I say to Bri, who is sitting in my lap. I'm trying to reassure both of us.

"Why are they so mad?" Brianna asks, melting backward into me as if I could absorb her fear.

"They love each other very much, but sometimes they get upset. People can love each other and still have fights."

The voices rise to a crescendo, then I hear the front door slam shut. There is an extra crash after that, and then everything is suddenly quiet. Both of the girls start crying. Frightened and confused, I walk up the stairs and open the door. The clock that hung above the front door has crashed down to the floor and broken. Steve is picking up the pieces.

Living with Holly and Steve I've felt safer and happier than ever before, but the relationship that they have with each other isn't so rosy. Their family had expanded quickly when I arrived right after Ruth was born. The financial support from the state is minimal, and since Steve lost his job, there have been reverberations in the household. They are arguing frequently. Holly has been spending more time away from the house. I don't understand what's going on, and worry that it's my fault. I clean and take care of the girls, doing anything I can think of to make their lives easier. I need this family to be stable; I can't bear to see them falter.

When Steve and Holly fight, they don't curse or throw things, but they're both emotional. Their voices rise and fall. Occasionally one tells the other to keep it down. I don't know what the fights are about, but Holly has been my savior, so I default to her side. When Steve notices that I've come upstairs, he drops some fragments of the glass and stands up, looking at me like I'm an intruder.

"*What?*" Steve yells. "What, David?" His voice is choked with frustration.

"Stop yelling at her! What's wrong with you?" This is the first time I've injected myself into their conflicts, but I'm scared that this family will break up, and I can't let that happen. "Do you think yelling is going to fix anything?" I admonish him. "If so, things would have been better months ago. Just go. Go the fuck away. I have two kids in the basement crying." I tell this man to leave his own hard-earned home, then turn away.

"Who the hell are you to tell me to leave this house?" He catches up to me and gets right in my face. "Don't speak to me like that. You have no idea what you're talking about."

At six foot two, Steve towers over me. Our faces are close; I can smell the cigarettes on his breath. A flush of anger climbs up his neck to his face.

In the arrogance of my youth, I look at this man in his simple Lee jeans, white Hanes tank top, fingers and hands speckled with paint and calluses, and I feel nothing but anger and contempt. It surges through me. I want to shock him. I want to wake him up. "Go ahead, hit me, I dare you," I say. Then I spit in his face.

Parents in my past have been dangerous, out of control, and unreliable, and I goad him in this way because I know that Steve is none of these things. I know Steve would never hit me. I spit in his face because I trust him. I do it because I love him. I do it because he makes me feel safe enough to be angry.

"Enough, David. Go downstairs," he says in a low voice without looking at me. He turns away.

I turn, too, quietly, and go back down to my room. The house is quiet now, and I put the girls to bed. I hear Holly come home, and their voices are hushed. Things have temporarily reverted to normal, and I'm glad for the calm after the storm.

When I come upstairs in the morning, Holly is getting Bri ready for school. I head into the kitchen and fix myself breakfast.

"Yesterday was hard, I know. We love you guys," Holly says, coming up behind me at the sink. She gives me an awkward squeeze and I feel like her hero, helping to keep the family together, proud that I stood up for her.

At school later that morning, a voice comes over the PA. "David Ambroz, report to the guidance office." I have no idea why I'm being summoned and am surprised when I walk into the office to see that the vice-principal, my guidance counselor, Fred, and Mel are all there.

"You're being moved," Mel says. "Your foster father says that you threatened the children. Your foster mother has asked that you be removed from the placement, immediately. I'm going to take you home right now to pick up your stuff."

"What? They're what?" My heart hangs loose, out of my body. I can't believe what I'm hearing.

"Have a seat, David," Fred says, easing me into an oak chair that has no give.

"I'm being moved?" My voice breaks. "They're throwing me out?" The panic and desperation mount inside of me.

"David, they are not throwing you out. You are being moved, that's all," Mel explains calmly. "The placement was good, but it's not working for them right now. We are going to go to their home and pack up your things."

All I hear are the words *"for them"* and *"their* home." I am no longer part of the family. My breath is shallow. I can feel sobs trying to come up like vomit. I push them back down and say, "I'm sorry. Tell them I'm sorry. I'll try harder."

"David, the decision has been made," Fred says.

"Holly wouldn't do this to me. Let me talk to her," I implore.

"David, no." Mel is firm.

"But I'm in school. I—" I stop. I can see from the faces looking back at me that nothing I say will change their minds. This is not a negotiation. "What do I do now?"

They stand up, and we walk out of the room. The kids we pass in the hallway stare, knowing that something has happened. I don't care what they think. Another placement means another school. I'll never see them again.

You're so fucking stupid. You got too comfortable. I drill it into myself. I should never have stepped in. I should have known better. *They said you were part of the family, but it's not true. Families don't get rid of their kids.*

In the car, I plead with Mel. "There is no way he believes I'm a threat. I read to Bri. I rock Ruth in the rocking chair. I would never hurt them. I was trying to protect them. He *knows* that."

"David, this is not the time for this conversation," Mel says firmly. "Right now we need to focus on next steps. We are going to go, pack your stuff. Then we'll stop at the office, and we'll get you to an emergency placement."

They want me out. Holly wants me gone. I can't make sense of what's happening. Holly and I picked each other. I arrived at her house, hungry for love, and she gave it to me. I trusted her. She saw me, the real me. She nurtured me and encouraged me. She was the mother I wanted and needed. Her change of heart feels like the biggest betrayal. My mother would never have kicked me out, never. When my mother hurt me, I reminded myself of her illness, something she couldn't help. But why is Holly hurting me? It is the most painful punishment of all—

to be locked out of the family home. It hurts so much more than fists. Every measure of safety I had begun to feel evaporates in the car. I was wrong to let myself trust her. Steve. Anyone. It was a foolish mistake to let them into my heart.

My whole body clenches up, tight into a knot. I stare out the window, the world a blur, and I push the pain into a box and put the box on a shelf. I can't let them hurt me. No emotions. I have to survive. I don't know where I'm going next. I have to be ready.

In her Pontiac Firebird, Mel drives me to Holly and Steve's to fetch my belongings. No one is home when we arrive. I use my key and let myself in, but I stop in the doorway. The house is silent and still. I know its smells, and I breathe deeply to remember them. I can't believe this will be my last time coming here.

"Let's move, David. We don't have much time." Mel hands me a black trash bag. I descend the steps and load my belongings into the bag. I've done this before, a trash bag, fifteen minutes to stuff a whole life into it.

"You got everything?" Mel asks.

I tell her that I need my toothbrush upstairs. I take the steps two at a time, suddenly wanting to be gone, to leave this house. In the bathroom, I stare down at the cup with Bri's brush and mine. *Bri*. "I'm sorry, Bri," I say to the empty room. Then I grab my toothbrush, put it in my pocket, and walk straight to the front door. Mel's there.

"Lock it up, and give me the key, David." I do as she says.

Back in her car, I'm silent. "I'm not going to lie, David. This is bad. I'm not sure we'll find a great placement. Not at first. You are going to have to work with me on this, okay?"

I nod, grateful for the candor. I don't want bullshit platitudes. It's not going to be okay.

We drive to the same office in downtown Northampton where she brought me when I left Mae and Buck's. She starts making calls to try to figure out where I'm going.

For weeks I bounce from house to house—Holyoke, Amherst, Hadley—enrolling and unenrolling in schools as I go. None are permanent, so I don't pay much attention. Instead, I shrink smaller and smaller. I close myself off from the outside world. I don't want to feel any of this, and I don't want to remember feeling anything. I will not trust; I will not emote; I will not let anything affect me.

Finally, Mel calls, sounding excited. "David, good news! Your brother and sister's foster mother, Brenda, has agreed to take you as a crisis placement." This means I won't be there for very long, just until they find me a more permanent situation.

"Really?" For a second I tilt from emptiness toward excitement. The thought of living with my brother and sister again is something I could never imagine coming from this.

"It turns out she has room since Jessica and Alex are away. They're on a trip for two weeks, and you can stay there in the meantime."

So I won't be with them. But even in their absence I can't help but feel relieved to be going to Brenda's. Alex and Jessica have been happy with her. She doesn't hit them or ask anything unreasonable of them. She's one of the foster parents who do it because they care.

Brenda lives in a subsidized town house down the street from Amherst College. It's a simple home, everything is clean and orderly—clothes folded, carpet vacuumed. "David, we are going to put you in Jessica's room," she says, leading me into a tidy bedroom with a single bed and Jessica's drawings of dragons on the wall.

I thank her, and she leaves me alone in the space. I lie back on Jessica's bed. Maybe this will work out, and I can persuade Brenda to let me stay here. I could share my brother's room—maybe social services would pay for a bunk bed. It's not hope that I feel, it's survival. I have only a couple more years in the foster care system. The best-case scenario would be to stay with my siblings and to do well in school until I'm off to college. But I know from years of experience that that's not how it works. The system has a way of its own, and it isn't always reasonable.

The next morning, Brenda makes me breakfast and gives me money for lunch. It's more than I need—enough to get a treat at the school store—and clearly a kindness. "Have a good first day," she says. "Please call me if you're not coming straight home from school." Brenda is exactly the person I need right now. She doesn't ask any questions about how I'm feeling or what happened. She's not the type to have deep personal conversations. She just wants me to be well-fed and to do what I'm supposed to do, and I'm fine with that.

My new school is the same one Alex and Jessica have been going to for years, and when people hear my last name, they welcome me, exclaiming, "You're Alex and Jessica's little brother!" Alex and Jessica are well-liked. Jessica is known for the public poetry readings she gives, and Alex plays basketball and is one of the cool kids. In this moment, I'm proud to be an Ambroz. I'm immediately welcomed because of my name. They don't ask why I've been going to a different school or why I'm suddenly here. They simply accept me and understand that I'm the little brother and we're a family.

"David, we got your transcript," the guidance counselor tells me on my first day of school. "You've missed some work, and we don't have the same curriculum, so it would be best to—"

"I know—I've been in this situation before. I can catch up. Just give me the makeup work. I'll do it."

"If you are anything like your brother and sister, I know you will," she says, smiling. In the past, when I've entered new schools without my transcript, I've been placed in special education or the equivalent until the adults figure out what to do with me. I eventually learned that the only way to be put in the right classes was to tell them where I belonged and insist that I could handle it.

One person who is especially happy about my move to the school is Marianna, who has been my girlfriend in a long-distance way for about a year now. She expects to see me more often and is excited that we get to spend time together at school like her friends and their boyfriends.

"It's so great you're here now," Marianna exclaims, squeezing my hand. "It's brought us so much closer." We've walked the short main street of downtown and stopped to sit on a bench in a small park. Marianna leans into me, her curls kept in check with a black headband. My hand looks ghostly next to her warm olive skin. I'm taller than she is, but seated we are the same height. Her perfume smells too sweet, like the watermelon or mango sprays popular with all the girls in our class.

"It's important we stay this connected." Marianna leans in for a kiss.

"Yes, it's great…being closer," I say. It's a lie. I'm worried about being closer. I'm not sure I'll be able to keep up this act on a daily basis. We kiss. She's Catholic, and for a long time I've been off the hook for most physical contact, but now that I've moved, I'm expected to kiss her. I dart my tongue in and out of her mouth for ten to fifteen seconds. I count them in my head: *One one thousand, two one thousand…*

I go through the motions. That's my only plan for the time being, and it's working. People have stopped asking me if I have a girlfriend. Nobody is calling me a fag. I am passing as straight, and that makes every moment with Marianna worth it. I hide my living situation, my sexuality, and my emotions. From what I can tell, hiding who I am keeps me safe, and it is how I will get where I want to go.

A couple of days later, Mel comes to visit me. Alex and Jessica are due to come home, and my time at Brenda's is running out. Mel's charged up, walking down the corridor of the school with a glow in her eye. I know she has a plan.

"David, you were doing great at Northampton. You were on the track team and student council. You belong back there, and I think you should return to the LeBeaus. They care about you, they really do."

Mel gives me time to think. She always has a way of being present with me. Like a plane landing, she is all sound and motion until she touches down. When I need her, she turns all of her attention to me, and I am seen. She knows my current situation. She fought to make the placement with Holly happen in the first place, she witnessed its failure, and now she wants to nurture a truce so that I can return to the place where she knows I was happiest. Mel has at least twenty other kids on her caseload, and her office is a vault of endless paperwork; nevertheless, she always puts her whole heart into her work.

"I believe your story of what happened," she says. "But you need to make peace with the LeBeaus. Do you want to be right, or do you want to finish high school at Northampton?"

I'm quiet. I miss the girls. I wish I could go back in time to when it was a good situation, when I trusted Holly and respected Steve and loved them all. Some excitement is trying to creep through me, but I must keep it in check; I must smother it. I'm still hurt, and I'm wary.

"Say you're sorry," she urges me. "Admit it, apologize, get punished for it if you must, but move on."

How can I confess to something I didn't do? In a way she sounded like Mae: *Just shut the fuck up and do what I say.* They want to dim my light. They want me to erase myself. I've rejected this lesson, resolving never to sacrifice myself again. But in this case, Mel is giving me the best possible advice. My longing for the family is mixed in with the hurt and mistrust, mixed in with the feeling that our story isn't over.

A few days later I'm sitting across a table from Holly and Steve in the DSS offices in Northampton for the reconciliation that Mel has arranged. "I'm glad you're here," Holly says warmly. Her familiar eyes are on me, searching to see if there's any damage, trying to see if we're okay.

"Thank you for the chance to apologize. I lost my temper. I'm sorry," I say, trying to hit a believable tone. Then I add, "I love you." I add it because it's true and also because I know it's needed. Holly comes straight for me, and she wraps her arms around me. It feels good, but I hold back. I can't make a wrong move or portray any feeling of resentment. I want to be back in Holly's house because I know it's the best place for me, no matter how much this has hurt me. I want to trust her. I want to believe her. But I can't. Being accused of threatening the children hurt to the core, and I'm not sure I'll get over it. But I'll pretend, since, more and more, that's what survival has come to mean. We make our peace. I return to Brenda's to collect my belongings.

"David, it's been nice having you. See you back here real soon," Brenda says, and with that, she wraps up one of the most tumultuous periods of my life as if it were just another day. There is no buried meaning in Brenda's comments. She keeps it simple; I know what to expect of her, and it's a gift.

Mel and I drive back to Northampton in a companionable silence. But as we get closer to the house, she starts to prep me. "David. Listen to me. This is tough, I get it. Remember what I said. They do love you, and you did well there. All this is behind you."

Behind me? I'm shattered, and I'm holding another black trash bag in my lap.

I tell her that I understand, but I don't try to be convincing. I already know what I have to do. I'm going to be the perfect boy, but only because this is the best situation I've had and all that I know. I'm going to keep thanking all the adults in my life as they move me around like a piece on a chessboard.

We enter the cul-de-sac and pull into the driveway. "You ready?" Mel asks.

"Of course," I say, stepping out of the car. Lights, camera, action.

I force myself to smile when Holly opens the door. I've told myself that if they hug me, I should hug them back, and I do. Bri is the first of the children to reach me, and she throws her arms around my legs.

"Hello, Bri. It's good to see you, honey."

"I got that," Steve says and takes my trash bag.

"I'm gonna take off. I'll check in with y'all later today. Be gentle with each other," Mel says, and she drives away.

The house is unchanged, perhaps a little less organized than I had kept it, but it's the smell that hits me, a mixture of body products, cleaning supplies, and meals past. It smells like home.

"Why don't you unpack, and we'll start dinner," Holly says.

I thank her and head toward my room in the basement, passing the very spot where Steve and I had our fight. I swallow my pride. I'm back where I belong. I have what I need and want. The dehumidifier is still carrying on its endless war against the moisture. My bed is made, and the possessions that were mine but not mine are still here—board games on the shelf, some books, the weights I was using for exercise. I turn out the bag onto the bed and arrange my clothes in the drawers of the armoire. Then I sit on the end of the bed and gather myself. This time I'm going to do a better job of protecting myself. I remind myself that I won't open my heart again. I am biding my time until I finish high school.

I step up onto the stairs, knowing the part I am going to play. By the time I go back upstairs, my perfect-boy smile is back on my face. The incident and my departure are never discussed again. Only years later will Holly tell me that Steve never accused me of threatening the girls. My social worker somehow got that wrong. I can't say if knowing that would have made a difference, but it doesn't change what mattered most to me—that in a moment of crisis the answer was to get rid of me, perhaps forever.

A few weeks later, on a pleasant spring night, I'm lying down on the lawn in front of the Yankee Pedlar Inn in Holyoke. Next to an antique horse-drawn wagon, I kiss Marianna and move my hands around her body like an alien on a foreign planet.

Pre-prom, we had gathered at Holly and Steve's along with Jessica and Sam. Marianna had called all the shots leading up to this night.

"Black. You'll wear a traditional black tux. I want a white corsage. Don't get me red, okay? Red is for sluts. I want white."

"I believe white signifies mourning or death."

"No. I definitely want white."

Holly's father owned a restored 1920s Mercedes, a convertible with a canvas top, running boards, whitewall tires, and a spare tire mounted on the side of the car. He parked it on the front lawn, and we posed for pictures in front of it. The prom photos look just as they should—me and Marianna, Jessica and her date—four teens having the quintessential prom experience.

On the dance floor, I played the part, grinding on her to Boyz II Men and TLC, conspiring as we snuck sips of booze from disposable cups. Then she led me out to the lawn, where we joined all the other couples, everyone making out. I could feel Marianna wanting to go further, wanting to make this night something it couldn't possibly be. I'm sure she could tell there was something different about me. What was more important to her was that I was a perfect prop. I fit like the perfect white corsage.

Near the end of my junior year, like all the other kids in my class, I meet with my guidance counselor to discuss my future. It's the conversation I've been waiting for since returning to Holly's house. My guidance counselor, Mr. Granger, has a daily uniform of tired slacks and a muddily patterned blazer. Displayed on his desk is a photomontage of a banal family doing banal things. It's either his family or the one that came with the frames. On the wall behind him, triangular pennants from educational institutions hang optimistically. He's the epitome of bland, but today he's the most exciting person to me. He tells me to take a seat and sits across from me, hands folded.

"Vassar College is my first choice. I also like NYU—" I start in right away, but he cuts me off.

"David, be realistic, you cannot get into Vassar," he says.

I'm confused.

"Remember what I told you? A two-year community college is a great starting point. Very affordable. You can live at home while you attend."

It's obvious to me what's happening now, and I straighten up, put up my guard. All he sees is a foster youth with no resources who has transferred four times in three years of high school, unenrolling and reenrolling twice at this school. I have a D on my transcript in pre-calculus, an incomplete in health, and other mediocre grades. He ignores the mitigating factors: the itinerant childhood, the trauma, the multiple guardians. He doesn't see my high PSAT score, my passion for learning, and my ambition. He blows past my political engagement and foster care advocacy. He doesn't understand that it's a miracle that I've managed to get this far. He thinks he knows what's best for me. As he goes on and on about the benefits of community college, its afford-ability, and the fact that I could remain close to my family, he becomes noise and air. I no longer hear what he's saying because he fails to understand that I'm going to go to a good school, one of the best. I'm going to make an impact. I'm going to have a job, a home, and a life for myself. I'm going to have a legacy. I've already mapped it out in my mind. It's what keeps me going. Vassar's brochure says it's the last train stop on the Metro-North from New York City. Some of the students work in the city and take the train to school. This will be me, and I no longer see Mr. Granger if he doesn't understand that.

"Does that all make sense, David?" he asks when he's done.

"Yes, thank you." I smile and walk out of his office.

I'm going to need to figure this out on my own. On my way out, I pick up every college brochure on display, almost as an act of defiance. Mr. Granger doesn't know how to guide me, nor does any-one else I've met. I stop to examine a bulletin board in the hallway. There are notices for various scholarships, grants, and study abroad programs pinned on this board. I rip off a flyer advertising a scholar-ship program for high school graduates to study in Spain. It includes a host family that will provide food and housing. That sounds good to me. I don't want to stay with Holly and Steve and finish out high school. The pretending is over.

Being fluent in Spanish is mandatory for the program, but I don't let that stop me. I ask one of Jessica's classmates, who is Mexican American, to translate the Spanish part of the application for me. A few weeks later I receive a letter stating that I've been awarded a scholarship to study earth sciences at Práxedes Mateo Sagasta, a junior college equivalent, in northern Spain. I'm not sure how I'm going to do it, given that I don't speak a word of Spanish. Also, foster kids are in state custody until the age of eighteen and aren't allowed to up and leave the country, but none of this matters to me. I'm going to find a way.

Chapter 20

How do we get him to Spain?" Mel asks my attorney, Sue. From the outside, I am functioning, but I've told Mel that I can't stay in school and at the LeBeaus'. I can't stand being in the system any longer.

"Spain? Damn, David. Really?" Sue says resignedly. "He can't leave the country without emancipating, and they're not going to let him emancipate at seventeen. He'll have to exit care."

Foster kids are in state custody until the age of eighteen, and, for the same reasons we're not allowed to go on sleepovers or play competitive sports, we aren't allowed to up and leave the country. Emancipation means leaving the system, and it is aptly named. When I am free I'm also not sure how I'm going to live. She addresses me: "And the only way for you to leave care is to be reunited with your mom."

There is no way I want to be back in my mother's custody. Then I have an idea. "Or father, right? I could be in my father's custody?"

Mel looks confused. Then she says, "You mean Alex Ambroz Sr.?"

"David, you barely know him," Sue says, quickly catching on. "And he's not your father." Alex Sr. has been back in our lives for over a year, and, though he's not my biological father, I'm the one who tracked him down. It wasn't as hard as I thought it would be. Using a phonebook, I looked up private detectives, and a few phone calls led me to a company called People Search. The very nice woman that picked up suggested I have a parent join me before we spoke.

"I appreciate you wanting me to have an adult on the line, but that's not realistic for me. I'm a foster kid. I want to find him to help... to fix that." I knew what chord to strike.

"You sound very determined," she said. To get a phone number is surprisingly cheap—I can cover it with my savings from working at the photo shop. Once we have that squared away, she says, "Okay, tell me everything you know."

I didn't have much to share with her: All I knew was his name, that he was a doctor, that he was married now, and that he had previously been married to my mom in New York City, but apparently it was enough because some weeks later I received a brief letter that included his phone number. Without pausing to think, I dialed it.

"Dr. Ambroz, hello. My name is David Ambroz. I'm Mary's son. Alex and Jessica are my siblings. I wonder if we can talk more about..." I trailed off. I was pretty sure he wasn't my father, but his name was on my birth certificate. He had to have answers—but I didn't know what my questions were.

"I can't talk now. Call me back at this number in one hour." He gave me a different number and hung up. I sat there a little stunned. I didn't know why I was doing what I was doing, but it was already in motion. What was the best I could hope for? What was the worst that might happen? I hadn't even warned Alex and Jessica what I was up to. But I'd come this far, so an hour later I called the other number.

"How did you get my number? What do you want? How are your siblings?" His questions were staccato.

I answered as best I could, and then I said, "I wonder if you'd be up for meeting us here in Western Massachusetts."

"Meet? In person?" he asked, more to himself than to me. "Yeah, yeah, that'd be fine. But you can't call here, do you understand?" We arranged a date and time to meet at the same mall where I often hung out with Alex and Jessica. Now I just had to tell them that I'd tracked their father down without considering their thoughts or emotions.

When I told Holly, she was cautiously supportive. "Just remember, he hasn't been in your life for a reason. You've found him, but that doesn't change him. I just don't want you to be…" There was a long pause as she searched for the right word. "Disappointed."

That weekend, at the mall, I blurted out, "I found your dad," in the food court. Alex and Jessica stopped eating their pizza and simultaneously looked at me with their heads cocked to the same side.

"Huh," Alex said.

Jessica nodded and said, "Okay." They didn't have much of a reaction—at least nothing on the surface. They, too, knew he hadn't tried to find us or help us over all the years. If anything, it was remarkable that he'd agreed to come.

A few weeks later, Holly drove us to the meeting. In the mall parking lot, before we got out of the car, she said, "Listen. This is big. I just want to make sure you know that Alex Sr. is just a man. He's not going to rescue anyone. You are all strong, and you've come so far. I understand you want to meet him, but don't expect anything from him." She had spoken to him on the phone before this meeting, and she looked me in the eye to make sure I understood, and then turned to the back seat to do the same to Alex and Jessica. We all nodded.

He was standing outside of Foot Locker at a fountain turned dirt patch in the mall. He looked to be in his late forties with some extra pounds on his torso and a thinning chestnut-brown hairline. His button-down shirt was too big, and he wore frumpy khakis. But beneath his thick glasses was an enormous smile, and as we got closer, I noticed that his eyes looked kind. He reminded me of Alex—an older, fuller version. Surrounded by the hum of a slow day at the mall, he stood in front of us, the man that Mom had always referred to as our father, whose name I carried. He greeted us with his hand extended.

He gave me a firm handshake, then shook hands with Jessica and Alex. We didn't hug. Did I want him to hug me? I wasn't sure.

"So you're the detective," he said to me.

"Yes, I'm David."

"You're not one of mine, you know."

I froze. Though his message wasn't unexpected, his words were a sniper's fire to my chest. Still, my smile didn't falter. I didn't want to ruin it. "I see" was all I mustered in response, and he turned his gaze.

"Alex! Wow," he said, marveling at how alike they looked. "It's like looking at myself back when I was a ladies' man. And, Jessica, you're a beauty." We walked over to the food court and sat down. There was an awkward pause until Holly said brightly, "Let me get us all some drinks and snacks at Cinnabon."

"How's foster care?" Alex Sr. asked us in exactly the same way someone might ask how school was going.

"Uh, okay," I said, not knowing how else to answer such a question from a person who was on all of our birth certificates.

"I thought this might happen," he said. "Your mother always had her issues. I did what I could." My hackles went up. This man had no right to insult our mother. She fought to keep us, and he walked away.

He continued, "You can't—you can't—you can't let her know that we're talking."

I didn't like how focused he was on hiding our contact from everyone, but Holly had warned us.

While I felt conflicted, like I wanted something from him that I knew he would never give me, Jessica and Alex just seemed excited to talk to him, to be near him, and to hear from him. They knew not to expect much from him, but I could tell a little bit of them hoped for it anyway.

"Do you have kids? Are you still married?" Jessica asked.

"Oh, I do. They're the best. A daughter, Jenny, and my son, Adam. They are a marvel, so smart." How could he gush over his two children while staring at his first boy and girl, whom he knew nothing about? I could hear Jessica's tone deflate, but she still wanted to know how old they were, what they were like, and whether they knew we were alive.

"They're aware," he said, "but I haven't shared any details. My mother, your grandmother Ella, asks about you, though. She lives in Trieste. That's in Italy. You have a lot of family in that area and in Slovenia, and they're always asking about crazy Mary's kids."

Crazy Mary's kids? So they did know we existed. And that's how they thought of us—we were Mary's, not theirs. Worse, they knew she was not well, and their response had been to insult her and to abandon us. My emotions swirled. In his candor, he was setting off countless land mines of emotion. We were gobsmacked, with two-dimensional smiles on our faces.

Holly intervened.

"Alex, why don't you tell your father about how great you're doing in school?" Holly said, and I could see that she wanted him to understand what he'd missed.

When our Cinnabons were gone and we'd exhausted the small talk, we rose from the table. We didn't want to be rescued—not anymore, not by this man. But we wanted a father. It was clear that this man was kindhearted, probably beloved by his patients and his other family, but he was weak and oblivious to what he had condemned us to. I wanted to ask him, *What's wrong with you? Why would you leave us with her?* But it was clear that he wouldn't have answers that changed anything.

I realized that I felt a sense of relief that he was not my father, sad that the question was still out there unanswered, and worried about what I'd unleashed in Alex and Jessica. Though they seemed happy and optimistic, I didn't know what was going on with them under the surface.

"I have to go," he said abruptly. "They...she doesn't know I'm here. You can't call, okay? Here, take some money." He pulled out a wad of cash.

"Dr. Ambroz—Alex—may I take a photo?" I asked.

"Um, yeah, okay. But don't share the photo." So the three of us surrounded him on both sides, and Holly snapped a picture.

Then he turned and walked away, just as he had when Alex and Jessica were babies. When he disappeared down the hall, Holly stood opposite the three of us and looked at us, concerned. "That was hard. Are you okay? Come here." She pulled us into a family hug. We made our way back to the van, and Holly drove Jessica and Alex back to Brenda's.

"You'll find him, David. *Your* father," she said when we were alone together, as if reading my mind.

As bad as the meeting was with Alex Sr., it did make me want to find my father one day. Maybe he would be just as disappointing, but maybe not.

———

I wasn't sure why I'd reached out to Alex Sr. in the first place, but all at once, talking to my lawyer about how I could get to Spain, his purpose in my life became clear.

"If he *were* my legal father, he could take custody of me. Then I'd be emancipated from foster care, and I could go to Spain, right? Because if he claims to be my father, I guarantee no other father is going to step forward to argue." Sue and Mel reluctantly agree that this might work, so I try out the idea on Alex.

"Bro, shouldn't you finish high school? You missed enough already." Alex is sitting on his bed at Brenda's. He's a senior, and he's been accepted at the University of Massachusetts and will be rooming with one of his friends from high school. He's very eager to go, but he's already getting nervous about how to pay for his education. While he's gotten some financial grants and waivers, it's not going to be enough to cover his costs of food, housing, books, and just life. He's been working at Amherst Laundromat, trying to save up money.

Jessica, who's leaning against the door, says, "I just want to make sure you have thought about this." She, too, has college plans. She's going to Regis College, a private college outside Boston. She wants to study psychology and to become a social worker. She wants to work with kids. Since both of them are already facing the financial realities of college, they want to make sure I understand that if I emancipate, the system will no longer provide me with health care, housing, food, and clothing. I'll be on my own with no idea where my next meal is coming from.

I can't explain why I need to get away from the last seventeen years of my life. It's not my foster family, we've reached a loving peace. I can't stand the system, with its social workers, visitation schedules, state therapists, approvals for every step I want to take. I'd been wearing a fake smile for seventeen years just to get by, trying to be the perfect boy to get the basics, and I just want all of it to stop. I need to preserve the kernel of myself that still exists. I've been taught over and over that the only person I can rely on is me. I want my legal status to reflect that. I want to be emancipated, free.

"I'm not sure I can ride out this placement. It's not Holly and Steve—things are way better with them."

"They love ya, man. You know that."

"I know they do, but I've just got to get out. I can't do foster care anymore. It's crushing me."

"Bro, Alex Sr. isn't going to help you," Alex insists, always the truth teller. "The best we get out of him is a random short visit, and some cash once in a while. He blames it on his wife—says she won't let him talk to us. Yeah, right." However disappointed Alex might be in his father, he wants what's best for me, and he wants me to get what I need. I know that while he's tempering my expectations, he's probably considering if and how he can get Alex Sr. to help me. The three of us are still one for all.

"Maybe I can convince him to do this one thing, to help me get out of foster care. He won't have to actually do anything except show up in court and sign some papers."

"I think you should go for it," Jessica says, "but think of a plan B."

"Good luck," Alex says, but I still hear the doubt in his voice. "If anyone can get him to, it's you."

When I call Alex Sr., he's not happy to hear from me. His wife doesn't want him to have anything to do with "Mary's children." I start in immediately about what I need, and I try to use his guilt to pressure him. "Look, I need this. I need to get out of foster care," I plead. "You left us with Mom. Please don't leave me in the system. This will change everything for me. It will help me make something of my life. I would be so grateful." All will be forgiven, I imply, if he just does this one thing.

He takes a few breaths before he responds. "I understand what you're asking. I'll show up, say that I'm your father, and take legal custody, but I won't actually have to take custody of you, right? You're not mine, and you definitely can't try to come live with me. Audrey will divorce me. Your mother did a number on her. So once I do this, you're on your own, you understand?"

"You'll take custody on paper, and then I'll walk away from you right away. You won't be responsible for me in any way, I promise."

"Okay, okay. But remember you can't call here. You can't live with me." I see nothing of myself in him, or my brother or sister. I have his last name, it's on my birth certificate, and in that way I'll have to live with him my whole life. He's not my biological father, but his continuous rejection hurts.

"I won't call. I promise," I say.

Once he agrees, I have all the relevant parties in agreement: my social worker, my attorney, my foster parents, and my pseudobiological parent. I know this is what the judge needs to see, and I'm proud that I've pulled it together.

When my court date arrives, I'm nervous that Alex Sr. will lose his nerve and won't actually make the drive from West Virginia to Massachusetts. He's given me no reason to believe he's reliable. So I am surprised and relieved when he walks through the door of the courtroom.

"You know, I'm not sure about this," he says.

"You are saving me. You have no idea."

Moments later, he's speaking to the judge. "Yes, Your Honor. David Ambroz is my son. It's on his birth certificate."

This man is not my father. He could have rescued us, and he didn't. All he is to me is an instrument to get what I want. The judge, in black robes, looks down at me from a slightly elevated desk covered with teetering piles of manila folders. He peers at me over his glasses. "David, do you understand the implications here? Will you be able to adapt and be under Dr. Ambroz's care?"

"Yes, Your Honor. I've always wanted to be with my father." The sincerity in my own voice and words takes me by surprise. I suppose the desire to be with my father—not this man but my real father—is coming through.

With custody transferred, I am officially released from the foster system. "Thank you, Dr. Ambroz...Alex," I say, when we exit the room.

"Yeah, yeah. Remember, no calls. You understand, yes?"

"I understand. Yes." I'm too happy to be disappointed by him again.

"Good, good. Here." He gives me seventy-five dollars and a pat on the shoulder. "Good, good." He turns and heads back home to his family.

My lawyer shakes my hand. "David, are you going back to the LeBeaus'?"

Now that I'm free, I can't imagine going back to live with Holly and Steve. They are supportive of my plans to go to Spain, and their home is open to me, but I want to begin my new life starting now.

"I'll be fine, Sue. I'm going to crash with Jessica. Don't worry."

"You take care of yourself, David," Sue says, patting my shoulder, and she walks away.

Just like that, I am standing alone on the courthouse steps. I look up and around, and what was crushing me lifts. No more group homes. No more foster homes. No more surprise moves. I'm fully in control. Being responsible for myself is a new weight, one that I accept gladly.

⟵

I spend the months before I leave for Spain sleeping on the floor of the two-bedroom apartment that Jessica has moved into with three roommates in Amherst. Their boyfriends come and go. There are no regular meals, and we often order in from cheap places. The women are gross and messy. Their hair is everywhere. I try to keep the place clean, but it's a losing battle. I love every crazy minute of it.

One day Jessica tells me that she got me some shifts at Amherst Laundromat, where she and Alex work. "It doesn't pay much," she tells me, "but people tip when they pick up their laundry. And, honestly, you just give people quarters, fold laundry, and tidy."

The laundromat is a quiet refuge, where folding clothes is a reprieve from the chaos of living with four women. I love the whole process of laundry, sorting colors and whites, using the right detergents, and especially pulling piles of warm fresh clothes out of the huge dryers. The summer months pass quickly until, at last, I escape to Spain.

"Ladies and gentlemen, thank you for flying Continental Airlines. Our flying time today will be six hours and forty-three minutes." This plane has eight seats per row, and I'm in a middle seat. Above me is my carry-on, a black gym bag that I bought with tips from the laundromat. I have my passport and cash in a flat money pouch that hangs around my neck, under my shirt. A movie comes on the TV mounted on the ceiling a few rows ahead. My headphones don't fit the jack, but I watch the movie anyway, without sound. Before I try to sleep, I reread a letter that the program forwarded to me. It's from the woman, Gabriela, who's going to be my host mother. My sister's friend translated it for me, and her penciled notes are written above the Spanish.

David,

I was excited to learn about you. I can't wait to share my love of my country with you. I know you're going to fall in love with it too. I have an adult daughter, Ava, who is studying English abroad right now. And I have a very big family . . .

In the same envelope is a four-by-six photo. It's a candid shot of Gabriela and her adult daughter in the kitchen. They are making something chocolate, and they're about to smear it on each other's faces. They're both laughing. Soon I'm going to meet this woman. I'm going to live in her apartment with her. I close my eyes and try to imagine my new life.

When we land at Heathrow, I hurry to find my connecting flight to Madrid. The second flight is short, and in this airport everyone around me is speaking Spanish. I don't understand a word. Luckily, my scholarship program has someone there to greet me.

"David Ambroz," he says, stepping forward as I walk out of security, but with his accent it sounds more like "Dah-veed Ambroth."

"Yes . . . sí," I say. And that is all of the Spanish I know.

"It's fine, I speak English. Come with me." He grabs my bag, leads me to a small van, and drives me to an orientation at a converted monastery. Along with thirty other grant recipients, I spend a day getting basic cultural training. They explain the currency, what to do in an emergency, and what kind of behavior is expected of us. The next morning, I'm driven to a bus station to really begin this adventure.

It's a six-hour bus ride from Madrid to Logroño, the capital of La Rioja, with stops along the way. I find a seat in the back of the bus.

We drive along smooth, wide highways, but soon we follow smaller highways that climb up hillsides. I tear into the sandwich I was given, watching the countryside become more and more desertlike, until I fall asleep. When we reach Logroño, I step out of a bus, and before I have a chance to look around, a big-breasted middle-aged woman comes up to me and says, "David?" She's wearing a T-shirt, jeans, and a soccer jacket. I recognize the woman before me from her picture. She is heavier and has just a little more gray; an unlit cigarette hangs from her lips and bobs when she talks, but the benevolent smile is the same.

"You must be Gabriela," I say, reaching to shake her hand, but she pulls me in and wraps her arms around me in a tight hug. She starts speaking in Spanish right away. I look at her blankly and throw her a big smile instead. "No Spanish?" she asks.

"No, mucho," I admit. I don't want to get kicked out of the program for not speaking Spanish, and I study her face to see if she's disappointed or going to report me.

"Oh, David," she says, as if I'm an old friend with a long-standing foible, and she gives me another warm hug. I follow Gabriela to her car, and she continues to speak in Spanish. I don't understand a single word, but I can tell she's kind. Her words are a soft white noise, and I try not to doze.

She lights her cigarette at the car. "¿Qué necesitas? ¿Comida? ¿Tienes hambre?"

Hambre. I think I know "hambre." Does it mean "man"? Oh, shit, no, it must be "hunger." "¡Sí!" I say excitedly. I am hungry. She laughs, and I don't know what's funny, but she must have read my mind because in the car she gives me a potato tortilla sandwich.

"Gracias," I say. My other Spanish word. The sandwich is delicious. She smiles and steers us out of the parking lot. An even greater sense of adventure fills me, clashing with the new feeling of jet lag. My world has gotten bigger overnight.

She drives us through a few small villages, down twisted roads bordered by epic rows of vineyards. We're heading to her home, and I can't believe I'll be living here, in these beautiful villages, for the next year.

It's dark when we arrive at her apartment. Two days of travel have exhausted me, and it's written all over my face. "Deja tu equipaje, lo recogeré más tarde," she says, and from the gesture she's making, I put down my luggage. "Duerme," she says, pointing to a twin-sized bed, and without a word, I gladly obey.

In the morning, I wake up facedown, still wearing the clothes I've had on for two days. She's covered me with a light sheet. Gabriela must sense that I'm awake because she immediately knocks and enters. She opens the window in my room. Light pours in, along with the earthy smell of yeast from a bakery somewhere. "David, *ven*, come."

She leads me to the kitchen, but I see the bathroom and peel off to pee. I don't know what to make of the toilet—it has handles and a nozzle, but I have to let loose anyway. When I'm done, I lean forward to turn the handles, and water shoots straight up in my face. *Damn*, I think, *toilets work differently here*. Then I notice that next to this receptacle is a recognizable toilet. I've just peed in what I'll find out is the bidet.

After I wash up, I find Gabriela bustling around the kitchen. It's small with a square oak table in the middle and a half-sized European refrigerator, which I'll learn is all you need when you buy fresh food at the market every day like Gabriela and everyone in the village. A sunny balcony looks out onto an interior courtyard. A clothesline is stretched from one end of the balcony to the other, and colorful linen napkins are hung on it to dry. Gabriela gestures for me to sit down at the table, then puts a plate in front of me heaped with Spanish tortillas—a thick, frittata-like dish with potatoes, onions, peppers, and garlic—salad, and freshly baked bread. I've never had anything but supermarket bread, and the crackly crust and moist, airy interior blow my mind. I devour her food, and she sits across from me and eats a little bread while looking intently at me. "Mira, hijo, tienes que aprender español, pero rápido. ¿Me entiendes? Está bien. Aprendes conmigo." She waves her hand back and forth between us. I assume she's saying something about teaching me or talking to me. I nod in agreement in between bites of the fresh bread.

The junior college where my program takes place is two villages away. The first day, Gabriela drives me to her variety store, where she sells magazines, candy, CDs, and other random things. It's a narrow storefront in a long string of retail. From there, it is a two-mile walk to school. In front of the school is a white stone statue of Dante, sitting like Rodin's *The Thinker*. I notice that there's a cigarette, freshly lit, in his hand.

"David?" An older woman who is smoking on the steps calls out to me. "Hola, soy Lourdes. Ven conmigo." She abandons her half-smoked cigarette in an ashtray as she leads me into the school. There's still so much left to smoke that I reflexively think I should pocket it for my mother.

Lourdes escorts me to the door of my classroom. I take a seat in the back row to avoid being called on. The teacher introduces herself and begins to speak. I don't understand a word she says. All I know is that I'm supposed to be learning earth sciences with an emphasis in biochemistry.

"¡El americano!" says a young man on the way out of class. "Hola, soy Mateo. ¿David, sí?"

Mateo is gorgeous, with black hair, a solid build visible through his T-shirt, and a wide smile. I'm somewhat startled by his friendliness, but the moment is salvaged when the rest of his posse comes up. He introduces them: Talya, Esteban, Sofía, Martín. When they meet me, they air-kiss both my cheeks, even the men. I love it.

On a break, Mateo says, "Ven, traemos quieres un helado? conos de helado." I stare blankly, so he draws an ice cream cone on the page of his notebook. I finally understand, but it doesn't matter—I'll go wherever he wants to take me.

We walk to the ice cream shop, and on the way they try out their English on me.

"You are americano," Talya says. Her long black hair is pulled back tight. Her shirt, tucked into tight, high-waisted jeans, barely contains her large breasts. "Do you love Spain?"

"Yo quiero España," I stammer, and everyone laughs. At the ice cream store, I listen carefully when they order, then do my best to imitate them. "Un coño de chocolate," I request with a polite smile. Mateo and his friends scream with laughter. I have no idea what I've done wrong. "Un coño de chocolate, por favor," I repeat.

Sofía is weeping with laughter. "*Cono*," she says. "No *coño*."

"This is *coño*," Martín says, helpfully pointing to Talya's groin. She slaps away his hand. I bury my face in my hands, completely embarrassed, but Mateo pries them away and hands me an ice cream cone.

"Un...*cono*...de...chocolate," he says slowly with a smile, prompting me to say it with him, and my new friends applaud when I get it right.

"¡Eso es!" Sofía chimes in. The awkwardness that was a struggle for me in Massachusetts comes across differently here. When I don't know what to say, people cut me slack. They assume it's a language barrier, not a life barrier.

After classes end, I walk back to the store where Gabriela works.

"Vamos, David. Ayúdame." Gabriela gently nudges me to help her lock up the store. Then we make our way home for siesta. At 4:30 p.m., everything shuts down for a good three hours before reopening in the evening. It's strange to me, but I could use a break from trying to understand earth science in Spanish.

Gabriela serves me a simple meal of lentejas—lentils made in a pressure cooker, and croquetas—fried corn fritters. We eat together in the living room. It's a nicely lit room with three windows looking out on the street, and the couch has warm, well-loved blankets. Gabriela pushes a book toward me. It appears to be from the series of simplified versions of the classics that they sell at her store. She tells me to read to her in Spanish. I don't understand any of it, but she says, "Lo harás, lo harás. Solo sigue leyendo." *You will, you will, just keep reading.*

I've never seen someone more patient. In the evenings, Gabriela teaches me to cook. We make paella and pimientos, roasting the red peppers, peeling the skins while they're still hot, and preserving them in olive oil. I've been wanting to become a vegetarian, and here in farm country, where there are pig legs—jamón—hanging from restaurant ceilings and people drink wine out of a goat's bladder on special occasions, I find a new resolve. I can't fathom eating the chickens after seeing them run around in front of me. Gabriela finds this amusing. She starts to call me *lechuga*, which means "lettuce." I've struggled with food issues in the past, but Gabriela teaches me her passion for "la tierra, la comida, y la vida." *The earth, food, and life.*

On the weekends I go with Gabriela to the village's plaza. The village is a warren of narrow streets, but the main plaza is wide open, anchored by a tan sandstone church and the adjacent church buildings that have been converted to stores and other new uses. There is a fountain in the center of the stone square, and bars and restaurants with colorful flap curtains hanging over the doorways to deter the flies. Out front, there are tables full of people, and that's where we sit. Gabriela and her friend Carmela sip wine, smoking incessantly and talking nonstop. Carmela owns the tiniest tobacco store—a closet off the plaza—and she has the hoarse voice and leathery skin of a devoted smoker. The smell of tobacco hovers around her. They talk about everything and nothing—what they've seen, what they're going to do, what they're having for dinner, and politics. The native ethnic people of this region are Basque, and to be Basque is to be politically aware. I enjoy nodding along like I understand, and Gabriela often slows down to repeat something and asks me to respond. Folks meander through the tables, pausing to chat or argue with Gabriela and her friend. This is a village, and everyone knows each other. Conversations that began ages ago continue every day in the plaza.

On most weekends, Gabriela insists on taking me on adventures. I tell her that she doesn't have to—I can stay home and study—but she wants to show me España. I get a kick out of how she treats me like I'm eight years old. Thrusting an arm in front of me to keep me safe when I'm crossing the street, hugging me to give me comfort if she thinks I'm nervous. I quickly understand that Gabriela was born to be a mother. She's an empty nester, and she isn't done mothering. In me, she has a newborn; Spain is new to me, and I am ready to learn everything. I'm the complete focus of her life. There's something about the way she loves me that fills a void for both of us. Her eyes on me are always caring, attentive, and a home of sorts.

Her pride and love of her people and country are infectious. The two of us go on long drives on the roads that wind through the lush green valleys, passing Basque vineyards with bright green grapevines planted in orderly lines that follow the contours of the hills, and quaint medieval villages with mazes of cobbled alleys. One day, when I've been with her for about a month, we take a one-lane mountain road up to the foothills that bleed into the Pyrenees.

"Ay, David. Qué va. No. No puedo volver a escucharlo," Gabriela pleads when she sees me inserting the one cassette tape we have—the soundtrack from *Forrest Gump*. *I can't take it again.*

"Madre, no te pongas histérica." *Relax*, I tell her. We've heard the tape so many times on these drives that even she could sing the songs in English.

"¡Joder, para!" Gabriela commands me to stop the car. In the middle of the road stands an enormous cow. The road is cut into a hill, with steep rock on the right side, and a sheer drop on the left. Where the cow came from or is going is a mystery. The cow stares at us indifferently. She doesn't move, and we're stuck. I step out of the car. I can see my breath in the air, and it smells of rain and earth and cow.

"A fumar," Gabriela says, defending her right to light a cigarette because she knows I'll protest. This is our usual dance. She takes out a cigarette, I say no, and she promises to stop. So far I've gotten her to agree to not smoking in the house and when I'm in the car with her, but she grunts, "Cabrón americano," *American bastard*, every time I remind her. It's a strange reversal because I was my mom's cigarette supplier. Deep down, I know that I'm still doing the same thing; I haven't changed. I mother my mothers. Away from everyone in the US, I begin to learn these things about myself.

Eventually, the cow ambles past, expertly owning the few feet of clearance, like the mountain cow that it is. We get back into the car, this time with me at the wheel. We chug up toward the highest peak we can see. I belt out the songs of *Forrest Gump*, and Gabriela rolls her eyes at me, shaking her head but grinning.

She loves me, even when I drive her crazy, which makes me adore her more. I can't think of any other relationship when I've allowed myself to be this person. Kind of like a kid, I think. Perhaps it's that I'm not just learning the language of Spanish but how to be a child too. At Holly's, I was emerging from a traumatic situation that made me think behaving like a servant would protect and ingratiate me. Holly had started me on the journey to understanding that love is not earned through labor, and that there would not be repercussions if I made a mistake. Holly did so much, but it is taking me time. Maybe it's learning a new language, or maybe it's because everything is new, but here, I'm allowing myself to learn to walk, one clumsy step at a time.

The higher we climb up the mountain, the more we can see the taller mountains beyond. Snow and small rockslides pile onto the edges of the road. We trace the shape of the mountain, curving in toward the mountainside and then turning back out and being rewarded with views of the whole valley. I roll down my window and stick my head out to feel the freezing wet air. I'm away from the foster parents, the abuse, the system, and the poverty. It's all behind me. I'm soaring, I'm free. I chose this. I inhale it.

"Estamos aquí, hijo," she says. *We are here, son.*

Gabriela parks the car. We are maybe a third of a mile from the peak, accessible up a rutted fire road. The ground up here is frozen mud. The wind is fierce. We start to climb.

"Para, niño." Gabriela beseeches me to slow down.

I tease her for smoking too much, grin, then put my arm in hers and encourage her along. She smiles back. What we thought would be a simple walk turns out to be more like a mile. Near the peak are the remains of a stone shed, built from watermelon-sized rocks. "Este era un refugio para pastores," Gabriela explains. This was a small shelter for shepherds. Gabriela waits while I climb its walls and sit on the roof at the very top of the mountain. A sweeping vista spreads before me. Down below is a verdant valley, dotted with farms. It is bright green down there. Up here the mountain air is fresh and cold. There are no more trees. I turn around and see the snowcapped mountains stretching into the horizon. The contrast is so stunning, my heart swells. Gabriela smiles up at me, wrapped in her windbreaker, her cheeks red like apples. Her smile is pure. I am in love with this mother, this moment, this mountain.

When I step down, Gabriela hugs me fiercely. At first, I think it's just that she's cold, but then she says, "David, es tuyo." *David, it's yours.* She gestures toward the mountain. I look at her, puzzled.

"De ahora en adelante este es el monte de David." *From now on this is Mount David.* Gabriela gives me this mountain. "Siempre puedes volver a casa. A tu montaña." *You can always come home to your mountain.*

This mountain is mine. The mountain is forever, timeless, and it's where I belong. My mom gave me life, Holly gave me love, and Gabriela gives me the earth. Together, we look out toward the snow-covered mountains, wind tearing across the rocky grass. I feel her love and see my own mother in her. Physically, they are both short, full women with short hair and always a cigarette within reach. But in Gabriela I also see who my mother might have been if she weren't cursed by mental illness.

The mountain is almost big enough to fill the void that my mom left in my heart, and in some way Gabriela is too. "Hace un frío que te cagas," Gabriela says, and she's right. It *is* cold as shit.

"Oy, madre," I say with love, and we get back into the car for the long ride home.

Gabriela's mission is to show me her love of Spain, and a few weeks later she starts badgering me about an upcoming weekend wine festival to celebrate the grape harvest—Las Fiestas de San Mateo in Logroño. She keeps asking what my festival plans are and which of my new friends will be taking me to the festival. When Mateo mentions it, I suspect Gabriela may have put him up to it. I'm nervous about spending a whole weekend with my schoolmates. A night at the bar is fine, but a whole weekend? Gabriela is a Basque Spanish woman of the wine country—resistance of such a force is futile. I say yes.

Beep, beep. "*David!*" I hear through the open windows. I look down and see Mateo on his scooter, having stopped and pulled out a cigarette. He is only about five eight, but in my mind he is ten feet of sexy. He's wearing jeans, a loose T-shirt, and a helmet. One muscular arm clutches the handle of his scooter. The other is thrusting a second helmet up at me.

"¿Quieres ir conmigo?" Mateo asks if I want to ride with him to the festival.

"¡Sí!" Gabriela says before I can respond. I look at her to see if she's onto my crush, but she just gives me a big smile and hands me some pesetas.

"Gracias, madre," I say and lean into her hug.

"*¡Eh! ¡Pásalo bien!?*" Gabriela commands me to have a good time. *Let down your hair, relax, and drink,* she says, not with words so much as her eyes. She pulls out of the hug and puts her hands on my shoulders. "*¿Sí?*"

"Sí, madre, sí." When I get outside, Mateo has lit a cigarette and removed his helmet. His cheap Spanish cigarette, a Ducados, hangs out the side of his mouth as he kisses me once on each cheek. I climb up behind him and sit with my legs wrapped around his hips. I lean back to hold the bar behind me, but Mateo says something that I think means I should hold on to him. *Oh God, yes.* I put my hands around his chest, tentatively at first, then gripping tight as the scooter zooms ahead. He flicks the cigarette, proclaims, "Vámonos," and off we go.

I'm still not sure about the festival—I barely know these friends—but I know it's right to be here, on Mateo's scooter, pressed into his back. Mateo speeds through the vineyards, land that is deep tan and sprawling with ancient, lush vines. The vineyard rows roll over the hills in perfectly symmetrical patterns. The road dips up and down gradually; the bike is noisy and vibrates with speed, but I am focused on the heat of Mateo's body, holding him tightly as we lean into turns, penetrating the heart of the old city.

Soon there is a break in the vineyards, and we meet up with a freeway that follows the Ebro River into town. It is crowded with scooters, cars, and people—the traffic is nearly at a standstill as everyone pours from the countryside into town.

Finally, Mateo pulls the bike into a *chamizo*, a storefront that our friends have rented for the weekend. I'm a little sad that the journey has ended and there likely won't be much more alone time with Mateo. As we push through the door, a cloud of cigarette and hashish smoke fills my nose. It looks like a languorous Roman dinner scene with scruffy tables, dusty couches, and half-collapsed futons, haphazardly placed around the room. Mateo throws an arm around my shoulder and guides me toward Talya and the rest of our small posse—Esteban,

Sofía, and Martín. "Venga, hola…" "Qué hay…" "¡Lechuga!" "Ven aquí…" I barely know these classmates, but they treat me like an old friend or a beloved pet.

Someone pulls me onto a sofa. I land half on Esteban. "Joder, David," he says, laughing while pushing me off. Squished as we are, that push brings me closer into Sofía. She throws her arm around me and hugs me to her side.

"Está bien, David, puedes senterte aquí," she says in a fake sultry tone, and the pat on her lap helps me across the language barrier.

Martín, who likes to be the center of attention, stands up in front of the group. "Mira…" *Look.* We turn to him, but now that he has all eyes on him, it's unclear if he actually has anything to say. He pivots into what I think is a joke, although the Spanish is so rapid and accented that I can't be sure, but I laugh along with the others at his joke or story. I'm not fluent in the language, and that helps me muddle my way through the language of friendship. A bottle of calimocho is passed my way. It's two parts room-temperature red wine to one part Coca-Cola. It loosens my tongue, and I join in the rapid Spanish being thrown around. I'm drinking a lot for the first time, and it numbs my anxiety. I'm less self-conscious, my Spanish gets better, and I come a bit farther out of my shell.

"¡El americano! ¡Él necesita más vino!" says Martín, always the jester and life of the party.

It's as if he's speaking English. "¡Sí, por favor!" I shout. "¡Más vino!" *More wine.*

"¡El americano! ¡Él necesita comida!" says Sofía. *He needs to eat.* She's the mother of this group and sees I'm getting drunk too quickly. Suddenly everyone stands up. The American needs to be fed, so we're going to the festival. It's already night, and I can see only darkness outside. Arms locked, we make our way down the old streets, weaving deeper into the old city. The wine has worked its magic, and I see why it deserves this celebration. I don't feel truly known by these friends, but I feel welcomed and accepted and like part of it all.

"Para...comamos un poquito." Mateo halts the group at a bar. We push our way in. The clear glass cabinets along the bar are filled with *pinchos*, little snack sandwiches and tapas.

"Ay, Martín, pero bueno, déjalo. Que guaro." Sofía condemns Martín for eating more than his fair share.

"Déjame en paz," Martín responds, reminding her that he paid for the food.

We fill up on small squid, countless preparations of *jamón*, and for me, *tortilla de patata*. Then we go off to the next bar, and then the next, running into other people, making new friends. Every person in the city and the surrounding villages that can be here is out on the streets tonight.

"Está bien, puedes decírmelo...Ella te gusta?" I say, nudging Mateo toward Talya. *Tell me, do you like her?* Talya and Mateo have an ongoing flirtation, and I'm secretly curious about what he'll say. Will he deny it? Maybe if he does, that will signal something about how he feels about me.

"No me jodas, David." He denies a crush on Talya. "Toma," he says. *Take it.* He takes a puff of his cigarette and then indicates that I should take a puff. My mouth is where his just was. *I'm tasting a bit of him as I inhale,* I think. *Oh God, yes.* Sharing a cigarette is as close to kissing a man as I've come. I want the moment to last forever, but it ends when he ends it.

Later, back at our *chamizo*, everyone collapses onto futons. I fall asleep, the wine and food now settled in me. After an unknown amount of time, I feel someone shaking me. I open my eyes, and Mateo is standing over me.

"David, ahora o nunca..." he says. *David, now or never.*

"¿Qué hora es?" I ask. *What time is it?*

"¡A bailar!" Talya and Sofía sing out. *Let's dance!*

I look around and see everyone getting ready to go again.

We weave our way to a makeshift club. Lights illuminate the smoke in the air. The music pulses, *thrump, thrump, thrump*. We form an amorphous circle. *Thrump, thrump, thrump.*

Mateo is next to me. "¡Que pasó, David! ¿Estás bien?"

"¿Cómo?" I can't hear a thing.

"*¿Que pasó?*" he yells again. He draws me in by my shoulders, close to him. Our faces are inches apart.

"Qué cosa," Talya says, placing herself between me and Mateo. "Quédate conmigo." She pulls Mateo to her. *Stay with me.* I smile at him and drunkenly wink.

"Te veo pronto, David," he says. *See you soon.*

I nod okay and catch up with everyone else who's going back to sleep at the *chamizo*.

The next morning, Mateo strides out of the bathroom, bare chested, using his shirt to wipe his armpits after his sink shower. I pretend to avert my gaze, but as I do, his eyes meet mine and he smiles. His lips, full and dark red, pull back to reveal the gap between his front teeth. There is a small patch of dark black hair in the middle of his chest. The waistband of his briefs is visible above his jeans, a bold red.

When the group is ready, each of us ties a red handkerchief around our neck, and we go out onto the streets. The crowd throngs toward the center of the old city, and there are so many people out that we can barely walk.

"Aquí, venga." Mateo summons us to line up single file so we can power through the crowd. I'm right behind him, and he grabs my hand and puts it on his waist. Behind me, Talya does the same to me. We are a caterpillar, crawling forward until we lurch to a stop as close to the epicenter as we are going to get. Large trucks are parked along the street, giving out containers of red wine. The sky is pure blue edged by the buildings surrounding the plaza. Esteban hands out water guns and large empty farm jugs that we will fill with wine. My water gun is an enormous, multichambered, fluorescent-green-and-orange

Super Soaker. It has three reserve tanks. I laugh like a kid; how beautifully absurd.

The sides of the trucks drop partway so that we can fill our guns and containers with red wine. There is a mad scramble. Someone dumps an entire container of red wine on me. I taste its tangy residue. This wine hasn't aged at all—it's tart and sickly sweet. From now on I'll be able to recognize our regional table wine. Adrenaline shoots through me, pulsing with the energy of the crowds.

"Say hello to my little friend." I laugh, pumping my enormous squirt gun at a perfect stranger. She's feet away, her own posse behind her. We square off, and I'm doused by streams of wine from all sides. I lose my group, but I don't worry about keeping everyone together. I don't worry about losing everything. I can just be in the moment. I turn and see Talya right behind me. They have not lost me. I aim and shoot forth a stream of wine.

"¡Cara culo, David!" she bellows, catching the wine right in her face. Buckets of wine arrive from all around. When I slip and fall square on my ass in a puddle of red wine, strangers' arms appear to pick me up, broad smiles on their faces. Their shirts are drenched in red wine, and their hair drips on me as they help me to my feet. My gun is cracked and useless. I leave it where it fell. Searching around, I find an abandoned wine container. I dip it into a refill tank and launch the wine out into the crowd, giddy with wine and joy.

"David, aquí estas. Qué haces? Qué cosa." Mateo has found me. He's soaked too. He lifts me up in the air until my pelvis is at his chest level, and then lets me slide down his front. Our world shrinks. Our chests press together; we are face-to-face, alone among thousands of people. I can smell his breath, the hashish, his cologne mixed with wine and sweat. As he stares at me, his smile fades to a deep look. He grabs my hand. "Venga, chico." He leads me through the crowd, his hand tightly around mine, keeping us connected. Wine rains down as we find our way through and out of the plaza and down a narrow street.

"Aquí." We step through a small entry cut out of an enormous old door. We are in an underpass that leads to the courtyard of an ancient home. It's dark and silent.

"David, no puedo. No soy…no…" he insists, as if protesting a move I haven't made. I know he means he's not gay. But he leans into me, pressing me into the wall with his full weight. The kiss is firm and intense, and I feel it everywhere. My hands are at my sides, palms pressed into the rough stone wall behind me. An informal troupe of musicians walks past the open door, playing ballads on local instruments at top volume. He pulls back. "No, David, no. ¡No soy gay!" I'm not sure if he is saying this to me or himself. He pushes me hard, but not with anger. I'm already pressed against the wall, so his shove launches him backward. He turns and, without looking back, steps through the door and disappears. I sink down to a squat, place my head between my knees, and take a deep breath. I can still taste him.

"I am gay, Mateo," I proclaim quietly to the ancient stone walls. It's the first time I've spoken it out loud. I am gay.

Chapter 21

Eʟ Vɪʟʟᴀʀ ɪꜱ Qᴜɪᴇᴛ ᴛʜɪꜱ morning. To the north, the clouds are orderly, herded by the Mediterranean air mass that sweeps in from the sea and confronts the air mass brought in from the Atlantic's Cantabrian Sea. I step out of our apartment onto a street carved a thousand years ago to begin my circuitous run through vineyards—ten miles from El Villar to the picturesque village of Laguardia.

Up and over the vineyard's burnt-amber dirt hills I push myself hard. On my right are the mountains, and on my left are soft rolling hills, fields divided by stone walls, old vines, and some olive trees.

Towering above the main plaza is the village church with barely a window, its old walls three feet thick in places. Small patches of grass grow from cracks. Its door is open, and the smell of incense wafts out as I run past and back out another gate. I take the hilly main road, where there are no sidewalks and no other runners or bicyclists. This is a working community of hardscrabble Basques. Even after I've been doing this for almost a year, small diesel trucks still slow down when they see the odd spectacle of a man running for no apparent reason. I push onward. Today is a big day, and I need this run to relieve my nerves.

Before I left America, I had requested brochures and applications from colleges, and several months ago I sat down to fill them out. At the typewriter in my small bedroom, under an American flag that Gabriela had hung up for me in jest, I typed them out. Gabriela's typewriter was old but functional. Each time I made a mistake, I retyped the whole page. I didn't want to give the unknown person receiving this package any reason to reject me. To add to my overall stress, there was no one to ask questions about the colleges, no one to review my essays, no one to help me with the FAFSA, the form for federal financial aid.

The first hurdle for foster kids like me appeared when the applications requested detailed information about my parents—their names, addresses, and financials. I didn't know how to respond. I had a mother, but she was homeless and mentally ill; I had foster parents, but they had nothing to do with me financially. I didn't know my real father, and Dr. Ambroz had been crystal clear he'd have nothing to do with me. I was unsure of how one could put all of that in a college application, when there was no space for it. Flummoxed, I sat in my room in this farming village and pondered how to prove that I didn't have guardians with resources. How could I prove their absence? Finally, I turned to my former social worker Mel for help. She was the only face that stood out of the crowd of social workers. We wrote back and forth to each other, exchanging letters as we drafted a letter from her that we thought would explain my situation. She sent me a final draft on Commonwealth of Massachusetts stationery, and I added a photocopy of it to each application.

The application fees were another problem. For spending money I'd been working at a bar and helping Gabriela at her store, but I couldn't afford the application fees. For each college, it was sixty to one hundred dollars, and there were no waivers. All I could think to do was write another letter and attach it in place of a check, explaining why I couldn't afford the application fee.

"To Whom It May Concern: I'm sure you've noted the absence of the required application fee. Unfortunately, circumstances beyond my control prevent me from providing it at this time. I hope you'll give me every consideration, nonetheless..."

In the end, I submitted fourteen applications. Each package felt like a lottery ticket, the unlikely dream of a future greater than a kid like me could expect, or even imagine.

As I jog to Laguardia, a hilltop village surrounded by a wall, I pass through Saint's Gate. Like El Villar, this village has narrow old streets, churches, buildings of fieldstone, and cafés everywhere. Flipping my tape for the third or fourth time, I begin back through *Forrest Gump* again. Stopping at a public fountain that runs constantly, I bend over, cup my hands to sip, and splash some on my head like the farmers do to cool off. Here, I notice that the villagers are less startled at the sight of a runner, but they still stare as they walk by, clutching freshly baked bread. It's the hour of the doñas, a time when the widows and senior ladies walk around the plazas just as they do in El Villar.

It's been months now since I filled out the applications. Of the fourteen colleges, four had immediately returned my entire application along with a letter saying that they were unable to process it without the fee. In the last few days, I've received both rejections and admissions from others, but I can't afford the ones that have admitted me so far, some of which have financial aid packages relying on parental loans. But surely the rest will come today, and maybe one of them will offer me enough financial aid that I can attend. Without parents, an inheritance, a family, I believe my future life relies solely on what comes in one of those envelopes. I start to run again, fast. The hills fall behind me, one by one. I increase my speed until my lungs burn. When I return to El Villar, it's illuminated in late morning light. This place has transformed me. Completely isolated from everything I've known, away from the systems that failed me, Spain has been my first venture into a world of my own making, without the smudges of poverty defining my fate. I feel ready to take the next step—but to where? I hurry home to see if the mail has arrived.

Mail is a funny thing here, sometimes arriving early, late, or never. Today, it's early. When I reach the front door of the apartment, Gabriela is there to greet me with a thick envelope in hand.

"¡Lechuga!" she says as she holds the door for me. "Aquí." She pushes the envelope into my chest. The return address is printed in maroon. Vassar College. I tear it open on the spot and withdraw a letter and a folder. I read the first words of the letter: "We want to welcome you to the Class of 2002…" On the folder is a picture of a professor, his beard as white as the envelope, paused on his bike to speak to two students. Framing them is a gorgeous tree, and in the background is a Gothic edifice. The campus looks like a paradise. I see my future.

But "We want to welcome you" is not enough. *How much how much how much…?* "Vassar College," the letter tells me, "has a *need-blind* admissions process, and we will make sure you have the where-withal to attend." Need-blind admissions means that no matter what my financial status, I am in. Accepted. And through a combination of scholarships, federal student loans, and student work programs—they'll make it work financially.

"Lo hice, madre. Después de todo, ¡lo hice!" I scream to Gabriela. *I did it, Mother. After all this, I did it.* How can I communicate to her the depth of what this means? How do I express that I know, and always have known, that college is the only way to break the cycle of poverty and that I'm finally out.

"David, nunca dudé de ti." Gabriela assures me she's never doubted me.

"Lo sé…ya, lo sé." I know she never has. I crush her in a hug. She has such a firm belief that I will do great things. There is no better person to celebrate this moment with me.

The remaining months of my stay in Spain last forever and pass all at once. I'm eager to begin college, but I also love this place. Too soon, it's time for me to say goodbye to Spain, to Gabriela. She's driving me to the airport in the same outfit she picked me up in, impeccably clean; even her jeans have been ironed. She's smoking her third cigarette in violation of her promise not to smoke in the car, but I'm not going to give her a hard time on our last drive together. Her red Peugeot, stick shift, climbs from the plains of La Rioja, up the mountains, north across the Pyrenees, toward the airport in Bilbao.

"David, tienes que cuidarte, ¿me entiendes, hijo?" Gabriela says sternly. *You have to take care of yourself, do you understand, son?*

"Sí, madre, te entiendo perfectamente."

"Hijo, ya sabes que te quiero. Tienes un hogar aqui, siempre. Sé que amas a tu país, pero España puede ocupar un espacio en tu corazón también," Gabriela says. *Son, you have a home here, always. I know you love America, but Spain can have space in your heart too.*

"Sí, madre, sí," I say. "Te quiero mucho, y a España, por supuesto." I confirm my love for her and this land that has welcomed me.

I watch the ash of her cigarette grow longer, impressed that it doesn't fall. For a year, Gabriela has been a source of unreserved love, food, warmth, devotion. Her world has revolved around me. She has taught me Spanish, and how to live and cook. She's taught me how to love.

Spain has been a place of healing, of laughter and carelessness.

"Ay, joder, no me lo puedo..." Gabriela says when the ash drops from the cigarette.

The cassette tape ends. *Click.* I reach over and push eject, and out comes tape one of the *Forrest Gump* soundtrack. I flip it to side B and push it back in. Gabriela still professes to hate it, but on more than one occasion I've caught her humming along. Now her warm hand grasps mine.

"David, cariño, cuidate mucho, pero bien, okay?" Gabriela pleads. *Dear David, take good care of yourself.* A tear runs down her cheek. Her relentless, expressive love has chipped away at my heart, but I still can't cry. She knows this. Gabriela knows that she has cared for a broken boy.

I sit taller in my seat and put my hand on her neck. "Todo está bien."

The highways are smooth, and too soon we are at Bilbao Airport. She parks to walk me in. I hoist my duffel from the trunk and shoulder it. I have saved everything I can to remember this trip: the books from my classes, the thick sweaters that Gabriela gave me to get me through winter, the American flag she insisted I bring home.

She stops me outside the entrance to the airport. "David, tu país es hermoso, tu gente hermosa, pero no puedes dejar de lado todo lo que ganaste aquí. Hay muchas maneras de estar en el mundo. Mira a tu alrededor. Te vas para comenzar algo nuevo y tienes una opción. Puedes ser alguien que sufrió. Puedes ser definido por eso. O puedes ser tú mismo. Todavía no sabes quién es, pero encontrarás al hombre que he vislumbrado." *David, your country is beautiful, your people gorgeous, but you cannot let go of everything you gained here. There are many ways to be in the world. Look around you. You are leaving to begin something new, and you have a choice. You can be someone that suffered. You can be defined by that. Or you can be yourself. You don't know who that is yet, but you will find the man that I have glimpsed.*

We walk into the large atrium and approach the check-in counter. Printers whir behind the attendant. "Pon tu bolso en la báscula." *Put your bag on the scale*, she directs me.

I'm still not a genius at thinking in kilograms, but I know that my bag must weigh nearly double the maximum. The attendant tells me the overweight charge.

"Esa cantidad es ridícula. ¿Qué te pasa? Este boleto cuesta el alquiler de un mes. ¡Ahora quieres más sangre!" *That amount is ridiculous. What is wrong with you? This ticket costs a month's rent. Now you want more blood!* Gabriela rips into this woman.

"Madre, está bien. Pagaré. Tengo mis libros, son pesados." *Mother, it's fine. I will pay. I have my books—they're heavy.*

"*Que no*," Gabriela commands, and pulls out her credit card.

I smile in thanks and hand the woman my passport and Gabriela's credit card. Relieved of the bag, we walk toward the security line. My arm is around her shoulders, and our steps are slow.

"Cariño, tienes tortilla española. Eso debería llevarte todo el camino a casa," Gabriela says. *Honey, you have Spanish tortilla. That should get you all the way home.* She has made me three of them, cut them up, and stuffed them in my backpack.

"Está bien, madre. Estaré bien. Estarás bien. Gracias por su hospitalidad, por compartir su amor por España, por el País Vasco, por La Rioja. Gracias por su paciencia. Gracias por mostrarme una vida diferente a la que he conocido. Gracias por amarme. Volveré pronto, lo prometo," I say. *It's okay, Mother. I'll be fine. You'll be fine. Thank you for your hospitality, for sharing your love of Spain, of Basque Country, of La Rioja. Thank you for your patience. Thank you for showing me a different life than I have known. Thank you for loving me. I'll come back soon, I promise.* Tears are streaming down her cheeks. I know she wants a cigarette. I hug her tightly, kiss her cheeks, and then pull out of the embrace, pick up my backpack, and sling it over my shoulder. One final squeeze, and I turn. A few steps later I turn back and mouth the words in my heart, "Te quiero, madre." *I love you, Mother.*

PART THREE

Chapter 22

In Amherst, on the couch of my sister's summer rental apartment, I open an envelope from Vassar to find a directory with the photos and addresses of each incoming first-year student. I flip to my photo. It's one I had taken at a train station in Spain while Gabriela waited outside, smoking and impatient. It had taken several attempts to get a shot I liked, and despite our being emotionally all over the place about my leaving, I look friendly and eager. I'm wearing a beige Basque fisherman sweater that Gabriela bought me and a big smile. I'm fattened up with food and love. I fit right in alongside all these others. You'd never know what it took for me to get my little square photo in that book, and I'd like to keep it that way.

I am no longer an outlier. I'm staying with Jessica for the summer and getting ready for college the way any kid does, with some modifications. I shop for my dorm room, meticulously checking off the items on the college's suggested packing list. The money I use is from my summer job back at the laundromat, and I stretch it by collecting coupons and price shopping at Caldor, Ames, and thrift stores. Without knowing exactly what a "bathroom caddy" is, I go into the Salvation Army and ask if they have any.

At the end of the summer, a two-car caravan transports me, all of my worldly possessions, and a small group of people that care about me west on the Massachusetts Turnpike to Vassar. I'm in the back seat of Jessica's old tan Mazda, Alex is in the passenger seat next to her, and we're all drunk with this moment. After dropping me off, my sister and brother will return to their colleges. It feels like we've all made it through the war that was our childhood, and we drive along giddy with victory.

Sometimes behind us, sometimes in front, is the cherry-red minivan of the LeBeau family: Holly and Steve with the girls—Brianna, now nine, and Ruth, three—all here to see me off.

I went over to their house to see them at the beginning of the summer, when I first got back from Spain. Brianna was the one to open the door.

"*David!*" she yelled, unabashedly joyous to see me. I hadn't been the best letter writer, but our connection was still powerful.

"Hey, hon. Ughhh, you're squeezing the life out of me!" I laughed.

"It's so good to see you," Holly said as she and Steve came in for a giant hug. Squeezed in somewhere in this circle of familial love was Ruth.

"Come on, I made tri-tip steaks," Steve said. Cooking was his way of showing love. I didn't want to ruin the moment by telling him I'd become a vegetarian, so I knew I'd just cut the food and move it around the plate.

"You did it, David, we are so proud of you," Holly said when we were gathered at the table in the dining room. I didn't know if she meant going to Spain or getting into Vassar, but the year away had made me a different man. In poverty and in foster care, the immediacy of the present had been my whole world. I was always in survival mode. Spain had shown me the size and scope of the world, the different lives that people choose, and that there is more than one way to be.

"You've done good," Steve said. "Now let's eat." Through their consistent love and support, Holly and Steve were teaching me that families can have problems and trauma and regret and forgiveness, that love can survive the hard moments. Though we didn't agree on who caused the rupture, we did want to be in each other's lives. We wanted to love each other again.

"You know, I think you'd really love Gabriela if you met her," I said to Holly.

"I'm certain of it," she said. "Now, what is the plan for getting your butt to Vassar?"

The plan was this caravan that has now brought me from Amherst to Poughkeepsie. Across the entrance to the Vassar campus is a banner of maroon letters against a white background that announces, "Welcome Class of 2002!" We pass through a Gothic stone archway, and a parklike vista opens up. Verdant lawns. Bold flowers of all colors highlight entryways. Leafy trees are interspersed with elegant lampposts. There are even lakes and streams on campus. Beautiful young people and their families move about with purpose, arms loaded with boxes, almost all of them smiling. It's hard to believe that my presence is expected here. That this will be my home for the next four years.

I've lived in streets and shelters and more apartments than I care to remember. I've attended countless different schools, arriving late, unprepared, and unexpected. This year I will start school on time, as planned, at a prestigious institution, with no chance of being transferred or going to school hungry. I don't have to live in the now of survival—I can see the next four years laid out ahead of me. I will be here, and I intend to suck the marrow out of the experience.

We pull up to my dorm, Davison, and are conducted into a parking spot by rabidly enthusiastic students. Sophomore RAs in matching Vassar T-shirts descend on our car to welcome us with hugs. My caravan is carrying more love than stuff. Clothes, books, two sheets, two towels, a pillow, a blanket, a collection of basic school supplies, and the winter clothes that got me through Spain. Besides my duffel, most of what I've brought is in trash bags, my signature luggage, but inside it is clean and neatly folded.

Davison is a late-nineteenth-century building. My dorm room is on the fifth floor in what used to be the attic, and the one service elevator either is being held at one floor or is out of service. My family climbs the stairs, past doors propped open to reveal parents fussing about, helping to make beds and set up rooms. The Dave Matthews Band blares out of more than one set of speakers, competing with the soundtrack from *Bulworth*.

It's clear to me at first meeting that Lucas and Rick, my roommates, are not exactly my people. Rick is six foot four and hardly interested in classes; Lucas is a soccer-playing white dude wearing a hemp hoodie. I can't afford to be picky. I just want to be liked. There are introductions between the families, and I say, "This is my brother, Alex, my sister Jessica, my sister Brianna, and my sister Ruth." I introduce Holly and Steve as my parents, but they are clearly too young to have parented all five of us. "Foster parents," I say to clarify, but that's as far as I'm going to go. Nobody probes.

The bed closest to the window is clearly the best one. At first, we all politely unload our belongings into the middle of the room, but then, suddenly, Rick's parents claim the premium bed for him. Lucas and I look at each other and shrug.

"Which bed do you want?" I ask him.

"I don't care," he says.

"Me neither," I say. There's a pause, and then I choose a bed using shelter-honed criteria: the one in the corner, farthest from others, so you can see the whole room and nobody is behind you. While the families make conversation, I set up my space as I always have, making the bed neatly, refolding my clothes and putting them in the dresser, and lining up the pencils and supplies on the desk. Days after we move in, anyone looking at the three desks in the room would be able to point a finger at them one by one and say, "Disaster. Disaster. Homosexual."

Lucas and Rick pull out their stereos and laptops. I clutch my yellow Walkman tighter. Then Lucas and Rick or their parents start to discuss necessities that they've forgotten. Lucas's parents think he needs a desk lamp. Rick has forgotten his toiletry kit. Their parents are going to take them shopping to fill in the gaps—a kid from downstairs is going with them. Someone invites me to come along. This whole concept is unfamiliar to me. Having addressed the packing list I felt obligated to follow, I don't go buy other things so casually. What I have, I have. What I don't, I don't.

When there is nothing more for my family to do or say, they fuss and linger, lining up books on shelves and organizing my desk needlessly. The only window in the room is at eye level when I'm standing up. I look out, and Alex and Jessica come to stand on either side of me, quiet. We don't say it out loud, but we understand that this day marks the end of our childhood. They've already started college, but I have always brought up the rear, making sure we all stick together, and I am finally across the finish line.

I put my arm around each of them, stare out the window, and say, "We made it. We survived." Whatever highs and lows we had come down to this: We survived, and we love each other. At the dormitory door, Jessica reaches her arms around me. And then Alex pulls us both into an oceanic hug. This is our goodbye.

Families are supposed to leave campus by a certain time, probably to help everyone cut the cords. I walk my family out to their cars. Holly hugs me close. Her pride in me warms my soul. Steve joins in unexpectedly. So much love and pain, zigs and zags, but these two have taught me the value and strength of imperfect love.

My roommates and I head to the All Campus Dining Center (a.k.a. ACDC) for dinner. The meal plan is included in tuition, so when we enter, I show my ID, and I am free to eat whatever I want. We all have the same IDs. Nobody can tell that I'm completely broke. I load up my tray and pretend to join the chorus of complaints about the food.

For the first week of school, dubbed Camp Vassar, we first-year students have the whole campus to ourselves so we can get situated. Everyone is trying to find a friend or a group or a hookup. The energy is manic. *Ready, set, make friends!* It's a nonstop game of speed dating, which brings me into unwanted conversations.

"Where are you from?" Lisa asks innocently. Do I say New York, Massachusetts, Albany, Spain?

"Northampton—it's in Western Massachusetts."

"Oh, wow. I applied to Smith. Northampton is such a cute town. Do you have any siblings?"

"Actually, yeah, one brother and three sisters." I combine my foster family and my biological siblings. "What about you, where you from? How many siblings?" I ask.

"It's just me. My parents are divorced, thank God. Mom is back in the city and my dad is in Westchester County. Have you heard of Chappaqua? I'm sure you'll meet my mom—she's going to be here a lot," Lisa says.

Now I'm in safer territory. "Tell me about Chappaqua," I say. I'm comfortable so long as we're not talking about me. I don't want to explain foster care or poverty or why my mom won't be visiting. I don't want what happened to me to define me.

A few nights later, Lisa opens the door to my dorm room and says, "Ambroz, we're getting sushi!" She's accompanied by a pack of fellow first-years. "We are going to split up and drive over, you in?" she asks.

I want to be *in*, but I've never had sushi, nor do I want to, nor could I afford it if I wanted it. But I'm worried that if I keep declining my classmates' invitations, they'll stop inviting me. I long for the ease I had with my friends in Spain and remember the adventures I got into with them just by saying yes.

"I'm in," I say. I won't eat, and I'll make sure I don't have to split the bill, but I'll be there.

When classmates invite me to join them on trips to the local Kmart and Caldor to pick up coffee makers, popcorn poppers, beer, or whatever, I also join as an observer.

"Going to need one of these," Lucas says, lifting a blender off the shelf of Caldor.

"Margaritas!" his new friend, Rick, crows. Lucas puts it in the cart without even glancing at the price. The pile in the cart grows, and at the checkout, I watch the total on the cashier's monitor climb. Lucas and Rick are chatting away, oblivious. I feel anxious and realize I'm clenching my fists. *You are not paying for this*, I remind myself. *Calm down.*

"Three hundred forty-six dollars and twenty-five cents is your total, hon," the cashier says. Behind us and in other lines other college students are doing the same thing. This cashier has probably watched similar carts get unloaded all day long. Lucas hands over a credit card, barely pausing his conversation with Rick.

"Do you want the receipt in the bag?" the cashier asks.

"Nah, don't need it, thanks," Lucas says, and we push the cart out to his Mercedes. Rick has an actual DeLorean, like the one from *Back to the Future*. I watch their unconscious consumerism closely, fascinated. They seem so comfortable in luxury cars, using credit cards, buying whatever they want. I find it impossible to imagine what it would be like not to spend any time and worry making sure I had the money, food, and supplies to get by, to take all of that and just let it go. How free I would be.

But I am not free. On Orientation Day, armed with my schedule of classes, I get into line at the bookstore with a basket full of the textbooks I need for my classes. The basket is heavy, and I put it on the floor, scooting it forward with my foot as I approach the register. The woman at the register is older, with a wash and set. Her lilac perfume is stifling. I breathe through my mouth and smile up at her.

"That'll be three hundred sixty-five dollars," she says.

I hand her my brand-new Vassar College ID card, the one that enabled me to sail through the all-you-can-eat dining hall. She looks at me and understands.

"No, honey," she says. "You can use this at the commissary, but not the bookstore. Do you have a credit card?"

I don't even have a checkbook, much less any real money in a bank account. Back in my room I have $120 in cash stuffed in a sock. I can't quite grasp what she is saying, and she can tell. She smiles kindly and says, "Leave your basket here and head up to Financial Aid."

But Financial Aid is closed for the day. I stand in front of the door for a moment, feeling as if it's been slammed in my face. Then I walk slowly out of the building, crushed. For my whole life I've had to connive, haggle, and force my way through the doors that are open for everyone else. I thought that was over. Vassar was the ultimate ticket, and I thought I was on a one-way train that would lead me out of poverty. But colleges have no experience with kids like me. That is, kids with no parents, no cash, and no home. From the beginning of the process, starting with the financial aid application, there had been a baseline expectation that students would be supported by family. Whether it was the family student loans with excellent interest rates, the cosigned loans to buy a computer, the cost of the books. It dawns on me that there will be expenses beyond tuition, and that with each expense I will have to visit the financial aid office to remind them that I have no family to underwrite me.

I go to the library. It's a beautiful Gothic building. There's a three-story-tall stained glass window that I know from orientation depicts Lady Elena Lucretia, the first woman to receive a doctorate, defending her thesis. I sit below her, feeling the weight of what she'd gone through to get to that moment.

It's 1998, and I'm not the only one for whom finding answers to a question online is a novel concept. The only digital search I've used is *Encarta*, Microsoft's CD-ROM encyclopedia, so a few days later I return to the library armed with a handwritten list of search terms: "foster," "orphan," "scholarship," "college," and anything else I can think of. I log on to Netscape and Yahoo and start searching. Eventually, "orphan" comes through for me. I arrive at a site for the Orphan Foundation of America. It's a small nonprofit in Virginia that provides support to foster youth in colleges around the country. I call the number. A woman named Julia answers, and I explain the situation.

"This isn't really how we work," Julia says. "We don't hand out cash. We have specific programs to help foster students achieve academic success." But years of dealing with bureaucracy has taught me not to give up.

"I would be the best investment you ever made," I tell Julia. An arrogant statement, but I believe it and don't want her to hang up. Finally, Julia agrees to help me. I'm so excited that I take the yes and get off the phone. Then I have to call her back to figure out the logistics of quickly getting a check from Virginia to Poughkeepsie, New York.

To supplement the financial aid Vassar has provided, I have need-based scholarships and merit scholarships. I receive funds from the Community Foundation of Western Massachusetts, and other small amounts from a variety of nonprofits. I even have a stipend from the Robinson family—the United Methodist parishioners who once sent me to sleepaway camp. When I first arrived at Vassar, I wrote them a letter to thank them. They had always seen me and treated me like a human being, and it meant something. Lee wrote back, and we began corresponding. Next thing I knew, he sent me a check, and from then on, he would send me Christmas cards and $250 at the start of each semester.

Until the stipend comes in from Julia at the Orphan Foundation, I use the library's copies of the textbooks, or borrow them from class-mates, or fake my way through class. One professor kindly photocopies the readings for me. As tight as money is, when the check finally comes in, I use a bit that's left over to buy a Vassar sweatshirt. It is a large gray hooded sweatshirt with VASSAR COLLEGE in bold maroon script. I wear it often, with pride.

October arrives and brings with it a deep chill. The redbrick buildings that surround the dormitory quad do very little to cut the wind. One night when I walk into my dorm, I see a lot of classmates heading into the multipurpose room where the big TV is located.

"What's going on?" I ask someone.

"They fucking crucified a gay kid in Wyoming," she says, and wipes angry tears from her eyes. "It's nuts. They strung him up on a fence post, tortured him, and left him there till he died." Without waiting for my response, she heads into the common room.

I follow, still cold from my walk across campus. I stand with my classmates and watch a cable news program where two newscasters are discussing Matthew Shepard, a gay college student from the University of Wyoming. I absorb the information without allowing any visible emotion to cross my face. I don't move. I feel like just by being in this room I risk being outed. It's irrational but how I feel. Nobody can notice that I'm here, or that I'm gay. Rigid with fear, I back out of the room and take the staircase two steps at a time, retreating to my room.

In the nights that follow, there are candlelit vigils for Matthew Shepard on campus, but I don't feel like I can risk participating. Being gay is still illegal in most states. And clearly it's dangerous. I get that Vassar is a safe haven. It's "gay friendly." But these liberties don't apply to me. I have too much at stake. I am a Frankenstein of financial aid, fellowships, and scholarships. It's always on my mind that if I come out as gay, some of the support I'm receiving could evaporate. With all of the faceless committees making decisions about my scholarships, I would never know the real reason they were declined. So even though I see other LGBTQ students out and proud and mourning Matthew Shepard, I don't feel like I have that option. I have to decide what is more important to me—to live as my full self or to preserve the tenuous foothold I have in the world of the college educated.

My life on campus is a balancing act that is unexpectedly threatened by Christmas.

"We are staying in the city, but my mom promised we'd at least see one Broadway show," Rachel says.

"That's great, which one?" I ask.

She doesn't seem to hear me. "At least I'll get my mom to do my laundry, but we usually get to travel, sometimes to my grandparents' place in Tampa. Would I love to be in the ocean right now! What are your plans?"

"Um. Not much. Going to stay local, got so much work to do. You know."

"That sounds awful. I can't wait to get away from here," Rick says. "We're going skiing in Breckenridge."

"Where's that?" I ask.

He gives me a funny look. "Colorado." Then, as if he's decided I was making fun of his destination, he adds, "For some reason my dad likes it better than Aspen."

The dorm is closing for the holidays, and everyone seems to be going home. This presents a problem: I do not have a home. Alex has transferred to a college in West Virginia, where he's living off campus. Jessica is at an all-women's residential college a state away and is going to her friend's house for Christmas. My mother, to the best of my knowledge, is homeless in DC. Holly and Steve are still a warm presence, but I haven't figured out what our post–foster care relationship is. So my plan is to hide out in the dorm.

Three days before the campus closes, the dining hall hums with pre-break excitement. I start to hoard food from the cafeteria. After dinner, I quietly slip items from my tray into my backpack. I take anything that won't go bad. I need it to tide me over the long break.

We return from the dining hall to find a new sign on the front door of the dorm: DON'T LEAVE PLANTS IN YOUR ROOMS. THEY WILL DIE.

"What am I supposed to do with all my plants?" Rachel moans.

"You can bring them to the residential life office. Hopefully they won't kill 'em," Rick suggests.

"Why will the plants die?" I ask.

"Over the holidays, they turn down the heat in the dorm to fifty-five degrees, just high enough to prevent the pipes from bursting," Rick answers.

This building, my corner of the attic, is the only home I have, but it looks like I'm going to have to figure something else out. I can't bear to go back to the financial aid office yet again. The shame of my poverty and background keeps me silent.

The day before the dorms close, I give a campus tour, walking backward, sharing how great the school is. "The social life is amazing, there's always something to do...we have state-of-the-art science facilities...there are five a cappella groups..." I tell a group of prospective students and anxious parents. After the tour, I go straight to my shift at Friendly's. Plastering on my please-dear-God-tip-me-well-because-they-pay-me-$2.25-per-hour smile, I've been saving money for food, but I still don't know where I'm going to sleep.

I come home from Friendly's to an emptying dorm. My roommates have already taken off for the holiday, and their crap is all over the place. I spend the evening cleaning up their areas. I fold their clothes, make their beds, and organize their desks, getting everything I can under control, but behind my industrious front, I have no idea what to do. The cafeteria is eerie—there are very few students and fewer meal choices.

On the day that they're turning the heat off in the dorms, on my way to Friendly's, I pass a cheap motel advertising a special if you book a room for a week or longer. Scraping together my tips and "borrowing" a little cash from my roommates' desks—payment, I tell myself, for my cleaning services—I book a room. After work, as the heat in the dorm drops, I load up a duffel bag with my clothes and the food I've hoarded and move into the motel.

The room isn't all that bad, given my standards. The maroon carpet has some mysterious stains; the synthetic bedspread isn't quite warm enough. I turn up the heater to full blast. It rumbles in protest and smells slightly like burning plastic, but it blasts out heat. When I'm not at Friendly's, I go to the library or loiter at Dunkin' Donuts, trying to study and refilling my coffee until late.

It's as if I've been living a dream. I'm back in my real life now, the one where I'm isolated, living out of a duffel bag, sleeping in a temporary bed, passing my days at Dunkin' Donuts, catching the jingle of holiday carols and faraway glimpses of other people celebrating Christmas. No matter what I do, no matter how much of my dream I make come true, this life is always a possibility, always waiting for me, always looming. Rising from homelessness and poverty is a fight against gravity. I am learning to cajole, connive, and earn my way forward, but if I stop playing that game, I risk ending up right where I started.

Chapter 23

Penn Station, where I spent many a night as a child, hasn't changed. The homeless people spread out, instinctively keeping a certain distance from each other. In the narrow, windowless corridors, the air is thick and industrial. The floor, the surfaces, everything is dirty and worn. I pull out my wallet to buy a ticket, remembering my mother reaching into her bra, negotiating discounts. "One ticket to Miami."

I'm putting the change back in my wallet when I hear, "Sir, can you give me a dollar?" I look up to see a child. A boy. My heart hammers. I look him over. He's anywhere from nine years old to an underfed twelve. His clothes don't fit. His cheeks are drawn. He looks at me, hopeful, resigned. "Sir?" he says to me again.

He is me, maybe ten years ago. At his age, I stood right here, in a sea of commuters, begging for a dollar. I remember the people surging toward me, faceless in crisp, generic business attire. I planted myself right in front of them, my hand outstretched. But they parted to pass on either side of me without a second glance. Their indifference made me feel invisible. I was not of this place, this time. My obvious poverty gave them permission to dehumanize and ignore me.

"Sir?" The boy jolts me back to the present, and I remember where

I am and where I'm going. I pull a twenty out of my wallet and hand it to him. It's a paper Band-Aid on the hunger that eats at one in five children in the United States. He smiles, an impish grin, snatching it away before I can change my mind. I think I hear a "Thanks" and he is gone.

The train from New York City to Miami chugs down forgotten routes, interrupting the quiet intimacy of backyards. I'm a sophomore now, so it's been a year since I spent Christmas alone in a hotel room. This time I'm going someplace warm. But that's not my only objective. On campus I appear confident and popular. I lead tours, join committees, see plays; I'm a member of the Vassar College Democrats, the rowing team, a theater troupe, and the premed club. I go from classes to work, to the library, to work, to the dorm. I move full speed ahead, generating an impressive blur of achievement. The faster I spin the less I have to look at myself.

There is a part of college life that is all around me, but that I don't join: the hanging-out-with-friends part. Briefly, in Spain, I managed to relax, but at Vassar I ignore the alienation I feel even when surrounded by friends. I see my classmates doing what they want. They follow their desires, passions, and dreams. They sleep with people, make mistakes, blow up relationships, have a few drinks, start all over again. They seem so oblivious and brave to me. But I also see them all as having safety nets. Their parents will always love them, even if they fail a class or break a rule or run out of cash or need a place to stay. Every step I take is a strategy to make sure I don't lose all that I have gained. I have made a bargain with God and the universe that I won't do anything to jeopardize my own success. I'll channel all my energy into work, school, and achievement.

Yet I can't spin fast enough to ignore my sexuality. I am compelled to answer this pulling inside of me, the longing to connect with another man. I can't afford to make a mistake, so if I have to be gay, to answer some of the questions that haunt me, then I am resolved that nobody can know. I want to be gay, at least for a weekend, but I want to do it far, far from campus where no one I know will find out.

In the brutal winter of Poughkeepsie, I decided on Miami as the right place for my sexual awakening. Miami is far enough that I won't know anyone, and they won't know me. And it is warm. I take on extra hours and save up enough cash for a train ticket and a cheap hotel. I'll barely have enough money to feed myself, but, before the heat begins to drop in the dorm rooms again, I am en route. I am eager and scared and clueless. After twenty-four hours of travel, two thousand miles from here, I will finally be gay. What will that mean? What will it feel like? How will I find my people? Am I cute enough? The train plows forward, slow and relentless in contrast to my tumultuous mind.

I brought some of my course reading assignments, but their dullness doesn't help distract me. Giving up, I adjust my yellow Walkman, searching for decent radio stations. When I find a good one, I listen until it evaporates as the train moves along. I've had almost no sex ed, and certainly nothing that addressed the needs of LGBTQ youth. I've watched porn, but I know that's not what real gay sex is. My desire exists in a void. How will I know what to do?

I land in a remote, dank hotel near the train station in Miami. To get to South Beach I have to transfer buses, but if there's anything I can easily master, it's a public transportation system. I follow the tide of tourists to the wide, golden beach, where I can immediately see clusters of men in Speedo bathing suits. I spread out the striped towel I brought from my hotel close to, but not too near, a group of beautiful men and sit, watching the ocean. I walk down to the water and say hi to a couple of guys as I pass them. They return the greeting, not unfriendly, but I don't know how to start a conversation. Back at my towel, I try to psyche myself up to go talk to people. Maybe I'll ask to borrow suntan lotion. Or maybe someone will come over to find out what book I'm reading. By evening, I still haven't managed to speak to a soul beyond a hello. I walk past restaurants and bars where gay men are obviously congregating, and peer in longingly, but I can't afford to buy food or drinks. I've got to budget carefully. At the end of the day, I head back to my hotel disheartened. What am I supposed to do to find gay people that I can approach? Nobody else I see is here alone. But I've always been alone. I've taken care of myself. I've managed my own survival. This part, the part where another man and I recognize each other and forge a connection—it's a mystery.

Another day passes like this, my plans and hopes setting with the sun. What I need is for someone to notice me. Someone to approach me and take the lead. Then, on the long ride back from the beach to my hotel, the bus nearly empties out. I'm facing one side; he's facing front. His skin is a beautiful light brown color, his black hair a pleasing contrast. I look without looking. How does this work? He looks directly back at me, sending a jolt through my body. Is it a look, or a *look*? How do I express interest? What if he's straight? What if he's the angry straight type that beats up queers? Wait, is he smiling? Yes. He's smiling at me. His teeth are startlingly white. I find myself smiling back.

With a slight nod, he gives me the instruction I need. *Come here.* A few others are left on the bus. How am I supposed to go over to him? People will notice. What will they think? *Okay, I'm doing this.* I stand up, clutch the hang bar for a minute, and casually make my way back. When I reach him, he pats the space next to him. I sit. He looks older, maybe thirty, shorter than I thought. His firm thighs come out of his blue shorts—legs covered in thick black hair. I want to touch them. His shorts fit snugly, barely able to contain what appears to be a massive bulge. He nods again, no words spoken. Just the nod, this time toward his cock. I'm not sure what to do. Am I reading this right? Is this how it is to be gay, a language of nods? How did I not know this simple language?

He gives a firmer nod. *Okay, I'm going to do it.* My left hand hovers over his bulge. I can feel the heat emanating. Then his hand is on top of mine, pressing my hand onto him. His eyes close. His hand massages the top of mine, causing me to massage him. Okay, I can handle this; I like it. I can smell him now. Coming from work, he has a mild funk overlaid with a fading cologne. We grope each other while mostly looking straight ahead. The bus lurches block to block, too often detained at a light.

"We are almost home," he says, and I understand that we're heading to his place. Eventually he nods again, we rearrange ourselves, he pulls the string, and we disembark at his stop. We make small talk as we walk: *How long are you here for? Where are you staying, with friends?* I feel both aroused and petrified. I don't want to know him. I don't want him to know my real name. I'm afraid that if one person knows I'm gay, everyone will know. On the train ride down, I came up with my cover. I'm "Zeke from Chicago." I've never been to Chicago, but I assume it's enough like New York that I can fake it. But he asks nothing personal, and that is an enormous relief.

His apartment is neat but not fastidiously so. The walls are a burnt yellow, the sofa pillows have a cheerful leaf pattern, and on all the walls and shelves are brightly colored artwork and knickknacks. We sit on the sofa, and, finally in private, we make out. Kissing girls felt like going to the dentist, necessary but unpleasant. This is completely different—an irresistible pleasure, pulling me like a magnet. His breath is not fresh, but tolerable. His hands are all over me. I pull back, wanting him to slow down just a little. I try to say so, but he presses his face into me, his tongue darting and insistent. He bites my lip, too hard. As he is kissing me, he yanks down my pants. I like it, yet I'm scared. I've seen porn, but I don't know what's supposed to happen here. Without warning, he turns me around aggressively, and I'm facedown in the couch pillows. My ass is exposed, and I try to push myself up.

"No...I'm not...No..." I protest, but he pushes me back, his hand pressing my head down into the cushion. His cock stabs into me without lubrication or gentleness. I don't have a chance to ask him to wear a condom. The pain is sharp, wrong. I feel a violent tearing, and before I react, he pulls out of me. Then he thrusts forward again. The pain is a supernova, blinding me.

I yell, "No!" and try to right myself, but he pushes me down again. His brutal thrusts never stop. I struggle, the pain and fear are extraordinary, but I am also confused. Maybe this is what it means to be gay. Maybe this is what the therapists were warning me about. I stop struggling, hoping it will end soon. I manage to turn my head to the side—a badge he was wearing has dropped, and I stare at it. He works at the airport. This man has a job. Why is he doing this to me? Am I going to die like Matthew Shepard?

At last, he is finished. His weight lifts off me, and I'm still facedown on the sofa, sweating and in pain. He steps away, pulling up his shorts and briefs. I find my way to my feet, pulling up my underwear. He returns from the kitchen, using a moistened dish towel to wipe down his groin. He throws it at me.

"Here, clean up and get the fuck out," he says.

I pull up my shorts, trying to be gentle with myself. Then I'm out the door. When I look back at him, he is sitting on the sofa. He gives me a nod and a satisfied smile. Does he have any idea how much he hurt me. Is this my fault?

I smile back, afraid that if I make a wrong move, he'll do it again.

I walk down the exterior staircase, clutching the railing. My rectum aches with each step, but I find the determination, and I start to run away. I run in no particular direction, just away from this monster.

When I get back to my hotel room, I'm bleeding. I stay inside the room for the remaining three days, one of which is New Year's Eve. I order food delivered but can't eat any of it. The TV is on, but I'm not watching. I'd like to leave early, but it doesn't occur to me to change my train ticket. I sit like a zombie waiting for it to be time for me to go. Each bowel movement is agonizing, but there is less and less blood.

Late at night, the memories and voices threaten to drown me.

You see that. You see them, Hugh. They are dying because they are faggots, Mom states, pointing at the others in the shelter, dying with purple lesions.

Is this what you want, homo? Enrick stares down at me, broom in hand.

It's not right, David. Homosexuals die. It's disgusting, my therapist's voice echoes in my head.

Sodomy is still illegal in most states, the guest speaker says in our political science class.

The question is whether or not a "gay panic defense" is sufficient to excuse their murder of Matthew Shepard. It must have been shocking to have a gay man hit on them, the speaker on cable news says.

There are out gay men on campus, and I have heard other voices—Holly's—but they are a minority, and quieter than the army of people telling me that what I am is wrong.

And now, I've proved them right. Everything they told me is real. This is what I deserve. I'm going to die of AIDS.

I'm angry with myself more than him. I don't know how to be safe and find a safe partner. How to love and be loved. There is nobody I can talk to, nobody to ask if I should feel what I feel, nobody I can ask if what I experienced was rape. These are questions that go unanswered for many gay people of my generation, but in my mind the barrier is heightened by the fragility of my hold on normal. Security, stability, safety—these are my priorities. Desires, needs, identity—these are for other people, people like my Vassar classmates. The ones with credit cards and vacation plans and their parents' hand-me-down Mercedes and blenders just for making margaritas.

When I get back to Vassar, I tell my friends I had an awesome time. MTV had a beach concert when I was there, I tell them. I got to see Enrique Iglesias perform. I tell my siblings I watched the concert standing up to my knees in the ocean at South Beach. I tell everyone it was the most amazing concert of my life, a perfect way to start the new millennium.

Love, for me, has to stay a dream scratched into the side of someone else's truck. But there is more that I want, another dream that has been building steam, and this one I'm ready to chase.

Chapter 24

THE QUIET BANALITY OF GETTING ready for the semester helps me put away Miami. I need to figure out my courses, meet with my adviser, set my work schedule, pick up books and supplies. When I stop attending to these simple tasks, my mind returns to that bus, that living room, the leaf-patterned pillows, so I don't stop. The line at the bookstore is epic—everyone is purchasing their second-semester books. I wait my turn, lugging a heavy basket of the hardcover tomes that will somehow prepare me for med school. I lift out the largest of the books—my textbook for advanced chemistry. The cover art is awful. It's heavy in my hand, and in that weight I feel the burden of something I don't want. I don't want to be a doctor. I take the book out of my basket and shove it onto the closest shelf. I feel instantly lighter.

I consider the rest of the books and one by one remove them from the basket. The realization comes slowly, and then all at once: I shouldn't be majoring in biology. I don't want to be a doctor. It was my mother's dream for me, and for so long whenever anyone asked what I wanted to be when I grew up, I've said "a doctor," but it isn't true anymore. Something changed last summer, and it's time for me to admit it.

Six months earlier, I had spent the summer after my first year of college as an intern at the White House under Bill Clinton. It was an unpaid internship, so I had to stretch to make it work. I got a night job at the Hard Rock Cafe, and Fran, the woman who'd given me media training when I lobbied for the Chafee bill, helped out by finding me free housing. Returning to DC to work in the White House for the summer was an opportunity beyond my wildest dreams. I was assigned to the offices of Ann O'Leary, special assistant to the president for domestic policy; Sonia Chessen; and Bethany Little, an associate director for domestic policy. At first, my responsibilities were simply to file, answer phones, and work at events. But when I told her about my work on the Chafee bill and with the National Foster Youth Advisory Council, Ann O'Leary asked me to tell her what I would do if I had the opportunity to reform foster care.

Her office was small, more like an alcove with a door, but it was less than two hundred feet from the Oval Office. I was very close to where change actually happened, and I had an answer ready. "Foster parents are the key. But we need more potential parents so that social workers can make better matches, and we need more who have college degrees. If a child is in a house with someone with a college degree, they're much more likely to get one themselves."

"Yes, David, but how would you *solve* foster care? How would you make this happen?"

"I sometimes think about it this way. You have kids, right? Close your eyes for a second and imagine you had to put your kids into foster care. What does that system look like? Who are the foster parents? How many kids does their social worker have on their caseload? Would we have group homes?"

"*Yes*. That's it, David. That's what I need you to do. You have my ear, go and write up what it looks like when we reimagine it from the ground up. And then tell me how we could make that happen."

In between photocopying, I looked for solutions to these issues. From the White House offices, I had access to anyone and everyone, and there was nothing I loved more than saying, "Hi, this is David Ambroz. I'm calling from the White House." I spoke to state foster care system leaders, former elected officials, and people from research institutions and nonprofits around the country to learn more about how foster care worked and what ideas they had for improvements. Then I put together a proposal. Clinton's COPS (Community Oriented Policing Services) program had successfully funded one hundred thousand additional community police officers, so part of my proposal was modeled on that. What if we had one hundred thousand more social workers? What if they got paid more? What if, after ten years of service, they could waive their student loans?

When I'd written up my proposal, I went over to Bethany Little's office in the Eisenhower Executive Office Building to present my ideas to her and a few other members of the Domestic Policy Council. The building looks like a Roman temple, a beautiful space overstuffed with desks and filing cabinets in every nook and cranny. After I shared my vision, they asked me lots of questions, then thanked me. They made no promises. Change doesn't happen because you're right. It's an ongoing slog. A million conversations that build to a moment of opportunity. I knew then that I wanted to carry the ideas I'd developed through my education and into the world. I had to make change. Change came through the law.

Now, in line to buy my textbooks, I remember what it felt like to be in the halls of power in DC. I want to understand the language of law. The laws that kept my family in poverty. The laws that moved me here and there, from placement to placement. The laws that operate in all parts of my every day. I want to be fluent in that language, and I want to use it to change the system. By the time I get to the front of the line, there is only one book left in my basket: Lewis L. Gould's *The Modern American Presidency*. It's time for my education to match my calling. I change my major to political science, switch to prelaw, and never look back.

I've stayed part of the National Foster Youth Advisory Council ever since it began when I was a high school junior. In spring, I take the train to the annual meeting in DC. I arrive at Union Station and walk less than a quarter mile to the offices of the Child Welfare League of America, where we have our meetings.

"Okay, everyone, let's focus in. Guys. *Guys!*" Debi, the facilitator, quiets the room. "We have big work to do here today. This is year four for the National Foster Youth Advisory Council, and we have a lot to build upon. Let's thank our host and sponsor, Child Welfare League of America." Debi pauses so we can all give a cheer, but I'm impatient. I'm missing classes for this and don't want us to waste time congratulating ourselves. I look around the boardroom. Twenty-four youth, mostly people of color, sit around the conference table, accompanied by some of their foster parents and other chaperones. A wall of glass looks out on Union Station, and Congress is only a block away. There are notepads and pens in front of each of us, and everyone has a bottle of water sweating onto a coaster. There are several easels with large pads of paper and markers poised to document our keen insights. This organization clearly has resources, and the energy is high, but I'm frustrated from past meetings in which our ideas were enthusiastically received, summarized, distributed, and then ignored. I want action.

"Okay, I want everyone to close your eyes. Take a deep breath. Deniah, please take this seriously. Close your eyes…close…there is no judgment here," Debi says soothingly. It's clear to me that Debi did not grow up in foster care, where closing your eyes makes you vulnerable, where painful visions haunt the quiet moments. "With your eyes closed, I want you to picture love," Debi begins.

That's it, I'm done. "Debi, I appreciate the orientation exercise, but with all due respect, we are here to change foster care, not to tap into a spiritual place. I'd like us to focus on that task."

All eyes snap open, and she smiles tightly. "Very well, Mr. Ambroz. Let's skip to a quick introduction, then. Would that be acceptable?"

"Yes, thank you. It's just that we have such limited time," I say, then take command, anointed by no one. I turn to a woman I know from previous meetings. "Celeste, would you start? Just a quick intro, any organizational affiliation, your connection to foster care, and one outcome you want to see from today or this body in general."

"Sure, I'm Celeste Bodner. I'm from Seaside, Oregon. I just started a website called FosterClub to help improve the lives of kids in foster care. I want to help foster kids go to college, that'd be my one thing. Oh, yeah, and I'm a foster mom to this one right here. Honey, you go." Celeste nudges her foster son lovingly.

Hunched shoulders and a curly blond crown of hair are all that is visible to the room. Her son mumbles, "I'm Terry," and stops.

"Oregon Ducks, huh?" I say, noticing the logo on his T-shirt.

He looks up. "Yeah, I love football." His face is cherubic, but there is a hollow look I recognize in his eyes.

"Me, too, man. Although, really, the Ducks?! Kidding, they're having a great year," I say, having no idea if they are or even when the season is. "Thanks for coming, Terry." I nod to his neighbor.

"Hi, y'all, I'm Sue An. Just one *n* and no *e*. I'm from Kentucky, and this is my brother Louis. He's already a dad. He's doing better than our mom did. So, what was the question? Oh yeah, I want to make sure siblings get to see each other, even when they live in different foster homes."

"Sue An, one *n* no *e*, thank you." I turn to her brother. "Louis, Sue An did some of your intro, but I know there's more."

"Sure, I'm just really excited to be in DC. I've never been outside of Kentucky. I flew in from Louisville. I got three little ones of my own. They're with their mom and my in-laws while I'm here. Courtney, Derek, and my youngest, Billie. Let's see, what do I want? Well, I wouldn't mind more help. I left care at seventeen. They sort of forced me to emancipate early, and it was real hard. Would have been nice to have a little more time to grow up, maybe health insurance at least until I was eighteen," Louis says.

"We're already having some great ideas. Sibling visitation, health insurance, maybe even extended benefits like food stamps, rental assistance, access to college, vocational education," I say. "Now let's break up into smaller groups, where we can talk more."

At first, my breakout group is silent. I have so many ideas, but I don't want to force-feed them to everyone, so I start us off by asking, "What are some of the problems most of us experienced firsthand?"

"Every home I was in, they were always struggling. Why don't rich people foster?" Tammy asks.

This is one of the issues I've thought about a lot. I am grateful for the many kind, generous foster parents out there, but where are the middle-class or wealthy foster parents? "How could we attract them, those other foster parents?" I prompt my pod. "If we want middle-class people to foster, I think we gotta figure out what else middle-class people care about. What's stressing them out?"

"Retirement," says Celeste. "My husband and I both have jobs, and we can barely save anything."

"What if, after ten years of good service as a foster parent, they got a pension?" I ask.

"That'd be game-changing. I think a lot of my friends would foster," Celeste says.

"What else do you think these folks are worried about?" I ask the group.

"Maybe if they have bio kids, they're worried about how they'll pay for college for their own kids. That might be why they don't even consider it for foster kids," Robyn says.

"*Yes*. For sure." This is exactly the conversation I want us to be having. I don't want to tweak foster care around the edges, making sure foster kids get to go to prom or get to go on sleepovers. I want the whole system to be reconsidered from the perspective of the child. Foster care, as it stands, is focused on reunifying the family. The idea is that kids rightfully belong to and with their parents, and the goal is to try to get them back there. But what if the system were refreshed to center on what is in the best interest of children? Change is impossible, until it isn't. I just have to believe that if people like us, youth advocates across the nation, if all of us start to share the same vision for reform, then our ideas will take root, and whenever there's an opportunity for change, we'll be ready.

"In some states foster kids get tuition waivers so they don't have to pay for college, even if they get adopted. What if in a foster family both biological *and* foster kids could go to any university that received federal support for free?" I ask.

"Wouldn't that just mean foster parents would be doing it for the money?" Erin asks.

"I don't care why they do it if they do a good job," Robyn states. Her gaze is fierce, and firm, only partially obscured by floppy bangs.

"It's okay to care about money. Money matters. People consider the salary when they take jobs that they love," I say.

"It's not just the parents, you got to get better social workers," Erin says, getting into this.

"Say more," I prompt.

"They got too many kids. They come and go. They're burned out. I never see mine."

"Burnout is real. I liked mine, but they ran her ragged. She left after only four years working in the system," Dennis says, speaking up for the first time.

"Maybe if we capped the number of kids they have and help them with their issues, they'd stay longer and provide better care," I say.

"What issues do they have? We're the ones in the foster house," Erin protests.

"I think it's the same stuff as middle-class folks. They can't afford to buy homes on their salaries. They have student debt from getting their degrees, and the pay is crappy," I say.

"Then let's do something. There won't be better outcomes for kids like us if the people in charge are turning over and inexperienced," Robyn adds.

Debi clears her throat at the front of the room. "All right, y'all. Let's reconvene and share what we've come up with."

Two hours and one bathroom break later, we've hit all the points I want to drive home: helping social workers with the caseload, recruiting diverse foster parents, and getting foster kids educated in order to break the cycle of poverty. Debi has aggregated our ideas on one master list. "Great work, everyone. During lunch we're going to hear a presentation from someone new, Rob W. So grab your grub and come back."

We take sandwiches and drinks from the credenza, and when we sit back down, Debi introduces a man who is as bald and white as a mountaintop.

"Everyone, this is Rob. He works with the Child Welfare League and wants to talk to you about a project he's got going. I think some of you are going to be really interested," Debi says and winks at me.

Looking down at my agenda, I see "Rob W. CWLA & Lambda Legal."

Rob stands up and smiles at us. "Wow. Can I just say wow? You guys nailed the most important issues. I know—I've been working in foster care for a long time." He pauses before shifting to his agenda. "Please keep eating, and I'm gonna tell you about a project we are starting. I want your ideas, and maybe your help. I work at a place called Green Chimneys in Boston. It's a group home for runaway youth—runaway gay youth."

The crinkling of wrappers and general rustling stops. Eyes look at him or turn away. *Did he say "gay"?*

"Not sure how much you all know about this, but gay kids—I mean LGBT kids—are really suffering in foster care. Many are thrown out of their bio families' homes, and the kids end up on the streets. Some end up in foster care, and some end up in places like the residential program I run, Green Chimneys. We specialize in helping meet the unique needs of these youth. And that's where you come in. Child Welfare League of America and Lambda Legal—that's a legal organization specializing in defending the rights of LGBT people—we want to work together to improve the outcomes for gay foster youth," Rob says.

This man is standing in the front of the room talking about being gay in foster care. I'm stunned. *Are folks looking at me? Do I look gay?* Until now, I've been de facto running this meeting, but this topic catches me off guard. It's not a problem anyone has brought up. It's not something I dared to flag in DC. I agree that it's a problem, possibly the biggest problem I've encountered, but the fear of being outed has kept me from ever bringing it up. I'm still afraid. I sink lower in my chair.

"I know you all are forming committees to work on your ideas, and I wondered if we could get a liaison—that is an ambassador—from this group to help us help LGBT kids," Rob says. *Am I red? Does Rob know? Did someone tell him?*

"I ain't gay, dude," Keon says.

"You don't have to be gay to help. CWLA has been around a long, long time. About fifty years ago, they put out a policy that encouraged state foster care systems to 'cure' gay kids. Well, that has not gone well, to say the least. Lambda and CWLA are partnering not just to repeal that, but to develop policies that help LGBT kids be healthy and happy."

"Nah," Keon responds. "I still ain't gay."

There is snickering. I hear someone mutter, "Fags don't need my help." I look up and meet Rob's eyes. In that brief moment he sees me, knows the truth, and smiles in sad recognition of the fear that is holding me back. Understanding that—out of homophobia or fear—none of us is going to volunteer, Rob puts down his pen as if he's about to call it a day. After being told my nature was a perversion, after being forced to listen to therapists and foster parents who tried to change me, I'm thinking of Matthew Shepard and everything that I could lose. But here is Rob, openly gay, fighting for what I've always wanted. I sit up, rigid. I place both hands on the table in front of me. Then I raise my hand and say, "Rob, I'd be glad to be the ambassador. I've shared some of my ideas today, and everyone else had really great ones, but there's one thing I really want to change. I wish they hadn't tried to cure me of being gay. No kid should live through that, especially not at the hands of the state." I speak clearly, my eyes not leaving his face.

"That's great, David. I think your experience will help. Let's connect on the next break," Rob says, but I can tell from his smile that he and I both recognize what is happening in this moment. I'm gay. I've said it out loud before, once, to a stone wall at a wine festival in Spain. Now, for the first time ever, I've said it in public. And I have finally acknowledged to myself that it isn't something that's wrong with me. All those years it was the people around me who ridiculed homosexuality who were wrong. It is part of who I am, and I don't want to fight it, change it, or deny it anymore.

"Okay, let's get to work," I say, knowing that at the end of the meeting, I will travel back to Vassar, where I am still in hiding.

Chapter 25

T HE CASKET AT THE FRONT of the room is open, and I can just see the silhouette of the man inside. I've never met this person, but his funeral is my reason for being in this small Connecticut town with a roomful of strangers. It's the beginning of my senior year, and my friend Nathan's father has passed away. As sophomores, Nathan and I were residential advisers for the first-years on our floor, and in an unspoken way we understood each other and became very close. His father had been seriously ill for a while. Nathan has shouldered a lot, always, so I'm here to support him.

It's been more than a year since the advisory council meeting where I came out, and I'm sharing a house with two friends, Mia and Sydney. We live together, but they don't know that I'm gay. Nobody knows.

Earlier today, Sydney, Mia, and I piled into my beat-up Chrysler, a car that I bought with a loan that the dean of Financial Aid personally arranged for me. It's been a boon, allowing me to drive to do odd handyman jobs to help cover my school expenses.

We pulled up to a nondescript building surrounded by an asphalt parking lot that had seen better days.

"Do we just go in?" I asked my carmates. I'd never been to a funeral before.

"Yeah, this is the wake, then the service, then the reception," Mia said. "It's old-school Catholic, you know," she explained. I didn't know, but I nodded as if I did.

"Do I look okay?" I asked, straightening my rumpled clothes.

"You're good," Sydney said. She was perky and energetic, but I was still figuring out how to get her to do her dishes. We walked toward the entrance and joined the line of people making their way into the building. A few other Vassar students met us in line. Conversations were hushed. I noticed that I was a little out of place in khakis and a blue button-down. Everyone else was wearing dark suits. The line snaked up and into the main room. That's when I understood that there was an open casket, and we were heading toward it.

"Do we go up? Up close?" I whisper.

"Yes. It's intense, but quick," Sydney responds.

"Why is the casket open? Why do we look?"

"It's tradition," Sydney informs me.

My sense of dread grows. I want to sneak away. Why does everyone seem so calm? "Have you been to one of these before?" I ask Kelly, a classmate.

"Yeah, my grandparents both passed and were old-school Catholics."

Sydney hushes us—we're close to the front. Then I look up and past the casket, and my eyes are drawn to a blond man who looks like he could be an Abercrombie & Fitch model. Our eyes lock, and my heart races in anticipation of coming closer to this man. *Good Lord, David. This is not the time or place. And he's probably not gay . . . or is he?* The distraction of my inner monologue makes it easier to approach the casket.

I pause to look down at this man I never met, and begin to understand the beauty and impact of this ritual form of goodbye. Then the line moves again, and I am standing in front of the family. I hug Nathan's mother, then his sister, and then Nathan. My friend, who is always so bright and witty, is muted and tearful. "Love ya, buddy," I say, and the edges of his mouth turn up slightly.

Once we've come through the receiving line, Mia says, "Let's wait in the foyer or outside to see about the service."

I look past her and see the beautiful blond man. He has drifted over toward the front door, and his eyes are still fixed on me. His look says, *Come with me*, or so I tell myself. My heart is in my throat.

"I have to use the bathroom," I announce, a bit too loudly.

"Thank you for letting everyone know about your biological needs, David," Sydney says.

"Meet you outside," I say, and dart after the blond man. Signs point to a second set of bathrooms on the floor below. Keeping a discreet distance between us, I follow him downstairs. In the presence of death, I feel something even more powerful—life, sex, connection.

He pushes through the restroom door, and I am hot on his heels. He steps up to the urinal, and I take the one next to him. We are both silent, staring straight ahead. As subtly as I can, I turn my gaze left and down, without moving any other muscle. It's immediately obvious that he's not just here to go to the bathroom. I touch myself, giving him a subtle sign that I'm here for the same reason. He matches my motion. *This is happening*, I think, and fireworks explode inside me. I've told myself I'll never do this, I can never let myself be who I am, but I want to more than anything.

Finally, we turn toward each other and meet, mouths open, thirsty for intimacy, for sex, for recognition. Inexperience gives way to instinct. I reach behind his neck, feeling his blond curls resting there. His hands come up to frame my face and chin, and he kisses me deeply. This is the wrong venue, but it feels right. We've both grown up in a world where sex is illegal in more than thirty states, where for generations gay people had to sneak around and hide, where Matthew Shepard has been crucified, where heterosexism has tried to force me to be some- one I'm not. Lust and love still happen this way because they must.

Upstairs, a life is being honored, and before long duty triumphs over lust—we have to go back up. It feels like we are two magnets, trying to separate but drawn back together. Then we both step up to the bathroom mirror, his eyes look at mine, and we smile.

"I'm Sebastian," he says.

"Ambroz...David. I mean, David Ambroz," I stammer. "Are you a friend of Nathan's?"

"Yes, we grew up together. Are you going for pizza later with the others?"

"I don't know...I will if you are."

"Come. I want you to come."

He goes up first. I wait a few minutes to make sure nobody will see us together, and then follow him up. I came down these stairs half a man, and I had accepted that. Now my whole body is full of something different, something bigger than my desire for this man. It is hope.

At the reception, Sebastian comes up to me and my roommates. "Hi, I'm Sebastian. This is Christine. You guys are friends from Vassar?" He pretends not to have met me.

I can't find words, and, thankfully, Mia speaks up. "Hi, I'm Mia, this is David and Sydney."

"You guys heading back tonight?" Sebastian asks the group, avoiding eye contact with me.

"Probably after the reception," Mia says.

"Well, if you want to, a few of us are going to get pizza afterwards. It's not far."

"*Yes.* Yes, we'd like that," I declare a little too enthusiastically.

My Vassar group looks at me oddly. Our plan had been very clear: wake, reception, home.

"Cool. We can leave together, you guys can follow my car," Sebastian says.

"*Great, yes, great.* That's the plan, then," I say, to the dismay of my carpool crew. As soon as Sebastian steps away, they close in.

"David, um, we are supposed to head back," Mia starts.

"We should stay. For Nathan. It's not right to rush off. He might join for pizza with his childhood friends, and I know he'd want us there." I didn't know anything about funeral etiquette an hour ago, but now I'm an expert.

Night is setting. There is almost no traffic on the roads, yet I tail Sebastian's car closely. I cannot lose him. The light of the pizza joint spills out into the parking lot. Outside, we converge with Sebastian and his crew.

"Hey, I think we might need a couple tables. There are a lot of us," Sebastian says, his eyes on mine.

"Fine, sure, yes," I say awkwardly. I'm afraid our chemistry is obvious to everyone standing there. "Let's mix it up, so we can all meet each other, and we'll save a seat at each table in case Nathan joins us."

"That's great," Sebastian says.

In the restaurant, Sebastian takes the seat directly across from me. The table is covered with a classic red-checkered oilcloth. We order pizza, pitchers of beer arrive, and while these people I've forced together do their best to make conversation, below the table a whole different conversation is taking place. Sebastian's foot, then leg, meets mine under the table, intertwining and pressing. Above the table, our pizza goes cold.

"How do you know Nathan?" I ask.

"We were friends in grammar school. It's a small town," Sebastian starts.

"Small town is an understatement! We're practically all related. Everyone here knows everyone's business," someone interjects, and it feels as if they are interrupting our date.

"Where do you go to college?" I ask them both.

"UVA...University of Virginia," Sebastian answers.

"In Virginia?" I ask stupidly.

"Ha, where else would it be!" the interloper helpfully points out.

Then I'm caught up in a swirl of conversation to my left, to my right, toward the other table. Too soon, dinner is over. My roommates ask for the check—they're more than ready to get back to campus.

"I forgot my wallet in my car. Be right back," I say to no one in particular, but my eyes drill into Sebastian. He'll find a way to excuse himself; I know he will. I walk outside and stand to the left of the door. Moments later, he is there.

"Hey, let's walk," I suggest, leading us away from the restaurant. "When do you go back to Virginia?"

"In a few days. I'm going to stay and visit my family." We gravitate toward a dark corner of the parking lot knowing we only have minutes before our friends reappear.

"I can come to Virginia if you want," I say, having no idea how or when I would do this.

"Yeah, you should." Sebastian stops at the edge of the lot and turns toward me, kissing me again. I pull him in closer, feeling his sinewy body beneath his pale blue shirt. We need to stop. We can never stop. We must stop. It feels like the first time I've been touched, the only time I've been touched. The sound of us coming apart must be like a suction cup breaking the seal. *Pop.* His hair is messy, my shirt untucked.

"Go ahead in. No, wait. What's your number?" I ask. I don't have a pen. "Write it down inside. Slip it to me."

That night I lie in bed feeling my body and remembering his touch. I feel nourished, full, alive. Something has been unlocked in me that will never be caged again. My narrowed life is expanding beyond my own dreams. The world is open and mine for the taking.

In the months that follow, Sebastian and I talk regularly. I wait till my housemates are out of the house to call. I don't know where his phone is, but I can tell he's in public because he keeps his voice low.

"Hi," I say, answering his call at the appointed time.

"Hi. How are you?" he asks formally. We need this warm-up almost each time we talk.

"Good." A moment of silence stretches.

"Wish you were here," he says.

"Me too. I could come down, like we talked about."

"It's far...hard to get to..." he stutters.

"I won't come if you don't want me to. I'm not planning to march with a rainbow flag onto your quad," I say in an attempt at humor.

"Come, then," he says, with a laugh in his voice, and we plan out my trip.

"I'm going to tell my sister. I won't tell her your name, but I think I'm going to come out to her when she's here for graduation. I have to—she's out in LA, and she's gonna help me get set up out there when I move for law school." I've gotten into UCLA, where I'm going to be in the Public Interest Law and Policy program.

"That's your show. Just don't out me as your boyfriend. Your sister knows Nathan, and Nathan knows my entire family."

"*Boyfriend?*" I ask. We haven't labeled our relationship.

"You are going to be a damn good lawyer, David. You don't miss a thing. Yes, *boyfriend*. I don't know what else I'd call us."

"I promise, I'll use my legal superpower for good," I say, laughing.

"I'm sure of that." He's serious now. We've had long conversations charting out our postcollegiate plans. He's going to work in progressive politics. My plan is to go to law school and then to work in politics afterward. Without addressing it, we both understand there will be no "us" in this next phase.

"All right, good luck, babe." He hangs up.

I have a boyfriend. I yell it in the empty house. "I have a boyfriend!"

In May 2002, Jessica and I are seated at the Beech Tree, a classic bar at street level with dark wood tables, leather seats, and the smell of hamburgers grilling.

"Two pours of tequila, neat," I say. Jessica gives me a funny look. She's in Poughkeepsie for my graduation, which will take place tomorrow.

"Wow. It's a little early for tequila, isn't it?"

My stomach turns, not from hunger, but out of deep anxiety. I don't waste any more time. "I'm gay."

Jessica is shocked. "Are you sure?" she asks.

"I'm dating a man. I have a boyfriend."

"Why didn't you tell me earlier? When did you know?" Jessica's voice breaks a little, and she starts to cry.

"Jessica, I know this is a surprise..."

"All right, here we go, two tequilas. Did you want lime?" the waiter asks.

"No. We're fine, thank you," I say.

"Did you all want to place an order for food?"

"No, but can we please have some water?" Jessica asks.

"You betcha. Do you want to hear the specials?"

"No. We are fine, thank you. Just the water," I say firmly. Then I tell Jessica, "I didn't tell you because, well, I'm telling you now."

The bartender delivers our waters. "You sure you don't want to hear the specials? We have an amazing summer gazpacho—"

"Thank you, no." He gives a tight smile and walks away. Half of Jessica's face is well-lit from the window, the other half is in shadow. In the daylight I see the sister I love and the person who had always tried to care for me the best she could, and in the darkness is the question of how she will react.

"You went to the prom with Marianna," she says, as if trying to puzzle it out.

"I'm gay, and I know it."

"Just be careful," she says. "I don't want you to die."

"Please don't say that to me," I say. My own stridence startles me, but "be careful" will be a phrase that I never stop hearing from friends and family, and it will always irk me. It feels tied to having the fear and danger of being gay pounded into me.

Jessica stands up and comes over to hug me. "I love you," she says. "I'm just scared for your future. You're one of the two people I love most in this world." I know why she's scared. We all were subject to my mother's homophobia. But my sister loves me, and I know she'll understand.

"How are you going to tell Alex?" she asks.

"In person. I want to tell him face-to-face. I'll tell him on his next leave." Alex couldn't make college work financially and has joined the military for the educational benefits it offers. Military service is a brightly lit path out of poverty—far more accessible than college. I'm grateful for Alex's service, but I wish it were more of a choice than a necessity for some of the foster kids who take that route.

"That might be a while, David. I'm not going to lie to him."

"And how often do you guys discuss my dating life?"

"Fair enough."

"It's mine to tell, Jessica."

"I know," she says, giving me another hug. "I'm glad you told me."

We walk back to her hotel, and I tell her I'll see her at graduation tomorrow. I'll also be seeing her a lot in LA, where she's getting a master's at the University of Southern California's School of Social Work. I walk back to my room feeling as if I've slid another piece into a puzzle that will be complete when I talk to Alex. Back in the town house where I live with Sydney and Mia, it looks like a bomb has exploded. I love my housemates, but their version of packing is to throw everything on the floor first—dishes, art, clothes, and pillows are scattered willy-nilly. We've been here together for only a year, but we assembled a life, and it makes me a little sad to see it dismantled without ceremony. They're shoving their belongings into bags. There's no graduate housing at UCLA, so I've rented the only space I can afford. I found it on Craigslist—it's a converted garage a few miles from the law school. I'll be able to walk or bike to classes. The owner has made it a point to emphasize how raw the space is, but even so I will soon learn that he's oversold it.

That night, at dinner in the cafeteria, a guy named Micah asks me, "Who the hell is Tony Kushner?" He points to a flyer announcing him as our graduation speaker.

"You know, the playwright? He wrote *Angels in America*?"

"They must be scraping the bottom of the barrel. Couldn't they get Oprah? Or at least an actor?" Lucas says.

I head back to my room, which is almost entirely packed up. There is nothing left on my desk but a stack of MapQuest printouts showing my route to LA. I put on my cap and gown and walk toward the hillside where we will graduate. On the way, I cross paths with the head of the college, President Fergusson. She is in full regalia, accompanied by a few people I don't recognize. I have been the student liaison to her office all year, and I realize this is my last chance to get a picture with her. I shove my analog camera into a man's hands, saying, "Would you please take a picture of me with President Fergusson?" So just before his speech, Tony Kushner does the honors.

Graduation takes place in an outdoor amphitheater built into a hill, with metal folding chairs leaning perilously forward in the grass. The sky is gray, threatening rain. We march in, capped and gowned. Vassar's colors, pink and gray, trim our gowns. Holly, Steve, Brianna, Ruth, and Jessica are somewhere in the audience, though I can't see them from where I sit. My mother isn't here. She has been homeless through most of my time at college and hard to keep track of, but I was able to reach her last night.

"I'm graduating, and it's because of you," I told her. I gave her credit to make her feel good, but also because it was partly true.

Given our upbringing, the fact that all three Ambroz kids had earned undergraduate degrees was a miracle. My mom played a part in both sides of that equation—the difficult childhood, and the value placed on education. She threw us overboard and gave us our lifelines.

"Why didn't you invite me?" she asked.

"Because I don't want you here, Mom," I said truthfully. "You'll disrupt the event. This is for me."

"David, that's not true. Well, I am very proud of you. I love you."

"Thanks, Mom."

Then she said, "I need money for a winter jacket, so if you get a chance, could you please send that to me?" I hung up feeling mixed emotions. Grateful to be free of her, sad that she was unable to experience this moment with me, and appreciating the irony that even in this moment, at the height of my achievement, she found a way to make it about herself.

I watch in awe as, in a fast-paced staccato, Tony Kushner delivers a riveting hour-long commencement address in thirty minutes. He urges us to be aware of what is coming in the post-9/11 world. It is a call to action for us to be aware and honest and agents of change. He implores us to organize, to be political, and to claim power, redistribute it, and legislate it into justice. His words converge with everything I've been thinking and working toward and fighting for my whole life. This is exactly what I am going to do. This is my plan. And what can drive us forward in a world that is full of people who seem determined to bring it to an end? He answers his own question: *Hope isn't a choice, it's a moral obligation, a human obligation, an obligation to the cells in your body. Hope is a function of those cells, it's a bodily function the same as breathing and eating and sleeping.*

It is hope that has made me brave. Hope that has kept me clawing for the surface when I was drowning, hungry, bruised, torn down, and almost erased. Hope that has preserved my fight and my identity and my soul. Relentless, insanely impossible hope that has gotten me to this chair on this hillside, with this black gown and awkward cap—my full family behind me and around me, I will drive west infused with that spirit and determination. I am, finally, my whole self.

The next morning, I slowly drive my 1994 Chrysler out the stone arch of the main gate and onto Raymond Avenue. Upstate New York is in full bloom; the trees and even the weeds are vibrantly alive. It's twenty-six hundred miles to LA and I am going to law school, not as a vessel of the trauma that happened to me, but as an out gay man determined to hasten change. Driving down I-95, the sun on my back and spread through my eyes, I think of all my foster siblings, and other foster kids whom I met along the way. Their faces flash by in my mind. My heart presses toward them, hoping that they've made it too. My soul holds on to a hope that some have even made it out of the poverty and violence. That they are all safe and determining their future. Hope should be theirs too. I know that I'm not going to law school for me, I'm going with the determination to help them. To help get kids like me off the streets, to make sure they are never put through a system that grinds away hope. This mission gives meaning to everything I have seen and experienced. It will give shape to everything I do. Out of all the darkness, it becomes my home.

Afterword

Poverty is never about the future. The poor are consumed with the now, as they must be to survive. Poverty is passed down from generation to generation. According to studies of intergenerational poverty done by the National Center for Children in Poverty, of the children who spend at least 50 percent of their childhood in poverty, nearly half of them will be poor at age thirty-five. When a child comes into our custody—"our" being the custody of the state— it is our chance to intervene with powerful strategies to arrest the cycles of poverty, violence, and all the ensuant misery, but we fail. As you can see from my story, the system as it currently stands doesn't do right by children, but it could.

I am forever a foster kid, like these others: Steve Jobs, John Lennon, Marilyn Monroe, James Dean, Cher, Eddie Murphy, Simone Biles, Tiffany Haddish, Greg Louganis, Coco Chanel, Nelson Mandela, Larry Ellis, Eleanor Roosevelt, Maya Angelou, Tammy Baldwin, Nancy Reagan, Ella Fitzgerald, Tina Turner, Carol Burnett, George Lopez, Michael Bay, Art Linkletter, James Brown, Francois Truffaut, Andrew Jackson, J. R. R. Tolkien, Edgar Allan Poe, Simon Bolivar, Aristotle, Jonathan Swift, and Leo Tolstoy. Our potential is unlimited, but foster youth have to fight our way out of the systems of poverty to achieve.

Like these others, I succeeded in spite of the system, not because of it. I endured many of the same things every youth served by the system experiences: abuse, mobility, mental health issues with parents, and a rotating cast of foster parents, social workers, and courts—some good, some bad.

At times I felt like I had no rights. I was subject to my mother's whims and then to the regulations and limitations of various agencies. What I learned was that if I wanted more, better, and different than the world that was handed to me, I would have to carve it out myself. The system did not make that easy. My desire to be educated and self-reliant should be something the system nurtures in every child.

In my work as an advocate, sometimes I ask people to close their eyes and imagine a child that they care about, and now I want to ask you to do the same. Think about your own child, your relative, your friend's child, your future child, yourself. What if you knew that this beautiful child would be placed in foster care? What would you want for that child? That is what we should be giving them now. My mother planted the idea of college in my head, a dream that I saw photographed on the folder of the Vassar brochure and that I fought hard to fulfill every day I spent on campus. When I close my eyes, I want every child to have a chance for some version of that. Every homeless and foster kid is our child, and we should design a system accordingly. While writing this book, my publishing team and my friends would ask me what I wanted people to do after reading my story. They asked, "What can we do?" I love that question because (as you've probably figured out by now) I didn't write this book just to share the hurdles I faced in my escape from poverty. I wrote my story with a deep hope that you will be motivated to do something. I want you to use your vote. We must vote to center the well-being and success of these most vulnerable, our children, in our politics. We can "solve," at least in part, the tragedy of youth in poverty by reforming foster care. Right now our foster care system is better than it's ever been. We still need fundamental change, but we are strengthening a worthwhile system, not starting from scratch.

I earned my doctorate in foster care reform not in the halls of a classroom, but instead during the years I spent in the system in countless foster homes, and among my foster brothers, foster sisters, social workers, judges, lawyers, and therapists that acted in and upon my life. In the years after I emancipated, I struck out to understand and find solutions to the foster care system. A solution to the myriad of shameful statistics emerging from the ranks of the 425,000 youths whose lives are touched daily by foster care. The solution involves social workers, foster parents, biological parents, and foster youth themselves. I want you to become one of the changemakers.

Consistent, empowered social workers are key to improving outcomes. We can increase the number and quality and retain an experienced workforce by decreasing their caseloads and increasing their pay and benefits by either a salary increase or alternative compensation such as meaningful student loan forgiveness, home loan assistance (similar to that for veterans), and access for social workers' families to preferred programs like early enrollment in college for their families. I want you to advocate for them and for those changes.

Great and diverse foster parents are the heart of a successful system. We need LGBTQ+ parents, single parents, married heterosexual couples, parents of different races and beliefs. Perhaps above all, we need to recruit more middle- and upper-income foster parents with higher education degrees. This effort is not to displace but to add to and diversify the incredible commitment of lower economic classes who are already fostering. Parents' level of education has a profound impact on the likelihood that their children will pursue higher education.

Also, these other economic classes bring in additional political power to push for change. The change we need in the foster care system is to make all foster parents eligible for a federal or state pension, add them to the federal employee health care plan, and make their biological kids eligible for free or subsidized tuition at state colleges and universities. Today, almost all of the cost of foster care is paid for by the federal government—this extends that commitment at minimal cost but with huge impact. By removing the biggest concerns of the middle class (health care, pension, and college tuition for their biological children), we can incentivize the masses to foster. I want you to foster a child, if you have the means, or to support someone or an organization that fosters.

There are approximately 450,000 kids in foster care. Each year, tens of thousands emancipate into independence. Imagine foster youth, by the thousands, emancipating from foster care not into homelessness, or poverty, but into higher education. In the last two years of foster care, perhaps they dual enroll in community colleges and high school at the same time—pursuing vocational certificates like nursing or plumbing or pursue their two-year associate's degree or transfer to a four-year college.

A significant obstacle to higher education is access to housing. More than half of foster youth will experience homelessness when leaving foster care, and less than 5 percent will secure a higher education degree. Instead, let's put the "community" back in the thousands of community colleges across the nation. I want you to push to build dedicated dorms at community colleges where current and former foster youth get priority for housing and early enrollment. We own the land the colleges sit on; these are the public's schools; and these foster youth are the public's children. Imagine a country where foster youth emancipate into a degree, acquiring a skill certification or vocation or having the chance to transfer to a four-year college. I want you to help make that future real.

Finally, let's take into account the biological families of foster children. Nearly 60 percent of the youth in foster care are entering the system because of neglect. Neglect is often rooted in poverty—

the inability to provide stable housing, food, and resources. The best way to reform foster care is to decriminalize poverty and help families remain intact whenever possible with wraparound support—be it jobs, mental health care, or whatever is needed. I want you to help these children and families obtain these resources.

Foster care is an inflection point where we can halt the systemic inheritance of poverty and violence. All of our children deserve this chance.

Acknowledgments

For thirty-eight years, a story grew in the dark. It came to light because of the profound contribution of a group of individuals that knew my story was worth telling.

Hilary Liftin, part-collaborator, part-therapist, full-time friend, and forever my "sister."

Krishan Trotman, of Legacy Lit and Hachette Book Group, thank you for believing in the power of words to change the world. Your consistent voice and wisdom meant everything.

Daniel Greenberg, my literary agent, for saying YES when all he had was a chapter and an outline. Your reputation and belief helped make this project become a reality.

This is "my story," but also the story of my family—all of them. An amazing collection of individuals that love me, challenge me, and keep me connected to my past. To my foster parents Holly and Steve, thank you for the powerful lessons of love; and to their daughters, my foster sisters, Brianna and Allie, for always making me feel like your brother. To Dan Ferguson for helping me become the man I am. To Vincent Bartle, who opened my heart to the love of a child, and in that healed us both. To every foster sibling I had, too numerous to name. I hope in telling my story, you see your own. You are not invisible. You are not forgotten.

Thank you to the following individuals whose love and support made this book happen: Judy Meyers, Tamar Abrams, Rachel Barchie,

Acknowledgments

Isabel Bermudez-Olano, Celeste Bodner, Larry Bolton, Kevin Brockman, Zelene Cruz, Eric Garcetti, Ana Guerrero, Dean Hansell, Sabrina Huffaker, Amina Iro, HJDA, Steven Levine, Stephen Massey, Eileen McCaffrey, David McFarland, Sarah McKay, Jeff McMullen, Charley Medigovich, Terry Mutchler, Leah Paulos, Brian Pendleton, Sheree Shu, Natalie Tran, Tammy Chow Weaver, and Rob Woronoff.